The Eclectic Odyssey
of Atlee B. Ayres, Architect

NUMBER EIGHT
Sara and John Lindsey Series
in the Arts and Humanities

The Eclectic Odyssey of Atlee B. Ayres, Architect

ROBERT JAMES COOTE

Color Photographs by W. Eugene George

TEXAS A&M UNIVERSITY PRESS

COLLEGE STATION

All illustrations are from the Ayres and Ayres Records,
The Alexander Architectural Archive, The General Libraries,
The University of Texas at Austin, referred to in the
captions as the Alexander Architectural Archive,
UT–Austin, or from the University of Texas Institute
of Texan Cultures, San Antonio.

The paper used in this book
meets the minimum requirements
of the American National Standard
for Permanence of Paper for Printed
Library Materials, z39.48–1984.
Binding materials have been
chosen for durability.

Library of Congress Cataloging-in-Publication Data

Coote, Robert James, 1931–
    The eclectic odyssey of Atlee B. Ayres, architect / Robert James
Coote ; color photographs by W. Eugene George.—1st ed.
       p. cm.—(Sara and John Lindsey series in the arts and
humanities ; no. 8)
    Includes bibliographical references and index.
    ISBN 1-58544-122-8
    1. Ayres, Atlee Bernard, 1873-1969—Criticism and interpre-
tation. 2. Architecture, Domestic—Texas. 3. Architecture,
Modern—20th century—Texas. I. Title. II. Series.
NA737.A98C66   2001
720'.92—dc21   00-012954

CONTENTS

ILLUSTRATIONS

PREFACE

It was with an architect's eye that I first admired the early-twentieth-century houses that yet today, at the beginning of the next century, still exist along the pleasant streets of San Antonio's suburbs of Monte Vista, Olmos Park, and Terrell Hills. I was especially attracted to those pale stucco houses with terra-cotta tile roofs, balconies, and filigreed iron balconies and window grills, reminiscent of Italian villas and Spanish farmhouses. To me, they seemed to be not only charming, but also appropriate to San Antonio's environment and to its historical and cultural heritage. Among many fine houses, those in which the architect Atlee Ayres had a hand stood out for their architectural elegance. As a designer and architectural historian, I became curious about the development of Atlee's design sensibilities and his eclectic approach of seeking inspiration and guidance from buildings of many times and places. Eventually I came to believe that a study of Atlee as an architect, and of a number of the houses in which he was involved, could provide a window on the issue of style, which is a continuing concern of those who design houses and those who experience them.

Subsequently I explored the extensive cache of Ayres material in the Alexander Architectural Archive of the University of Texas in Austin, and in the Ayres Collections in the Institute of Texan Cultures in San Antonio. Together with the houses themselves, the majority of which are in San Antonio, and a few others in South Texas, Oklahoma City, and Kansas City, Kansas, these collections were the bedrock of this investigation. I pursued the larger topic of eclecticism in the Battle Hall Library of the University of Texas in Austin, in the Library of the Royal Institute of British Architects in London, and in my own library.

Fortunately, the extensive Ayres Collection in the Alexander Architectural Archive contains original working drawings and specifications, which made possible detailed descriptions and analyses of Atlee's houses. His formation as an architect, the shaping of his design sensibilities, and his eclectic method were illuminated by a close examination of documents pertaining to his brief formal art training in New York, 1892–94, and by perusal of his extensive library of over three hundred volumes and more than five thousand prints and negatives of photographs he took or purchased on his travels in the United States, Europe, Asia, and Mexico. His clippings files of material, culled mainly from architectural magazines, contained pictures of important historical buildings as well as work of his contemporaries and information on materials and construction—all fuel for his own designing. His voluminous office correspondence and the houses themselves revealed much of his artistic preferences, his professional techniques, as well as something of his character and personality. Indeed, it is evident from the Ayres Collections in the Institute of Texan Cultures that Atlee emerged as a prominent and rather colorful figure in San Antonio society.

The pieces collected from the archives were also helpful in creating a voyage of reasonable invention of possibilities and probabilities that surrounded them, the contexts in which they existed and which they represent. For instance, although there are only a few remnants from Atlee's formal training at the Metropolitan School of Art in New York City—only a couple of worn notebooks, a few of his drawings, and an 1893–94 prospectus—it was possible through other books, newspapers, and periodicals to re-create with some accuracy the Fifth Avenue that Atlee must have walked to get to school in the old, red brick Metropolitan Museum on the edge of Central Park. Similarly, much can be known about the Southern California of the 1920s that Atlee photographed on his several motor trips, information that makes Atlee's work more vivid and intelligible.

After exploring the influences on Atlee's design sensibilities and the shaping of his artistic tastes, I made a series of detailed studies of twenty-five houses designed between 1898 and 1938, which seemed a logical cutoff point before the Second World War ended the building of the sort of large traditional houses that Atlee designed. These were selected from a much larger number done by Atlee from 1898 to 1969, first in partnership with C. A. Coughlin until 1905, then from 1922 with his younger son, Robert M. Ayres, in the firm Ayres and Ayres, Architects. Atlee practiced until his death in 1969 at age ninety-six. In the studies of the houses, I discuss them not only as representative of styles, but as architectural compositions—their plans, spaces, exteriors, materials, and structure. Style can never be completely independent of the reality of the thing. At its best it is symbiotic, integral, not applied. It is the sense of fakery that is offensive to an in-

formed mind and cultivated sensibility. Fortunately, all but one of these houses still exist, though some are much altered in external appearance, and even more so in interior furnishings.

My task of locating and identifying the houses to be examined was made considerably easier by a copy of Donald E. Everett's original newspaper supplement guide to the Monte Vista district. Stephanie H. Cocke kindly gave me my first guided tour of the locations of Ayres houses in San Antonio. I am grateful to those present owners and occupants who helped with access to some of the houses. My understanding of the Atkinson house, now the Marion Koogler McNay Museum of Art, was greatly helped by an informative tour given me by the house architect, J. J. Stevenson, and by a study by Darin Beidiger of the building's successive stages of development. In Kansas City, Robert and Sally Uhlmann were wonderfully hospitable and generous with documents pertaining to Ayres's Sam Roberts house of which they are the sympathetic owners. Kenneth J. LaBudde, George Erhlich, and Cary and Glenda Goodman helped acquaint me with Kansas City and its elegant early-twentieth-century suburbs. Richard Drummond Davis and Emily Summers have been similarly helpful in Dallas. Melvena Heisch of the Oklahoma State Historic Preservation Office assisted me in my investigation of the Brown and Buttram houses in Oklahoma City. I am especially grateful to Atlee's grandson, Robert M. Ayres, who kindly gave copyright permission to the Ayres Collection at the University of Texas.

I cannot express enough my appreciation for the unflagging support and encouragement given me by Nancy Swallow and Beth Dodd, in the Alexander Architecture Archive, and that of Tom Shelton and his colleagues at the Library of the Institute of Texan Cultures. I am indebted to many others for their contributions to the form and intellectual content of this book. These include friends and colleagues: Drury Blakeley

Alexander, Anthony Alofsin, Richard Cleary, Marian B. Davis, Susan Toomey Frost, Mary Carolyn George, Christopher Long, and Roxanne Williamson. I would have been lost without the patient technical assistance of Robert Swaffar, Jim O'Donnell, and Patricia Alvarado.

The end result, this book, is not to be taken as an exhaustive nor definitive account of Atlee Ayres's practice, much less a picture of the whole man, but as a special study of his search for style, his odyssey of eclecticism. It is, as one of my original readers felicitously described it, "a kind of artistic biography." In all, I have tried to avoid puffing him up on the one side, and of underestimating him on the other.

The Eclectic Odyssey
of Atlee B. Ayres, Architect

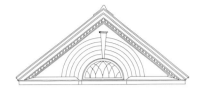

CHAPTER I

An Eclectic Inheritance

"The twentieth century has had to rediscover what the
nineteenth century learned so painfully: eclecticism is
the vernacular of sophisticated societies: architecture
begins where function ends."
—J. Mordaunt Crook, *The Dilemma of Style*

In the seventy-one years of his professional career that lasted from 1898 to his death in 1969, at age ninety-six, Atlee B. Ayres, with his son and partner Robert M. Ayres from 1922, was involved in more than five hundred architectural projects principally in San Antonio and the counties and towns of South and Central Texas, but also in Kansas, Oklahoma, New York, and Mexico. These encompassed a wide range of types of buildings that included major civic structures such as San Antonio's Municipal Auditorium of 1926, done in conjunction with the firm of Jackson and Willis; the Smith-Young Tower, also of 1926, which was San Antonio's first skyscraper and the tallest building in Texas for several decades; and the Administration Building at Randolph Air Force Base, whose shining white tower and blue and gold chevron-patterned dome was nick-

named the "Taj Mahal" by the airmen who trained there. Atlee was appointed state architect of Texas in 1915 and was responsible for the State Highway Building, the Land Office Building, a remodeling of the Capitol, as well as the Engineering, Law, Pharmacy, Women's Dormitory, and ROTC buildings on the campus of the University of Texas, all in Austin. The firm of Ayres and Ayres was the architect of seven Texas county courthouses, at least forty office buildings, sixteen schools, and several libraries and churches. Much of Atlee's professional success resulted from his position in San Antonio where he was viewed, as he viewed himself in part, as a pillar of the community. As a member of a conservative, elite, old guard society, Atlee would typically be president of Fiesta, be photographed in a parade as he rode by in the Texas governor's car, and, wearing a bowler hat, as he jauntily drove his one-cylinder Ford down the street (fig. 1). It was, however, the nearly two hundred houses that Atlee had a hand in designing that remain among his finest achievements.

When Atlee began his long practice in 1898, he boarded an already moving ship of design heavily freighted with the residue of the past.[1] At the beginning of the twentieth century, the fabric of American residential architecture was already a complex patchwork of styles. It had an eclectic history, not unnatural in a relatively new and rapidly changing country. Well into the nineteenth century, America's residential architecture had largely reflected the country's English heritage, both England's traditional vernacular buildings and those inspired by the classical world of ancient Greece and Rome, and their successor, Renaissance Italy. By the middle of the century, in the flush of economic expansion after the Civil War, American architecture proliferated in exuberant, flamboyant, sometimes bizarre eclecticism, producing piles of rock, brick, and wood filigraine, masses of turrets and pregnant bays—inventions not without charm but somehow lacking dignity and authority, the pedigree of

their European predecessors. Throughout the nineteenth century, in the decades of Greek and Gothic Revivals, Italianate, and French Second Empire styles, but especially in the Stick and Shingle styles, and the fanciful Queen Anne style, the European and English inspiration was remote and used freely, even promiscuously, producing unique amalgams of Victorian ostentation or charming eccentricities depending on one's point of view. *Holly's Country Seats* (1863) "pleaded for an American domestic architecture that 'culled' from the structures of all ages and countries."[2] By 1870 "architectural anarchy had reached a point at which disorder had resulted almost in physical brutality, and ugliness conducted a constant assault and battery wherever one turned one's eye." "Yet this period had established, by violent reaction against the past, a coarse vigor and self-confidence in its own lights, which are necessary for any kind of architectural creativeness."[3]

In the latter decades of the nineteenth century, the privileged few at the top of the economic ladder sought something far more grand—something to rival the great houses of England and Europe—in a great display of wealth to create the aura of high culture suitable to their social status. In 1881, Richard Morris Hunt, the first American architect to be educated at the École des Beaux-Arts in Paris, completed a mansion on Fifth Avenue for W. K. Vanderbilt. Its inventive eclecticism—informed by the monuments of the late Gothic period in Belgium and France, obliquely reminiscent of the fifteenth-century house of Jacques Coeur in Bourges and the sixteenth-century Chateau of Blois—precipitated a fashion for drawing on the past with a scholarly and cultivated taste shaped by education and travel abroad. Later, in 1895, Hunt designed for George Washington Vanderbilt a French chateau whose foundations covered 5 acres of the 130,000-acre domain in North Carolina's Great Smoky Mountains.

Others followed Hunt at the École des Beaux-

Fig. 1. Atlee B. Ayres in his one-cylinder Ford, c. 1904. The UT Institute of Texan Cultures, The Atlee B. Ayres Collection

Arts where they became acquainted with the practice of eclectic transformation of the classical tradition and the intelligent use of classical composition adapted to contemporary uses. Most students took the opportunity to explore the architectural riches of Europe first hand. Even if they were neither schooled nor traveled in Europe, American architects studied the plates of books on the historic buildings of Western Europe and England: French chateaux, Italian villas and palaces, Flemish townhouses, German cathedrals, and Tudor manors. These were inspiration for those designing lumbering dark Romanesque mansions and gleaming chateaux of Caen stone for the rich—houses that were admired and emulated by the middle classes as well. By the end of the century, a generation of architects trained at the École were in prominent American practices and on the faculties of the most influential schools of architecture in America.

The triumph of a clique of Beaux-Arts–trained East Coast architects at the 1893 World's Columbian Exposition in Chicago firmly established the fashion for an academic eclecticism, largely based on European precedents. These architects and teachers established a way of thinking about architecture that centered on a form of eclecticism that drew on historical styles not in order to imitate or reproduce them exactly, much less to misuse them with late-Victorian abandon, but to reinterpret them with scholarly understanding for a contemporary American audience. It was an attempt to restore literacy to architecture through an educated eclecticism that used not just superficial motifs and details, but which also had a concern for scale, proportions, composition, and authentic detail. Some of the houses of the "Gilded Age," the pre-income tax years of the beginning of the twentieth century, were of overweening opulence of size (e.g., the 110-room Widener mansion near Philadelphia). Their façades were lavishly ladened with paired columns, swags and cartouches; their interiors marbleized, gilded, and frescoed; their vast lawns

and formal parterres designed to emulate those of Versailles. Some were monuments of eclectic invention. James Deering's Florida winter residence, Vizcaya, accommodated rooms in a number of styles: an Italian Renaissance hall, a Robert Adam library, a Biedermeier guest room, and others, all perfectly executed within the shell of a convincingly Italian villa of the seventeenth century. The summer residence of George Gould was "an attempt to put a French chateau's roof on a Georgian house."[4] The grand civic buildings and handsome houses of Delano and Aldrich, Carrerre and Hastings, and John Russell Pope set standards of accomplished eclecticism that revealed a deep understanding of older European styles adapted to the present. Atlee could see the work of these architects in the major architectural magazines and in the books of his library, which included large portfolio monographs of the work of the prominent New York firms of McKim, Mead and White, Charles Platt, and Dwight James Baum. Chicago's Howard Van Doren Shaw and the slightly younger David Adler built large Italian villas and French chateaux for the second-generation social elite of Armours, Swifts, and Ryersons. Similarly, Mellor, Meigs, and Howe built for the elite of Philadelphia's Main Line.

The influence of academic eclecticism permeated the profession, gradually filtering out through the rest of America. In the latter part of the nineteenth century, American architecture also reflected an interest in America's Colonial past, an interest partly stimulated by the United States centennial of 1876 in Philadelphia. Perhaps it was also a matter of nostalgia for "the good old days" before the exhilarating, but exhausting and confusing, years of post–Civil War America. However, the dominant style of residential building from 1880 to 1900 was the Queen Anne style. Vitality and rampant individuality suffused the curiously named style (curious because it had nothing to do with the eighteenth-century English queen). The half-timbering and tall chimneys, the shaped gables and carved brickwork, cheerful balconies and verandahs of white-painted woodwork, and large, many-paned windows—made popular in England by Richard Norman Shaw and William Eden Nesfield and others—were imported and translated into an American version that proceeded easily from the earlier "Stick" style in the use of balloon framing and wood cladding. The popularity of the Queen Anne style lay in its inclusiveness, its eclectic inventiveness, its appealing eccentricities: a profusion of angles, secret niches, towers and bays, brightly polychromed surfaces of wood siding and scalloped shingles, exotic ornament and "gingerbread" trim (made cheaply available by the newly invented turning lathe and accessible via the new railroads). The style was made distinctly American with inventive American spindlework and other pre-cut architectural details. Fanciful and charming, commodious, and available at any size, Queen Anne houses enjoyed great popularity well into the first decade of the twentieth century.

In the first decade of his practice at the turn of the century Atlee looked first to the American Colonial tradition, in order to transform irrepressible Queen Anne individualism into something more dignified and in fact more reminiscent of the American past, perhaps a resurgence of nationalism and nostalgia stimulated by the 1876 centennial. The transition was one of subtle changes. In the first years of the century, it was a matter of slightly more accurate Colonial details applied to the asymmetrical volumes, porches, and turrets of Queen Anne houses. Gradually there appeared historically accurate classical Tuscan Doric and Ionic columns and capitals, dentils and modillions, Adamesque swags, and other motifs derived from the American Colonial and Federal vocabulary. Gradually the exuberant complexity was reduced to much simpler volumes; symmetry ordered the façades—at least those facing the street—with the rear ones usually being more functionally unruly.

In the first decades of the twentieth century, there were other alternatives to attract Atlee's attention, in particular the work of the Chicago architect Louis Sullivan and his highly original protege, Frank Lloyd Wright, only five years older than Atlee himself. Wright had declined Daniel Burnham's offer of four years of study at the École des Beaux-Arts, plus another two in Rome. Wright wanted to find his own way, "to preserve the freedom of the picturesque while subjecting this to the discipline of the emergent movement toward formalism."[5] In his early houses of the 1890s he assimilated academic formalism. More important to the development of his organic architecture and the Prairie style were the example of the Shingle style, and the related Arts and Crafts Movement with its extensive interest in Japanese art. Atlee also had at hand the *Craftsman* magazine founded by Gustav Stickley in 1901, with its illustrations of the plain, sturdy, unornamented furniture that Stickley designed and produced, which furnished many a relatively inexpensive and very comfortable bungalow. But except for a few houses in 1914–16, Atlee never adopted these innovations wholeheartedly. However, he could see the freedom in the open plans of interrelated interior spaces flowing into one another and out to verandahs, terraces, and lawns.

For a while after the First World War, Atlee looked to Europe for inspiration, especially from Italy and Spain. The war created a widespread interest in English and European buildings that heretofore had existed mainly for the privileged classes. Architects were expected to be skilled in many different styles and to command an eclectic vocabulary that drew on many so-called "period" styles of the whole spectrum of English and European history. Architects built their vocabularies by studying examples in books and magazines, and, better yet, by traveling to see the buildings, making drawings, and by taking and collecting photographs from archival sources to serve as inspiration when they returned. The judicious use of a castellated parapet or oriel window could create a romantic *mise en scene* that satisfied a desire for a home that was one's castle. Many a small American house presented a small porch with a sweeping roof, tall living room window with tinted glass, a bit of stone veneer or false half-timbering, as American architects tried to adapt foreign prototypes to the scale, pattern, and building conditions of American living.

After 1922, perhaps chafing at the exacting restrictions of the formal Italian Renaissance style, with its insistence on strict symmetry and formalized proportions and details, perhaps recognizing the increasing costs of the rich materials and elaborate moldings required for emulating palatial Italian originals, perhaps seeking a style more suitable to the South Texas climate, landscape, and Hispanic-Mexican past, Atlee turned from his books and plates of monuments. Several trips to Southern California exposed him to the American Spanish style, which by the 1920s dominated all categories of buildings there. The 1915 Panama-California Exposition in San Diego, and the Panama-Pacific Exposition in San Francisco had promoted considerable interest in the architecture of Spain, especially in California, Arizona, Texas, and Florida where examples of original Spanish Colonial buildings remained. The romantic and theatrical style seemed to Atlee not only right for California, but potentially so for San Antonio. To fuel his new brand of eclecticism, he traveled to Spain itself. What interested him was not so much the Spain of formal Renaissance styles—the flowery Plateresque, nor the baroque Churrigueresque styles—but rather the vernacular buildings of the countryside and villages. The wonderfully picturesque, asymmetrical stucco and stone farmhouses inspired Atlee to adopt a Spanish style for some of his finest houses.[6]

By the 1920s, there was an increasingly violent debate among architects about the merits of Traditional Eclecticism versus Modernism. There were those who were itching to get on more fully

with the present and the future, who saw no point in dressing up in the trappings of the past. In 1929, some architects believed architecture to be "still prey to the dangers of sentimentality. . . exposed to the poisonous infection of silly magazine articles, written by romantic creatures to whom art means affectation, to whom architecture means stage scenery, to whom imitation and reality are of equal importance, if indeed they do not prefer imitation."[7] The positions taken by many American architects in the 1920s and '30s reflected the uneasiness posed by European Modernism that brought into question historical eclecticism and traditional styles. Some reacted violently to the "grave danger of youthful rebellions," to the "childish things that affront all canons of good taste, essentially vulgar." One of the deans of the American architectural profession, Ralph Adams Cram, found the stark new buildings of Paris "dull hideousness, artificial and grossly ugly."[8] Modernism was found to be "belligerent, without manners or courtesies, bereft of delicacy of statement." These reactions may have been based on the common feeling that "we long to turn our backs on our rigid, grimy warehouses, on the geometric hives we call our offices, on the harshly efficient plants where many of our working hours are spent, and fly for solace to Fairyland" described as a suburb of enchanted houses of "towers and turrets," of "the quaintest little dormers." "The strong vigorous rational design . . . may be all right for 'high brows,' but life is fraught with too many cares already to make thinking in our leisure moments attractive."[9] And yet, the same author wondered, "Is it so easy to make the right choice? There are so many lovely flowers by the wayside."

Nevertheless, fresh incentives for change came from Europe where modernist desires were finding form. America had felt the influence of the 1925 Paris Exposition Internationale des Arts Decoratifs et Industriel. Art Deco motifs drawn directly from Paris—chevrons, arcs, sunbursts, stylized maidens, and flower sprays—now became available as stock, prefabricated items from American manufacturers. Atlee approached Modernism with some caution. However, in October, 1928, he wrote to Helburn, Inc., in New York, for some books on "modern architecture" to look over. A few weeks later, he received some that he sent back the same day. Later, in 1935, he contacted Vincent, Freal & Cie for catalogues and prices, as "I am considering purchasing some portfolios or books containing illustrations of good, not too radical architectural modernistic designs."[10] The American professional architectural journals of the 1930s published Modern designs virtually exclusively. Nearly all the twenty-four hundred entrants in the 1935 General Electric Architectural Competition offered flat-roofed, cubist houses of innovative construction in steel and concrete, with aluminum strip windows. But the rigors of the International Modernism style—the flat roof, the plain surface, the demands for an orderly life without clutter, the fact that the houses aged badly and were oddities in most communities—were unappealing to most of America. In the 1932 "Better Homes in America Small House Architectural Competition" President Hoover presented the gold medal to Royal Barry Wills for the design of a traditional Cape Cod cottage, chosen because it had an air of domesticity, fine scale and composition, a familiar use of materials, careful details, and the spirit of the locality in which it was built.[11] These were qualities that Atlee continued to seek.[12]

Perhaps the most influential celebration of early American building was the reconstruction of Colonial Williamsburg, Virginia, in 1932, where four hundred buildings of recent construction were removed, seventy-nine Colonial buildings were reconstructed, and sixty-three Colonial buildings restored. It satisfied the American taste for replicas and reconstructed historical sites that "in the absence of authentic remains, reveals a fondness for make-believe that is one of the components of Eclecticism."[13] The 1938 annual meeting of the American Institute of Architects was held in Williamsburg.

Atlee's work from 1898 to 1938 was an eclectic odyssey that made its way through a succession of design influences. It forged an important link between the late Victorian architecture of Texas, the buildings of Alfred Giles and James Riely Gordon, and the vernacularly oriented work of David Williams and the younger, renegade protomodernist O'Neil Ford from 1930 on. In fact, when the local San Antonio chapter was disinclined to nominate Ford for Fellow of the American Institute of Architects in 1960, it was eighty-six-year-old Atlee Ayres who responded to Ford's personal request to endorse the proposal for his nomination, which fortunately succeeded. Atlee himself in 1931 was the first San Antonio architect to be named a Fellow of the AIA. He was a charter member of the Texas Society of Architects in 1913, and later of the West Texas chapter of the AIA. In 1937, with two fellow architects, he led the movement for state licensing of architects, and by drawing lots with the other two—Lester Flint of Waco and Raymond Phelps, Sr., of San Antonio—became the third licensed architect in the history of the state of Texas.

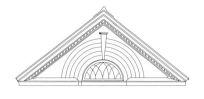

CHAPTER 2

Architectural Education: New York, 1892–94

In his youth, Atlee Ayres lived directly across the dusty plaza from the fabled Alamo, in a three-story limestone building, variously described as a hotel, an apartment house, and a lodging house, which his father leased and operated. The Ayreses had come to Texas from Hillsboro, Ohio, near Cincinnati, in 1880 when Atlee was six, first settling in Houston and then moving to San Antonio in 1888. As Atlee recalled many years later, "San Antonio at that time gave a very picturesque and interesting impression to the tourist and newcomer alike, with its narrow winding streets, old structures of Spanish origin, and chili stands on the various Plazas which were illuminated at night with varied colored lanterns, and the large wood fires heating the food and the chili queens in costume."[1]

Atlee had come to an old city founded in 1718

by a group of Franciscan missionaries. There were evocative, sadly neglected, eighteenth-century relics for him to see: the presidio captain's residence (since 1930 known as the Spanish Governor's Palace) on the Plaza de Armas; San Fernando Cathedral on the Plaza de las Islas, now the Main Plaza; and other reminders of the days of Spanish viceregal rule, Mexican ascendancy, and the short-lived Republic of Texas. As a teenager, Atlee could have seen across the plaza from his home the Alamo's golden stone façade with its distinctive curved parapet. At the south end of the plaza, the Joske Brothers opened their department store the year the Ayreses came to the city. Next to the Alamo, the Greek Revival façade of the Menger Hotel had faced the plaza since 1859. In the prosperity that followed the belated arrival of the railroad in San Antonio in

1877, a generation of architects—including Alfred Giles, James Wahrenberger, and James Riely Gordon—were building substantial commercial buildings in the latest styles. Shortly after he arrived, while still a teenager, Atlee could have watched the completion in 1891 of three of their commercial buildings, could have seen the elaborate compilation of Renaissance columns and arches of Wahrenberger's Turnverein building, the gently rounded cupola and tower of James Riely Gordon's Clifford Building, and the sturdy Romanesque Revival Stevens Building's brick, limestone, and granite rusticated pilasters. The building's arches and oriel windows with their curved glass panes overlooked East Commerce Street. A little farther down Commerce, there was more to arouse a young architect-to-be's curiosity: the horseshoe-shaped, Syrian arches of the big ground-floor window, the triplet windows above, the polished-granite Moorish columns of the entrance porch, and the little turbaned limestone tower that perched precariously on one corner of the Cyrus Eidlitz First National Bank. Ayres was also fortunate to be able to see St. Mark's Episcopal Church of 1875, which had been designed by Richard Upjohn of New York, one of the most prominent church architects of the nineteenth century.

There was the residential district along King William Street, lined with the mansions that wealthy Germans had built after the annexation of Texas to the United States in 1846. The neighborhood south of the old center of the city dated back to the 1860s. Earlier houses had been sensible and relatively modest one-story buildings with porches sheltering their thick stone and stucco walls. But by 1890 there was a splendid succession of suburban villas. The Wulff House of 1870 stood as a kind of gate lodge for the entrance to the street. Its tall, rough limestone body and asymmetrical Italianate tower were clearly inspired by the influential books of Andrew Jackson Downing. The fashionable Italianate style was represented by several other

houses, such as the Stevens House of 1881 and the Hummel House of 1884, both nobly dressed in Texas limestone but neither as grand as the Norton-Polk-Mathis House. Standing outside the ornamental limestone posts with a cast- and wrought-iron fence that enclosed the grounds, Ayres could have seen the imposing layercake of the three-story, pale cream tower on which a master craftsman had lavished great skill in carving the columns and pilasters, the capitals, arches, balusters, and dentils. Further along the street, the English-born architect Alfred Giles built one of his earliest houses for Edward Steves in 1875. Its curved mansard roof and lacy ironwork crest, and the fancy jigsaw work in the spandrels of the porch arches, brought the flavor of Second Empire Paris to King William Street. If Atlee had managed to get inside, he would have been able to see in the elegant fourteen-foot-high rooms the frescoed floral ceiling paintings, the mahogany and native walnut paneled wainscoting, sliding doors with cut-glass panels, elaborate cornices, and rope moldings. In 1882, Giles remodeled the Oge House of 1857, adding long, two-story columned verandahs as well as an exceptionally exotic Palladian window opening onto the upper porch. In the 1880s there were other houses whose stone walls were surrounded by porches of delicate millwork, rhythmic single and paired columns, elaborate baluster and bracket designs. By Atlee's day, new influences had appeared. James Riely Gordon built the Kalteyer House in 1892, the year Atlee was to go to New York to study architecture. Gordon, who is best known for his robust Romanesque Revival courthouses in Texas, created a powerful composition of polychromed arches, turrets and cupolas, and generous verandahs.[2]

In 1891, eleven years after arriving in San Antonio, the seventeen-year-old Atlee—having had a number of small jobs including that of draftsman in the office of B. F. Trester—was working for Mr. Cadwallader in his sign-painting shop when a visiting artist from New York, Edgar

Hamilton, suggested that Atlee go to Manhattan to study art and architecture. Atlee's parents arranged for him to go to New York City in March, 1892, to study at the Metropolitan School of Art. Because the school year did not start until fall, Atlee found employment with O. J. Gude & Co., then the largest outdoor advertisers in the world. He set to painting large billboards on housetops that would be viewed as the steam trains clattered along the elevated railways of Third and Sixth Avenues. Much later, ninety-four-year-old Ayres recalled his rooftop paintings as "large size Quakers with a package of oats, also large portraits of President Garfield advertising TEA [sic] which was supposed to relieve headaches and constipation."[3] Some years after he had graduated, Ayres was sufficiently nostalgic to commission a large photograph of the façade of the house at Eighty-third and Lexington where he had lived. He added an arrow pointing to one of the two dormer windows in the mansard roof of the sixth-floor attic and the note, "my room."

In the fall of 1892, he began his course at the Metropolitan School of Art, which was located on the ground floor of the Metropolitan Museum on Fifth Avenue at Eighty-third. The building Atlee saw was built in 1880, a freestanding pavilion in polychromed Ruskinian Gothic designed by Calvert Vaux and Jacob Mould. It had been extended to the south in 1888 and was in the process of being extended to the north from 1890 to 1894 while Ayres was studying there. The building sat rather awkwardly adrift on the edge of Frederich Law Olmsted's still raw Central Park. Although the extensions that adhered closely to the polychromy and massing of Vaux's central pavilion incorporated some classical detail, it was not until 1895 that Richard Morris Hunt's Greco-Roman addition was designed and not until its completion in 1905 did the present imposing monumental façade relate the museum to Fifth Avenue, grandly masking the old red brick building behind.[4]

At the time, the Metropolitan Museum of Art had Henry G. Marquand as president and a list of trustees that included some of the most prominent names of New York: Vanderbilt, Stuyvesant, Rhinelander, Choate, and Avery, as well as the preeminent architect Richard Morris Hunt. The purpose of the School of Art was to furnish instruction in drawing, painting, sculpture, architecture, and the industrial arts. The classes offered included (1) architectural drawing, (2) antique drawing, (3) advanced antique drawing from classical statuary and casts, (4) life drawing for women, (5) life drawing for men, (6) still life, (7) modeling, and (8) advanced painting—taught by the celebrated artist John LaFarge, whose rich paintings adorned the interior of Henry Hobson Richardson's Trinity Church in Boston, and the Quattrocento rooms of the 1888 Villard Houses in New York. In 1892, the majority of students, some eighty-two, enrolled in the classes to draw from casts of antique sculpture. Smaller numbers came to study painting from still life (twenty-one), painting from life (seventeen). In La Farge's elite advanced painting class, there were five students.

Atlee was enrolled in the class in architectural drawing, which had twenty-five students, thirteen of whom came from New York City, including George W. Kelham, who was to play a part later in Ayres's effort to acquire architectural registration in California in the 1920s. There were also three fellow Texans: two from San Antonio and one from Galveston. Atlee was proud enough of his Lone Star roots to label his copy of the school's prospectus "A. B. Ayres (The Man from Texas)." The prospectus stated: "It is the object of the class to give training in Architectural Draughtsmanship, so as to fit students either to enter offices as draughtsmen or to pursue to advantage more advanced studies in architecture or in the decorative arts." Atlee's teachers were George Bartholomew and Seth J. Temple. Bartholomew had been a pupil of Arthur Lyman Tuckerman, who, in addition to being manager of the Schools of the Metropolitan Museum, had

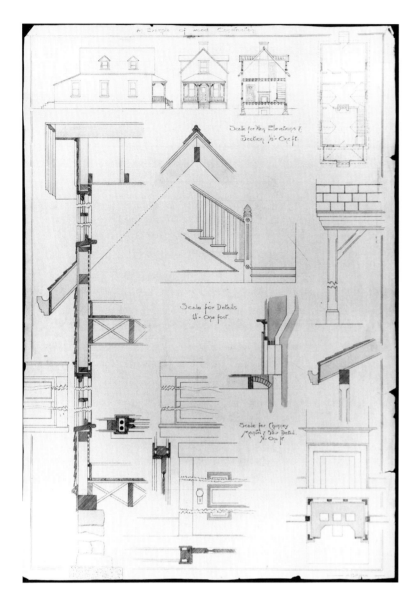

Fig. 2. Study of wood construction, 1892 student drawing by Atlee B. Ayres. The Alexander Architectural Archive, UT–Austin

dormer with a sculptured figure rendered in flat washes, india-ink washes, and a rendered elevation of an interior color study; eight plates of projections: points, lines, and surfaces, solids, cubes, pyramids, ellipses, and cones, intersections of solids and hollow cubes and spires; fourteen plates of shades and shadows; and twelve plates of elements of architecture, including the Tuscan, Roman Doric, Ionic, Corinthian, and Composite classical orders, moldings and cornices, pedestals and pediments. There was also a heavy dose of freehand drawings: forty plates, many from casts and plates of architectural form and ornament, as well as classical figures, drawings showing the techniques of constructing perspectives of buildings and shadows; fifteen plates in design of wood and stone construction (fig. 2), designs of hospitals, gymnasia, Renaissance capitals and portico, a casino with bridges, an artist's house, an entrance to a park, and a tomb. There was also a "Problem for Prize Competition for a Small Museum," requiring plan, section, elevation, perspective, and details.[5]

Some of Atlee's schoolwork was kept in a small, 4" x 6" notebook with a round-cornered, faux-tortoiseshell cover. Within, Ayres made faint pencil drawings. The first were copied from plates of classical architectural elements—column and pedestal, parts of the entablature, and ovolo, fillet, cyma recta, waterleaf and egg and dart moldings—all copiously laden with precise numerical notations of even the smallest parts, and ratios of proportions of the Greek Doric, Ionic, Composite Corinthian, Tuscan, and Roman Doric Orders. It is striking to the early-twenty-first-century eye, so untrained to perceive sophisticated proportional relationships, so disinclined to think in terms of numerical ratios, to see Ayres's notes for a table of intercolumniations of the Doric Order, with its columns of tabulations of fractions of diameters as the basic unit of measure. This concern for proportions showed up in careful, hardline plan drawings for a wooden gymnasium, clearly based on a series of

been instructor in architectural drawing and design and lecturer on the history and principles of architecture. Temple was a graduate of Columbia College's architectural program, at that time in the School of Mines. From these men, Atlee was to receive instruction in the use of the pencil, brush, and drawing pen, in the rendering of plans and elevations, and in details of construction and ornament. As examples, the prospectus listed the drawings done in the previous year: sixteen plates of brushwork, including elevations (enlarged and colored, from Scheult's *Recueil*), a squares, like the plan of the Renaissance church Santo Spirito in Florence. His small sketch designs of classical pedimented porticos showed construction lines based on radii from the points of an equilateral triangle. Later in the notebook, there were small, two-point perspective constructions with vanishing points and outlines of simple cubic forms.[6] These are indications of a classical, disciplined design foundation, similar to that available at most schools of architecture at the time, but otherwise there is scant evidence that Atlee's two-year course provided extensive or rigorous architectural design training of the caliber of the established architecture schools such as the Massachusetts Institute of Technology. It was surely considerably removed from the strict, formal training in composition and expression received by those Americans who attended the courses of the École des Beaux-Arts in Paris, on which most American programs were modeled. Still, the resources available to Atlee were not inconsiderable. The collections in the museum were an invaluable resource. He recalled that every week the class was taken upstairs to sketch scale-size plaster models of Egyptian and Roman architecture. Once a month, Professor Ware and other Columbia instructors would come to confer with Atlee's own instructors about his work and that of his classmates, and Atlee was permitted use of the architectural library at Columbia. In addition, the class made field trips to construction sites of banks, hospitals, and other new buildings.

Atlee made many studies of artifacts and architectural details in the Metropolitan Museum, technical drawings of structure and construction, freehand sketches and building designs, elevation studies and exercises in shades and shadows. The underlying theme was the past, in particular the lineage of the Western tradition from Greece and Rome through the Renaissance, the venerable legacy of Western Europe. Atlee's drawings included a 15" x 16" full-size sketch of Greek acanthus leaves, a pale pencil study of an acroterion,

another of a marble sarcophagus with putti and garlands, masks, chariots and horses, and further studies of the classical ornaments including the cyma reversa, bead and reel, egg and dart moldings. There was a wash and pencil study of a classical Roman male nude and of a lion's head. The Italian Renaissance was represented by a barely recognizable drawing of Donatello's famous David. Was this done from a reproduction in the Metropolitan or from a plate in a book? There were architectural drawings: a plan and two sections at $\frac{3}{16}$" = 1'0" of masonry domes and arches, a complex hemispherical dome on a cylindrical drum on spherical pendentives. There was a $\frac{1}{4}$" elevation in ink of a bay in a Queen Anne façade, and a freehand pencil drawing of a neoclassical French pavilion (fig. 3). Atlee rendered the domed building, with its neoclassical portico, frieze, moldings and statues in pale washes, terracotta roof, light-blue windows, and green grass and trees. He signed a two-minute sketch "A. Bernard Ayres," which he seemed to favor in his student days, perhaps as an "artist name." In fact, the Beaux-Arts training put great emphasis on the "architect as artist," through the rigorous expectations of excellence in drawing and painting, not only as a demonstration of technical proficiency in illustration of architectural ideas but also a certificate of artistic sensibility befitting the cultivated person an architect was supposed to be. Freehand drawing and rendering were very useful, as they would prove to be for Ayres, in establishing one's reputation in society.[7]

Outside his studies at the Metropolitan School, Atlee attended evening freehand drawing classes at the Art Students League, founded in 1875, which shared with the Architectural League of New York the galleries, studios, and classrooms of a recently completed building designed by the prominent architect Henry J. Hardenberg for the American Fine Arts Society, which was founded in 1889. At the new building at 212 West Fifty-seventh Street, Atlee had access to virtually every current important exhibition of art and architecture held

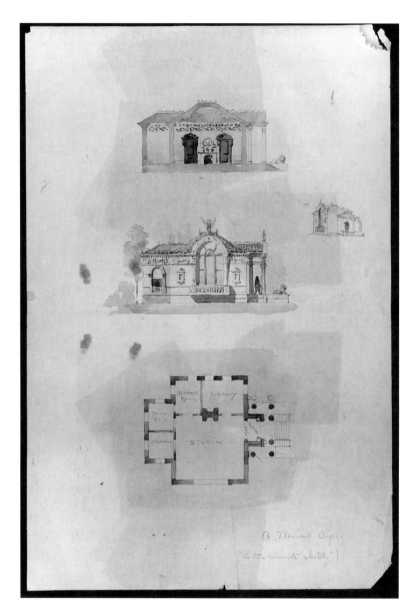

Fig. 3. Design for a pavilion, 1892, student drawing with watercolor wash, signed "A. Bernard Ayres." The Alexander Architectural Archive, UT–Austin

Atlee also took private oil-painting lessons on Sunday mornings with the painter Frank Vincent Dumont. On Sunday afternoons he often went sketching along the granite escarpments of the Hudson River and across the river to Staten Island with an illustrator friend who had studied in Paris.

Augmenting the courses of studio training, Atlee benefited from an agreement of the Metropolitan School of Art with the trustees of Columbia College, by which the pupils of the Museum School had free admission to certain lectures in the fine arts. These were given under the auspices of the college, some at the Museum, some in campus lecture rooms on Forty-ninth Street (prior to the move to the new Morningside campus then under construction). For example, in 1891, Professor Ware had given two lectures upon the transition from Ancient to Gothic architecture; Professor Hamlin, two lectures upon the Early Renaissance; and Russell Sturgis, four lectures on style in the fine arts. In the spring of 1894, Atlee attended thirteen lectures and recorded notes meticulously in a notebook that he carefully inscribed in elegant calligraphy "A Course of Lectures on the History of Ancient Ornament delivered by Seth Justin Temple to the class in Architectural Drawing at the Art Schools of the Metropolitan Museum of Art: Notes and Sketches." Ayres's copious written notes, oddly devoid of sketches, traced the development of architecture from ancient Assyria, Greece, and Rome, through Medieval and Renaissance examples, to the eighteenth century.[8]

As a student, Atlee met with some success in his course of study. He won a "First Award" of the Tuckerman Prize for his design of an "Entrance to A Museum of Natural History." At the end of his first year, in May, 1893, he was included in the school's First Annual Exhibition. The exhibition catalogue—hand-decorated with the signature "A. B. Ayres (The Man from Texas)," and by the enigmatic figure of a beak-nosed

in New York, including the annual exhibition of the Architectural League, a major event for the professional, student, and public at large. A student of architecture could learn much from the building itself, which was completed in the year Atlee arrived in New York, for it was a stately palace, its three central panels ornamented with delicate French Renaissance classical detail, important evidence of an emerging concern for academic correctness and urban grandeur. In addition to his classes at the Art Students League, instructress sternly admonishing a young lady—gave some insight into the essentially fine arts orientation of the exhibition. The students' paintings included landscapes of scenes along the Hudson, in the Berkshire and Catskill Mountains, and the beaches of Long Island. Some titles were youthfully romantic: "A Moonlight Reverie," "Idle Hours by the Sea," "Autumn Leaves," and "Pleasant Thoughts." There were several sundowns and twilights, still lifes of apples, China plates and Russian tea service, fans, and slippers. There were a few paintings of picturesque tramps, children catching frogs, a dog's head, and a small blue fish. Perhaps the most engagingly modest work was titled "A First Attempt." Atlee's own contribution was four paintings: "A Gateway," "A Pound of Grapes," and two "Sketches along South Beach." There were also architectural paintings by the students, such as a representation of the Roman Temple of Faustina and of the Egyptian Temple at Karnac. The instructors themselves lent paintings, including a study of the Tomb of Scipio Barbatus, and other more contemporary scenes such as "After the Opera."[9]

Atlee completed the full two-year course "with honor" and received his diploma on May 26, 1894. However, it would be a mistake to think that his limited formal training was his only education in New York. It was perhaps not even the major one. We may imagine the larger experience of this teenager from a remote and, by comparison, provincial, small Texas city, during his stay in what was then already the financial and cultural capital of America. Atlee arrived in a New York that was "a confused island of commercial towers, usually tricked out in classical dress, rising from a morass of utilitarian factories, shanties, warehouses, and docks."[10] When he arrived, it was a city in transition from the haphazard, unruly development of the thirty years since the Civil War in an enormous wave of expansion that created a city that—with the 1898 annexation of Brooklyn, the Bronx, Queens, and Staten Island—had 3.1 million inhabitants. When Atlee

was there, Manhattan had not yet become a city of skyscrapers, nor of the grand civic monuments that were to be erected in the early years of the twentieth century, the truly Roman scale of Carrere and Hastings's New York Public Library, built from 1897 to 1911, or of McKim, Mead and White's 1904 Pennsylvania Station, which was yet to come.

Much of Ayres's New York was a motley collection of late Victorian commercial buildings and tenements, a stylistic eclecticism, described in 1892 by an outraged Beaux-Arts graduate, A. D. F. Hamlin, as "the most horrible compositions that disfigure our streets, the most outre, barbarous, and illogical hotch-potches."[11] In the years before Ayres's arrival, influential critics like Montgomery Schuyler, a member of the editorial staff and literary critic of *The New York Times* from 1883–1907, along with Russell Sturgis—one of the lecturers at the Metropolitan School and a contributor to *Architectural Record*—had promoted the Ruskinian, moralistic, preference for Medieval structuralism and Romanesque fervor. In the twenty-five years since the Civil War, Manhattan had grown steadily north, the upper classes leading the way up Fifth Avenue, the immigrant poor crammed into the tenements of the Lower East Side. As the city growth followed the steam-powered, elevated railroads up Third and Sixth Avenues in 1878 and up the West Side Ninth Avenue in 1880, the fabric became an unruly mixture of eclectic villas, townhouses, and apartments. But the stylistic eclecticism that characterized the period from the Civil War to 1890 lacked a didactic or highly moralistic content. Instead, it was the product of a sensibility that sought the exotic and beautiful.

There were nevertheless major buildings for Atlee to see. The Metropolitan Opera House had opened in 1883 and Carnegie Hall in 1891 though both were hybrid combinations that included studios, offices, commercial space, and an apartment hotel. Stanford White's wildly exotic pleasure palace for Madison Square Garden, which had opened in 1890, was an architectural tour de force a part Northern Italian, part Spanish combination of white terra-cotta and pale buff brick, its tower evocative of the Giralda in Seville. The spires of St Patrick's Roman Catholic Cathedral, first designed by James Renwick, Jr., in 1850, were at last complete in 1888. It stood as an architectural anachronism among the flamboyantly eclectic, astylar churches of cosmopolitan New York and the extravagant synthesis of Gothic and Saracenic motifs of the Temple Emmanu-El of 1868.

By the time of Atlee's arrival, New York had already sprouted a few tall office buildings. In 1870, the peak of the Mansard roof of George Post's Equitable Life Assurance Building at 120 Broadway rose to 130 feet. In 1875, there followed his 230-foot tall Western Union Telegraph Building looking like some Hanseatic Northern European guild hall, and his vaguely Romanesque Union Trust Building in 1890. Within a year, his golden-domed Pulitzer Building's twenty-six stories laid claim to the title of "The Tallest Building in the World." In Atlee's years there, the tall building became essential to New York's image. Unlike the pragmatic expression of the Chicago utilitarian speculative office towers, New York's tall buildings were more often headquarters for national and international corporations and were thus clad in mantles of classical and European dress, especially the current, opulent, overblown classicism of Paris. These lessons were not lost on Ayres when in 1929 he came to design and install his office behind the Gothic-inspired ornament of the octagonal lantern of the Smith-Young Tower, for thirty years the tallest building in San Antonio.

In New York, Ayres was likely to have experienced in some measure the lively pageant of the street, perhaps have seen, at least from the outside, the restaurants, the theaters for light opera and burlesque, and the new hotels (the old Plaza begun in 1883 at the southeast corner of Central Park and in 1892 the twelve-story Classical Savoy and the vaguely Romanesque New

Netherland, at 234 feet, the tallest hotel in the world), the department stores with their free noontime concerts, the vast fabric of New York's surging social heterogeneity and inharmonious democracy. At one end of the scale were the exclusive private clubs, the new Metropolitan Club on Fifth Avenue, behind whose flat marble façades and splendid gate, a young architecture student might have had a glimpse of softly illuminated, richly paneled rooms or the marble stair hall that rose through the glass-topped interior court. He might have seen the impressive brand-new Roman triumphal arch of the Soldiers' and Sailors' Memorial in the Grand Army Plaza in Washington Square, or watched, on the heights above the Hudson, the construction of the Valhalla of Grant's Tomb based on Napoleon's Tomb at the Invalides. If he took an interest in the 1893 competition for a new New York City Hall to replace the old 1811 two-story brownstone that clearly no longer represented the reality nor the ambitions of the city, he could have seen the entry of the celebrated firm of Cram, Wentworth, and Goodhue, which was an eclectic synthesis of Wren, English Baroque, and fourteenth-century Siena. He may have seen the schemes for the new campus of Columbia College on Morningside Heights on the upper West Side. In 1892, in Atlee's first year in New York, the trustees had invited several architectural firms to lay out the new campus, including Richard Morris Hunt and McKim, Mead and White. Later, William Ware and Frederich Law Olmsted were asked to meld a new plan and McKim was hired in December, 1893. Construction went on until 1914, with the Avery Hall of the School of Architecture being inaugurated in 1912.

Atlee remembered walking through the snow up Fifth Avenue to school, a novel enough event for a San Antonio boy. But he also had the opportunity to see the very epicenter of residences for the city's rich and social elite. In the 1870s, old New York society lived near Washington Square on lower Fifth Avenue, the new rich a bit further up in the Thirties, in Murray Hill, in dignified and somber townhouses. But in 1879, William Kissam Vanderbilt and his ambitious wife Alva built a stunning exception to the brownstone fronts. On the northwest corner of Fifth Avenue and Fifty-second Street, there rose a glistening chateau of Caen stone. Though redolent of the late Gothic period in France, it was undeniably an original composition, not a replica, perhaps the first example in America of informed, scholarly eclecticism, freely adapted to American ambitions. It was said that Charles Follen McKim, one of Hunt's greatest competitors, "made a habit of strolling up Fifth Avenue late at night to gaze again and again at the Vanderbilt chateau. He said he always slept better for the sight of it: having taken a look at it, he was ready to return home for another cigar before going to bed."[12]

In 1884, Louis Comfort Tiffany had Stanford White design a mansion whose golden brown brick rose above a husky Richardsonian stone basement. By 1885, the very serious brownstone façades of the Villard Houses, on Madison between Fiftieth and Fifty-first Streets, captured much of the character of the Renaissance Roman Palazzo Cancelleria. The boom up Fifth Avenue overlooking Central Park began in 1890, the grandest houses occupying the corners of the blocks or, like the Frick Mansion, the whole frontage. The two miles of millionaires' houses evoked many historical associations through a variety of eclectic styles: Richard Morris Hunt's "chateaux style" for the Astors; McKim, Mead and White's Italian palazzi and red brick and limestone Anglo-American "Georgian" in successive years. Carrere and Hastings built the 1892 Richardsonian Hoe House on East Seventy-first; in 1893, the Herter House on Madison in a Regency style; and, in 1893–94, the H. T. Sloane House in a modern French style of inflated classicism with its exuberant columns, garlands, and cartouches. The trend toward an elaborate Beaux-Arts Baroque culminated in Montana Senator William A. Clark's ornate mansion at Fifth and Seventy-seventh Street, at $5 million. It was reputed to be the most expensive house in the United States in 1907.

In addition to the opulent houses of Fifth Avenue, there were the apartment houses, which, as in the great European cities, were the preferred residences of those who were neither poor enough to be crowded into tenements nor rich enough to have a detached or semidetached house. Some apartment houses were amply grand. The vast bulk of the Dakota Apartments on Central Park West loomed over the snowy landscape and skaters on the pond. The great broad pile of tawny brick trimmed in stone stood sentinel at Seventy-second Street, the only grade-level vehicular crossing through Central Park, a symbolic gateway to the West Side. The palatial building was surrounded by dry moats and iron railings. Its interior arrival court and fountain could be glimpsed through a majestic gate. By Atlee's time, in 1893, more than one million New Yorkers—seventy percent of the population—lived in multiple-family dwellings, four-fifths of which were tenements, commonly of a plan that admitted little light and ventilation. Still to come in 1918 were the ornate Ansonia and Alwyn Court, decked out in the latest Parisian fashion, and the studio apartments of the Hotel des Artists with its great two-story, north-facing windows.

If Atlee ventured further afield, across the Brooklyn Bridge to the seashore, there were Coney Island, which had been developing since 1875; the Hotel Brighton, built in 1875; the Manhattan Beach Hotel, built in 1877; and low, rambling buildings with asymmetrically placed mansard roofed towers, awnings, and long, deep porches for the breezes and promenades. It was a place for outings to the amusement shows, rude taverns, beer gardens, and bathing establishments of the eastern end of the island. Outside Manhattan lay the developing suburbs. As early as 1853, A. J. Davis had designed the English style Llewellyn Park in New Jersey. In 1878, McKim, Mead and White were commissioned to design a model home for the Short Hills Park Development. In 1892, Lawrence Park was opened north of the city in Bronxville, and Vandiver Park, in Flatbush. The latter was to be a wage-earners community of inexpensive wood-frame houses, with narrow gabled fronts and porches overlooking a small front yard. One had to go to Long Island, to Roslyn and Wheatley Hills, or into Westchester Country, to Hyde Park, to see the country houses of the rich, or to Newport, Rhode Island, where they were erecting their so-called summer "cottages" along the cliffs above the Atlantic. From the ocean walk, one could have seen The Breakers under construction, the monumental Italian Renaissance summer palace of Cornelius Vanderbilt, which was finished in 1895.[13]

Well, what of this Atlee actually saw in passing, or stopped and studied, or absorbed is not recorded. We do not know if or how he explored the city and its surroundings, nor how he traveled there from San Antonio—most likely by train via St. Louis. It is strange that there is no evidence of his visiting or even being concerned with the major architectural event of 1893, the World's Columbian Exhibition in Chicago, exactly in the middle of his years in New York. The exhibition had been the triumph of the East Coast establishment architects, whose eclectic work in New York was all around Ayres. Nevertheless, the eclectic sensibility to which Atlee had been first exposed as a student in New York permeated his own work through much of his practice. His continuing affection for New York showed when much later he wrote to his old teacher Mr. Bartholomew, "I will never feel entirely satisfied until I move back to New York. I dream of living there constantly,"[14] this, twenty-six years after graduation and after twenty-two years of successful practice in San Antonio.

After graduation in 1892, Atlee returned to San Antonio. Little is known about the four years of his professional apprenticeship there, nor about the year that he worked in Mexico City. In 1898, Ayres and C. A. Coughlin opened their office in San Antonio.

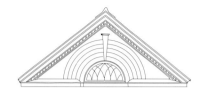

CHAPTER 3

Foreign Travels

England and Western Europe, 1911;

Around the World, 1914;

Spain and Italy, 1921 and 1928;

Mexico, 1924

By 1911, Atlee had not traveled outside the United States except for the year and one half he spent in Mexico City shortly after his graduation from the Metropolitan School in New York in 1894. From the time he opened his office in 1898, the practice had flourished in San Antonio's boom years of the first decade of the century. In those years, although Atlee was a very successful young architect, designing large houses, mainly in the currently fashionable Colonial Revival style, he lacked the sort of artistic range and polish that personal acquaintance with the great buildings of the world—Western Europe in particular—could provide for those who had experienced them first hand. Many of those who had studied at the École des Beaux-Arts, and others who had gone on the Grand Tour of Europe, had the opportunity to develop their

sensibilities, and to stock their warehouses of architectural images. That experience could lend scholarly authenticity and sophistication to their designs as well as authority to their professional and personal reputations. It was a time when the most reputable architects were those who could provide an increasingly knowledgeable and demanding clientele with buildings that demonstrated a convincing connection to the great buildings of the past, buildings that demonstrated an informed and educated eclecticism. It behooved Atlee—in order to go beyond his present level of artistic development and professional skill, and to enhance his reputation—to travel abroad, especially to Western Europe, to the cradle of Classical and Renaissance architecture, to experience what was then believed to be the principal source of great architecture. What he lacked in formal education, he could make up in first-hand experience.

In 1911, Atlee, at age thirty-seven, having accomplished thirteen years of successful and lucrative practice, planned his first trip abroad, for himself, his wife Olive, and his two young sons, Robert and Atlee, Jr. Their itinerary was gluttonous, at breakneck pace, which, for a first-time experience, was understandable and arguably the best. The itinerary included the following: Gibraltar, Genoa, Turin, Lake Como, Bellagio, Venice, Florence, Pisa, Rome, Naples, Pompeii, Sorrento, Capri, Amalfi, La Cava, Brindisi, Corfu, Athens, Constantinople, Constanza, Bucharest, Buda-Pest, Vienna, Prague, Dresden, Berlin, Potsdam, Amsterdam, Cologne, Heidelberg, Lucerne, Interlaken, Lausanne, Paris, Le Harve, Southampton, London, Lemmington, Kennelworth, Warwick, Stratford, Birmingham, Manchester, Glasgow, Quebec, Montreal, and Montreux.[1] Oddly enough, the houses that Ayres designed in the three years from the time of this first European trip to 1914 when the Ayreses went on a much longer trip around the world, seemed little influenced by his exposure to the great architecture of the past. Instead, the John Kuntz House of 1913 in Monte Vista reflected more an interest in the very American Prairie style that was emanating from the Midwest in the houses of Frank Lloyd Wright, Walter Burley Griffen, and others. One of Ayres's houses was described in the local newspaper as a "Specimen of Frank Lloyd Wright architecture—Drawn in offices of Atlee B. Ayres, Architect."[2] Ayres's 1914 Robert N. Martindale House on West Kings Highway was another departure from his earlier Colonial Revival houses—more open to the outside through asymmetrically placed openings and porches, resembling a little, the large suburban houses of the English architect Norman Shaw and other freestyle Tudoresque houses in vogue in England. It was however not truly pedigreed academic eclecticism, and by comparison with the work being done by leading East Coast firms

like McKim, Mead and White, rather awkward.

In January, 1914, at age forty, Atlee set off on his second trip abroad, around the world via Europe and Asia. The 3" x 5" brown hardcover books provided by Thomas Cook & Son outlined an ambitious tour of nearly six months that was to take Atlee and his family to ten countries around the world. Sailing from New York, Atlee, his wife, and teenage sons, arrived at Cherbourg on January 26, and spent the night at the Hotel Regina. They left the next day across the wintry landscape in their sleeping car, across the Alps to Genoa and down the coast past Rome to Naples, where they were to board a ship for Egypt. Arriving in Alexandria, which Atlee found to have no architectural interest, they went on to Cairo to continue their eight days in Egypt. From the train Atlee observed the "little villages constructed of mud and bamboo walls and gross thatched roofs surrounded by tall waving cocoanut palms." As they approached Cairo, he noted the "many minerettes [sic] and glazed domes of the mosques." The train station was something of a shock, as he saw "No regard for the architectural beauty of the interior at all," the walls completely covered with posters. In Cairo, their schedule included the Pyramid of Giza, the Sphinx, the tombs of the Caliphs, and the palaces, mosques, gates, and bazaars. Thomas Cook arranged for donkeys for the visits to the pyramids and for a private dragoman and carriage that bore them to lunch at the fabled Mena House Hotel. In his fifteen pages of typewritten notes, Atlee recorded the size of the 38" x 7' masonry blocks of the pyramid, the guide's athletic demonstration of the proper way to ascend the pyramid, and his own disappointment with the unexpected smallness of the Sphinx. He also described the bazaar's dusky, teeming, narrow streets overhung with latticed windows and thronged with natives in bright-colored costumes, with red fez, and pink and orange turbans. He found the buildings in the business and European sections "mostly modern and well-appearing, though none of them are fireproof." While he admired the hotel staff's becoming uniforms of dark blue coats and trousers, and large red sash with the name of the hotel over one shoulder, Atlee, like most western tourists, was unaccustomed to and offended by the omnipresent beggars whom he described as "like a lot of hungry coyotes." He also found that "The Egyptians are quite cunning in the manufacture of antiquities." The authenticity of their scarabs was not to be trusted. From Cairo, they took the sleeper train up the Nile to see "numerous tombs, temples, etc. all of which are interesting beyond description." At Luxor, Atlee wrote more about the bothersome flies and the persistent begging for tips, "bakshsesh" than about the temples themselves. He also seemed moved by the widespread afflictions of the eyes of the natives.

The Ayreses embarked for the Far East on February 10. Arriving in Ceylon, they began an eight-day itinerary, arranged by the local Thomas Cook & Son, who were officed in the Victoria Arcade in Colombo's York Street. They set off by carriage and train to the Moon Plains, the Hakgalla Gardens, and to Katugastota, "where the Temple elephants may be seen bathing at about 5 P.M." The helpful, solicitous travel agent also advised them that "The Temple of the Tooth facing the Kandy Lake is next door to the Hotel, and it is suggested that the Temple be visited at about 6:30 P.M. on this day." Of course, the Ayreses' days were also carefully designed around the proper British times for lunch and afternoon tea. The lush landscape of Ceylon dazzled Atlee, and he recorded detailed observations of the tea and rubber plantations and the processing of the tea leaves. He also wrote detailed descriptions of the people and their dress. He marveled at the rickshaw drivers' stamina to run in the scorching sun.

India was a different matter. The Ayreses next went to Bombay by ship whose stifling hold was packed with bodies fleeing the plague. The Ayreses spent over a month in northern India,

first Delhi, then to Agra to see the shimmering Taj Mahal (fig. 4). By March 10, they were in Jaipur, where it was arranged for them to go by carriage to the foot of Amber Hill, thence by elephant. After lunch there was to be the drive to the maharaja's palace, the Jeysingh's Observatory, and the museum. After the lush greenness of Ceylon, the desiccated and deserted city of Fatehpur Sikri and northern India surprised and disappointed Atlee by their dry barrenness, which reminded him of parts of Texas. They went east to the holy city of Benares to drift in a boat past the bathing ghats along the sacred Ganges, and later, to visit the temples, bazaar, and the palace of H. H., the maharajah of Benares, across the river. On March 25, they were scheduled for an excursion by pony or dandy to Darjeeling's Observation Hill. With his eye for intricate detail, Atlee described the "dandy" as "a queer riding affair which is constructed of four bamboo poles, two of which are about twelve feet long, and are spliced together about two feet apart by two shorter sticks of bamboo. In the middle of this bamboo frame a rectangular open top canvass covered box is placed." He went on at length to describe the interior of the box and the method of being carried. Atlee's impressions were ambivalent. On the one hand he noted with curiosity the men's colored beards, in his words, "luxuriant growth of whiskers dyed bright red, orange, sometimes green or violet," but he thought that their custom of coating their hair and bodies with coconut oil "made them look like greased pigs." He noticed the beautiful robes and jewelry of Indian women yet found that the yellow paint on their face and arms presented "a horrible effect." He admired the smart uniforms of the native police and their deferential attitude toward those who might be taken for British. In fact Atlee admired most things British: the wide, well-paved roads whose construction of crushed hard stone and asphalt he described in detail; the British and American automobiles; the railroads; the British public works, gardens, and fountains;

Fig. 4. Photograph of Atlee's family at the Taj Mahal in India, taken during their world trip in 1914. The Alexander Architectural Archive, UT–Austin

Fig. 4. Photograph of Atlee's family at the Taj Mahal in India, taken during their world trip in 1914. The Alexander Architectural Archive, UT–Austin

houses and private clubs; and their smart white drill suits, white duck shoes, and white sun helmets. But it is striking that he wrote little about the actual buildings in India, nor about those anywhere in his travels. He depended mainly on photographs he took and those he acquired from other commercial sources. With these he provisioned himself with a graphic "library" of architectural elements that he could draw on for inspiration and example in designing his own buildings. When the Ayreses eventually sailed for home from Yokohama, he listed twenty-six films and thirty prints.

Their days in India ended in Calcutta, where they were happy to leave India and set sail for a week in Burma, to see Rangoon's golden-topped pagodas, beautiful parks and drives, and elephants working in the lumber yards. Their original schedule had included Shanghai, Nanking, Peking, and Canton, but their actual stay in China was short and the pace brisk: three and one half days in Hong Kong, three and one half days in Canton, and three and one half days in Macao,

before they sailed from Shanghai for Nagasaki, Japan, which was to be their last country before returning to America. They stayed at the elegant Kyoto Hotel in the Eastern Hills, explored the venerable temples and gardens of Japan's old capitol and made excursions to Nara, Lake Biwa, and the Hodzu Rapids. On their way north, they stopped at the Fujiya Hotel, which sat at the head of Lake Hakone with snow-capped Mount Fuji floating in the sky. Early summer in the surrounding mountains was to be explored by electric cable car and rickshaws. Lastly, they went on to Tokyo, staying in the old Imperial Hotel. (Frank Lloyd Wright was yet to build the new Imperial Hotel in 1922.) As most tourists, they made the excursion north to the gaudy shrines at Nikko, and the giant Buddha at Kamakura.

The Ayreses sailed from Yokohama on June 18 and arrived in San Francisco on July 4. Before they sailed, while waiting at the Oriental Palace, Atlee enumerated their luggage, which consisted of twelve pieces: black wood chest, canvass-covered wicker trunk, white pine chest, two steamer trunks, four white pine cases, one roll of spears, one roll of bedding, and one roll-drum. They took to the hotel one camera, two suitcases, one wicker grip, one bow and arrow. There were also vases, watercolors, and a bronze. The baggage insurance was stamped boldly with "not including war risks," a sign of 1914, a nervous calm before the storm of war?

Sales receipts show that the Ayreses had made many purchases along the way. In Hong Kong there were tablecloths, tea cloths, and napkins; at the Kyoto Hotel, Satsuma ware vases, one fat vase and a pair of blue vases, bamboo trays, lamps, a red silk lamp shade, and one "blue fat figure." They bought shirts in Yokohama. Before they sailed, Atlee had written to an agent in Hong Kong for two chow dogs to be sent to Japan to accompany them on the ship to the United States. This proved to be impossible. Atlee made a careful accounting of expenses in neat columns—noting the number of days, names of stops, tips-guides, tips-hotels, tips-sightseeing, and incidentals. The whole trip cost $9,100, a sizable sum in 1914.[3]

Six years later, in January, 1920, Ayres again began writing the travel agencies, Thomas Cook & Son and Raymond Whitcomb, regarding travel in Europe. In the spring of 1921, Atlee, by then age forty-seven, and his wife sailed from Galveston to Gijon, Spain. They had planned two months in Spain, and another month in Southern France and Italy, before returning via Paris from Southampton to New York, a total of eighty-nine days and more than four thousand miles mainly by car. The trip eventually cost him nearly $8,000. Before going Atlee had written the distinguished architect Guy Lowell of Boston and New York, a serious scholar and author of books on Italy, to express his intention of writing a book on Italian rural buildings and to seek Lowell's advice. Lowell replied that his own second book had required fourteen months of almost constant travel by chauffeured automobile over large distances in Italy. He warned Atlee:

The Italian farmhouses and villas are not like New England farmhouses, visible from the road. You must hunt them out carefully just the way one searches for any antiquity. When you leave the highroad because a clump of trees, a garden wall or a red roof in the distance suggests something of interest, it is only one out of ten times possible that you are rewarded by finding something to picture. The best advice I can give is read, read, read, before you start out on the road, and after you get back. I am not making out a bibliography for you because it would entail a good deal of trouble and would only be worth doing in case you had serious intentions of following it through and had more than idle curiosity in such a list of books.

Lowell apparently saw Ayres as a casual, hastily prepared, and perhaps not really serious scholar. However, with patrician politeness, Lowell did recommend several itineraries to Atlee: an "A" List (the Roman Compagna, the Castelli Romani, northern Tuscany, especially around Florence and as far west as Lucca and Venetia, as far east as the Piave, as far north as the mountains, as far west as Vicenza), the "B" List (southern Tuscany and Siena, the various north Italian lakes, the bays of Naples and Sorrento), and the "C" List (Piedmont and Lombardy, the Ligurian coast, and eastern Sicily). Thus, in rather acerbic and lofty Brahmin tones, Lowell warned Ayres that finding fine examples of rural architecture was a difficult and time-consuming endeavor.

The Ayreses' itinerary made a circuit in southern Spain from Leon, via Salamanca, Seville, Cordoba, Ronda, and Granada to Madrid, thence north to Toledo, Avila, Segovia, Burgos, Zaragoza and Barcelona. From Spain they were to travel along the south coast of France, to Carcassonne, to Nice, and on to Italy from Genoa down to Pisa, Florence, Rome and back up to Perugia, Bologna, and Milan. Their list of buildings to be seen suggested an exhausting trip. It included some seventy "Small Italian Villas and Farm-houses," and nearly fifty villas, some very grand, and a few palaces. In the Veneto, the list included Andrea Palladio's Villa at Fratta, the Villa Emo, the Villa Porto, a villa near Schio and one near Rovigo, and the house at Cricoli, Andrea Palladio's first design, as well as villas by others at Quinto, Montecchio Precalcino, Breganze, and Asolo. Properties nearer Rome included the parterre, the house, lagoon, and view of the upper terrace of the Villa Lante near Viterbo and in Rome itself, the Villa di Papa Giulio, the Villa Madama, and the Villa Borghese. The country villas in the hills outside Rome, the great Villa d'Este at Tivoli, and the Villas Falconieri and Aldobrandini in the southern hills at Frascati were included, as well as those overlooking Florence, the Villa Gamberaia at Settignano, the Villa Medici, the Royal Villa at Poggia a Caiano, and the Villas Campi, Castello, Bondi, Salviati, Petraia among others. A few items of rural architecture, a Tuscan farm at Fiesole, a farmhouse east of Verona, the loggia of the Farm of the Convent at San Domenico, a farmhouse south of Bologna are included in an otherwise villa-studded list that does not seem to reflect Atlee's stated interest in Italian farm buildings. An entrance ticket confirms their visit to the Certosa of Pavia near Milan.

Although Atlee's travels gave him valuable first-hand experience of Italian architecture, he purchased many photographs from venerable commercial archives such as those of Alinari and Salviati in Florence. He assembled the black and white photographs in three large albums. The first titled "Italian: Doorways and Wrot [sic] Iron" contained thirty-three large Alinari photographic prints of Italian doorways from the eleventh to the sixteenth century. These Gothic and Renaissance examples came from diverse regions of Italy. There were Sicilian Moorish examples, an eleventh-century doorway from Bivona and a sixteenth-century marble entrance to a sacristy in Palermo. Rome was represented by the six-

teenth-century Palazzo Cancelleria, the early Christian church of S. Maria Sopra Minerva, and the delicate lacings of the pilasters on the tenth-century Church of S. Elia. From Florence, there were the fourteenth-century inlaid wood doors of S. Croce, the soft grey "pietra serena" stone of the Badia, and the Palazzo Vecchio. The large, glossy, precise photographs showed the sixteenth-century Palazzo Schifanoia in Ferrara, the bronze doors of the cathedral in Pisa, and the delicate, marble-trimmed pointed transoms and quatre-foil windows of a mellow brick gothic house in Venice. Of great use to Atlee were the photographs of architectural elements (columns, capitals, entablatures, pediments, pilasters, and moldings), decorative motifs (chevrons, barleytwists, corded ropes, acanthus, anthemion, coats of arms, friezes of garlands, cherubs, winged seraphim, and paneled, nail-studded doors with delicate intarsia patterns or carved medallions). In addition to the photographs of doorways, the album had eighteen plates of examples of wrought iron, intricate fourteenth-century chancel screens from Orvieto Cathedral, and examples of domestic ironwork for fifteenth-century Turin firedogs and a seventeenth-century Sicilian bedstead.

A second album, also marked "Italian," contained mainly plates of interiors of Italian Gothic and Renaissance palaces and villas. Within its pages were views of the heavy, wood-beamed and purlined ceiling and brackets of the fourteenth-century Palazzo Davanzati, its tile floors burnished like old leather, walls painted with geometric patterns, and robust, elaborately carved furniture. Also depicted were Savanorola chairs, canopied beds with silk hangings, painted chests, and monastic refectory tables, wrought-iron candleholders, and chimneybreasts alive with garlands and dancing cherubs. There were the palatial Renaissance interiors of the Palazzo Reale del Quirinale in Rome, the neoclassical Villa Reale della Petraia, and rooms of tapestries and elaborate friezes from the Vatican. Rossellino's fireplace in the Palazzo Picolomini was surrounded with pilaster chains of flowers and urns. In the Villa Poggio a Caiano near Florence, the frescoed walls were alive with portraits of contemporaries. In the dining room, frescoed, naked children played in the vines of a delicate arbor. The album included some of the major innovative churches of the Renaissance: the centralized San Biagio at Montepulciano and S. Maria della Consolazione at Todi. Some of the photographs seem to have been chosen because of some interesting architectural detail—a corner of a Gothic house in Venice chosen for its elegant, pointed, lobed windows lined with twisted marble ropes and alternating dentils, or its plain, planked, folding shutters, or the way the corner was lined with a thin cord of marble against the brick walls. Perhaps it was the way the exterior chimneys were corbelled above the canals. Was it the gently sloping tile roof, the exuberant tile-capped chimneys, the picturesque massing of the farm buildings in their dusty yards? Whatever it was, something caught Atlee's eye, something suggestive for his own work, something visual, suggesting the interest of a designer rather than a scholar.

A third album collection of Alinari photographs, titled "European," focused on Italian churches, from early Byzantine examples in Ravenna and Islamic examples in Ravello and Salerno, to the late medieval church of San Miniato and Renaissance church of Sto. Spirito in Florence. There were architectural details for heavy coffered ceilings, iron balcony railings, and pierced marble screens. A fourth album, misleadingly labeled "Spanish," contained more purchased photographs of Italian details.

Of what use could these handsomely detailed photographic images have been to Ayres, to a practicing early-twentieth-century architect? One typical example in his Italian collection was the Alinari print dated 1921 Firenze, titled "Casa dell'Opera del Battistero. La Porta con la statuetta d. S. Giovanni." It showed a dignified doorway, classically proportioned, a chaste frame with a simple entablature surmounted by a semicircular transom containing a small statue of the child St. George by the noted sculptor Rossellino and flanked by eagles. The door frame consisted only of shallow stepped bands of flat or slightly curved moldings; the transom, a series of narrow bands of egg and dart beads, and leaf moldings. The door itself had eight carved circular medallions and 1,028 nail heads arranged in regular grids. A small part of the large door opened for everyday access. The photograph could be particularly useful because there was a metric meter scale standing against the door from which one could know the actual size of the door and its architectural elements. The door was 1.755 meters (approximately 5'6") wide and 3.50 meters (approximately 10'6") high; the whole doorway was 2.50 meters (approximately 8'2") wide and 5.50 meters (nearly 18') high to the top of the semicircular transom. The nobility and presence of this doorway depended to a great extent on its size, its grand scale, its proportions, the simplicity and elegance of its handcrafted stone details and sculpture that adorned it.

What connection could that door have had to a moderately large and expensive house in San Antonio in 1921? Certainly, its scale would have been inappropriate to even a rather grand house, dwarfing not only the people who used it but also setting a standard of size impossible to match with the other elements of the house—the floor heights, the windows, the other doors. Even if the budget were very high, it would have been very difficult to have the doorway executed in stone or with the same degree of craft. But, it could have inspired some of Atlee's houses in the Italian Renaissance style, such as the D. J. Straus House of 1923, which—with its semicircular arch and decorated transom—resembled, at a much smaller scale, many Italian doorways. The flanking wrought-iron lanterns bore a striking resemblance to the lantern of the Palazzo Boccella, gia Conti, in Ayres's Alinari print P.I.N. 8319. The graceful arches of the loggia of Ayres's Rigsby house were distant echoes of early Renaissance Florentine arcades.[4]

In 1924, Atlee planned to go to Italy again, for two to three months, with a car and translator, to photograph Italian farm buildings for a book he hoped to publish. As it transpired, he changed course and went instead to Mexico for five weeks with a fellow architect, George Willis. They went there specifically to collect photographic material for a book on the colonial and vernacular architecture of Mexico (fig. 5). In April, 1924, they arrived for a week in Mexico City; thence they drove north to the picturesque towns of Queretero, Morelia, Aguascalientes, and San Luis Potosi, and lastly to Saltillo south of Monterrey. They were hampered, indeed thwarted, in their intentions to take photographs during the spring rainy season when dependable afternoon showers limited their time for taking photographs to the mornings. The rains made it necessary for Atlee to depend on photographs taken by others. For many afternoon views shown in his book, Atlee turned to professional photographers. Although he found that "none of these towns we stopped at outside of Queretero and Morelia were worth wasting time on as far as securing architectural pictures were concerned" and that few towns "had anything of architectural importance and it was really very tiresome to have to stop over in these places." Atlee still needed photographs for his book, so he asked John Mullins, a professional photographer in Mexico City, to get details and close-up views of columns and ornamentation on a church at Tepozotlan, as well as shots of specific details of the windows and doors of the Iturbide Hotel and the gate of the churchyard across from Sanborn's in Mexico City. Atlee marked these with a red outline or cross mark on postcards and photographs. Later, he solicited additional photographs from the chamber of commerce in Chihuahua. He specifically wanted close-up detail pictures in a glossy finish showing the ornamentation of early Spanish architecture. He pointedly wanted "no modern."

That same month, Ayres bought a 5" x 7" photograph of the Cathedral of Puebla from "'La Rochester' Avenido 16 September, Mexico, D.F." In September, 1925, Atlee again wrote Mullins wanting lighter prints of eleven shots, which he specified by number. Finally in October he wrote Mullins—by then at Calpini, Apartardo 703, Mexico, D.F.—to thank him and request a bill.[5]

Earlier in the summer of 1925, Atlee wrote a series of enquiries regarding publishing a book on Spanish Colonial architecture to several companies in New York. These included the Architectural Book Publishing Co., Charles Scribners Sons, Brentano's, Doubleday Page & Company, and William Helburn, Inc., the last of which published, in 1926, Atlee's book on Mexico under the title of *Mexican Architecture, Domestic, Civil and Ecclesiastical*. Although the title page indicated photographs and text by Atlee B. Ayres, his introduction gave credit to other photographers as well. Alas, by March, 1927, Ayres's book had sold only 240 copies and there ensued a war of letters as Atlee and Helburn tried to come to financial terms. At Atlee's suggestion, Helburn agreed to pay $500 plus royalties, but by September Atlee had still not been paid. The outcome remains a mystery.[6]

Atlee's disappointing experience with his Mexico book was not enough to discourage him from planning another in 1928 on the vernacular buildings of Spain. At that time, his interest in Spanish architecture was in full flood, and his residential practice entirely dominated by Spanish style. In fact, his major house in Spanish style, the Atkinson-McNay House, was under construction. As early as April, 1927, he had written to an acquaintance in New England that he was contemplating a trip to Spain with a view of publishing a book like his previous one on Mexican architecture. In February of the next year, preparing for a trip to Spain, he solicited from the executive secretary of the American Institute of Architects in Washington formal letters of introduction to important people in Spain. He

Fig. 5. A patio in Mexico, from Atlee's trip in 1924. The Alexander Architectural Archive, UT–Austin

advised the secretary that he was going to Spain "to secure photographs of the Rural type of Spanish architecture for the purpose of publishing a book on same."[7] The transition of Ayres's interest to rural, vernacular buildings—rather than the important civic and religious buildings of more formal Renaissance and Baroque styles—suggests a shrewd, practical accommodation to the practical limits of American residential building of the time.

In April of 1928, the Ayreses sailed on the North German Lloyd Steamship Line via Havana and the Canary Islands to Cadiz, southern Spain. They traveled, as always, first class, taking their car with them on board ship. This trip was planned for forty-five days in Spain, thence along the French Riviera for twelve days in Italy, six days in Switzerland, nine each in France and England. Again the weather hampered their plans, the rain in Spain making the muddy country roads impassable and photography troublesome. Atlee also found it difficult to get close enough to his subjects. Consequently, in May, 1929, he wrote two companies to enquire about a telephoto attachment or new lens. He described his present equipment as "a Carl Zeiss protar lens VII F.35 C. M. Mounted in a compur shutter. I use this lens in connection with a 5 x 7 view camera for architectural subjects." At the same time in a letter to Bausch and Lomb Optical in Rochester, New York, he wrote: "Have a Revolving back 4 x 5 Grafton camera with a Protar VII lens with 16 5/16 focus."[8] Atlee returned from Spain with only two to three hundred negatives and immediately planned a similar trip in early 1931, which he did not make. However, of the photographs he did take, the great majority, sixty-two, are exterior views of farmhouses, low sprawling collections of long tile roofs, gleaming white walls, dusty yards and trellises of crooked tree limbs heavy with vines. Some are big, two- and three-story farmhouses with arcaded ground floors for the animals and deep, columned porches shading the living quarters

above. Ayres's eye was caught by several round castellated stone towers, remnants perhaps of an earlier fortified age. He also photographed eleven façades of village town houses and seventeen exteriors of country churches. While most of his shots were from sufficient distance to capture the whole ensemble, a few were taken closer to focus on exterior detail—a pierced tile grille, an elaborated doorway, a fountain. None of the photographs were labeled, nor accompanied by any commentary, scholarly or otherwise. In fact, they seem to be the sort of thing that were taken not principally as scholarly research but rather to serve a practicing eclectic architect for inspiration. The photographs, shot entirely from outside, concentrated on massing, proportions, color and light—pictorial appearances in short. Few of the photographs seemed to be seeking information about materials, structure, or construction, nor about the buildings' relationship to the climate, nor how they were used or inhabited. As the frame of the photographs did not extend much beyond the buildings, it would seem that Atlee was little concerned with the relationship of the buildings to their surroundings or the larger landscape.[9]

Perhaps as a substitute for the photographs that he failed to make for himself, partly because the weather had been singularly rainy, Atlee bought a collection of 171 photographs of Spanish buildings. The collection included a few churches: one with a fancy Plateresque doorway; a tall, noble, Romanesque, stone country church; the lovely arcaded court of a church in Granada; and several parochial village churches. From viewing the collection as a whole, it becomes clear once again that Atlee was interested much less in major civic buildings, or even palaces or villas in Renaissance styles, than in the humble vernacular residential buildings, the casa particular (individual, private), the casa typica, the casa humilde (humble), the casa de vecinos (ordinary folk), the gypsy cave, and the country buildings, the casa de campo, the masia (farmhouse), and, occasionally, but rarely, the grander old casa señorial or palacio. The majority of photographs were dated 1918, 1924, and 1926, and were taken in the provinces of Gerona, Malaga, Cadiz, Salamanca, and Barcelona, in well-known towns like Ronda and many obscure and little-known villages. Of the 115 total number of photographs there were some 50 exterior views of whole façades of town buildings and farmhouses. Some of them emphasized particular details: a doorway with wide flat voussoirs arches, a handsome studded wood door, stone quoins framing windows, a Moorish curbstone of a well, corners and ironwork, gratings of wrought iron, elements essential to Spanish style. Atlee bought 17 examples of balcony railings and window grilles. Surpassing the number of exterior views, there were a greater number, nearly 65, interior views within patios, precisely the sort of places that would be difficult for Ayres to access himself and difficult to capture technically in a brief visit. The small domestic spaces were for outdoor living, casually arranged with benches, chairs, tables, stoves, charming eccentric spaces with exterior winding stairways, irregular stuccoed walls with rounded corners, spindly grape arbors and scrawny oleanders, flowers in hanging baskets and in pots attached helter-skelter over the white walls. Ayres also selected a dozen photographs of street scenes, a street of gothic houses of the fourteenth and fifteenth centuries in Gerona, two corners of plazas in Cadiz and Ronda where he got 5 photos of a typical street as well.[10]

Later, when Atlee prepared a Spanish itinerary for a friend, he suggested Anteguerra, "a very quaint little town" and Granada, where he recommended the Hotel Washington Irving as well as noting, with great understatement in the city of the fabled Alhambra, "there are a number of interesting things to see here." Seville was not to be missed as it contained an interesting lot of shops with artists' studios. "Architecturally Madrid does not contain much of interest." But in Segovia, in the tile factory in an old church, "they make a wonderful lot of tile, the best of Spain." Atlee's "A" list included Granada, Seville, Ronda, Burgos, and Toledo. Perhaps remembering his own abortive photographic expedition in 1928, he warned his friend of much rain in April.[11]

Ayres continued to travel after the financial crash of 1929, the bank failures of 1931, and the Great Depression, but it seems he did so without the focused intentions of his earlier trips to Spain and Italy. In the 1930s, academic Eclecticism was fading under the pressures of Modernism and Art Deco, which more directly reflected changing conditions of finance, construction, of servantless lifestyles, and of tastes. There was less demand for scholarly references to the European past, no matter how scrupulously correct or richly inventive. Correspondingly, it became less important for architects to travel abroad, especially those who were influenced by the radical leaders of the International style, men like Walter Gropius and Mies van der Rohe who came to America from old Europe professing to disdain history. It would be later, after World War II, that Philip Johnson would announce the obvious, that we cannot not know history.

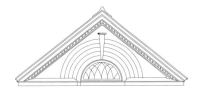

CHAPTER 4

"In Love with California"
1919, 1923, 1926, 1929

Although Atlee had made major foreign trips in 1911 and 1914, the latter around the world, it was his trip to the West Coast of the United States in 1919 that was to begin a very important—perhaps the major—influence on the evolution of his architectural beliefs and tastes, and the development of the Mediterranean, especially Spanish, style in his houses. Not only did California have a rich tradition of original Spanish building, but it was also in the early decades of the twentieth century an epicenter of new building in Spanish style.[1] In his own words, he became "crazy about the place."[2]

The affair began as early as 1919, when in writing to a former resident of San Antonio, Hugh Knight, Atlee reported that "Mrs. Ayres and I were out in California summer before last and went up to Seattle. It is a wonderful country and

I am very much taken up with it, and almost feel like moving there. My second choice is California and we would really move out there if I thought Robert would like the country." (His son Robert was then studying architecture at the University of Pennsylvania, and Ayres hoped he would join the firm, which he did in 1922.) Ayres's letter continued, "At the present time business is rather quiet on account of the unsettled labor conditions over the country. . . . Please write and tell me what you think of me coming to California."[3] Clearly a California aficionado, Knight responded with enthusiasm.

If you are contemplating taking Robert in with you and following architecture, then there is no second choice at all, Southern California is the place for you, for it is the mecca of every retired wealthy man—all the millionaires of the East come and build magnificent homes in Southern California, this is the opportunity for the real Artist-architect for they give you carte blanche and just go ahead and dream. What about Pasadena, So Pasadena, Altadena, Sierra Madre, Hollywood, Whittier, Santa Ana, Santa Monica, Newport, Laguna, San Diego, Santa Barbara, Montecito, Miramar, La Jolla, and a host of other places all through So California, nothing but palatial homes and with the new crop of millionaires made by the war there will be no end to them in the next few years. Furthermore, Los Angeles is growing faster than any other city in the United States, it already stands about sixth in population and will eventually be the Great Western metropolis, in time will even rival New Yoork [sic]. Here is the field for the architect without a doubt. . . . Come out to California, by all means, and get away from that execrable climate of Southern Texas, where when it isn't hot it is hotter, where all the vitality is sapped away and one has not sufficient energy to exist.

Knight concluded with more praises for "the finest network of concrete roads in the world, and the greatest system of interurban electric transportation in the world, and also the greatest hydro-electric power yet developed anywhere—where life can be lived to the fullest."[4]

This exuberant picture of the life and architectural possibilities of southern California seems to have planted a seed in Atlee's mind, one that grew more enticing during the decade to come. Still, it was eight months later that he wrote his former instructor, George D. Bartholomew, that he dreamed constantly of living in New York.[5]

In 1923, the Beverly Hills architect Roy Price sent Atlee photographs of the Thomas Ince Ranch, "Dias Dorados." The vast, rambling "farmhouse" for one of Hollywood's major movie moguls combined Mission style with

Andalusian touches: rustic wooden gates, pergolas with serried thick arches, grilled and latticed balconies, an octagonal dovecote. Inside, the motion picture projection room was designed to recall the deck of a galleon under sail.

In September, 1923, Atlee made his second trip to California. As he recounted to George Kelham, a classmate from the Metropolitan School of Art then practicing in San Francisco,

My trip to California made quite an impression on me as the work that is being done out there shows remarkable originality and character and with the surroundings they have, it makes your country very fascinating. To tell the truth I would like to live out there. Although we have a perfectly good home here, [a picture of which was published in Architecture in January] and a very good practice, I would be willing to give them up, if we could go out there and make a living. . . . My son, who is in business with me spent the month of August in California and after he returned my wife and I went out. Since we have been home we talk of California a great deal and my son seems to feel as we do about California, and as he is to be considered and there is more opportunity for him out there than here, I thought that I would see what the chances were for securing a license to practice architecture in your State.

Atlee went on to enlist Kelham's aid in getting registration without appearing there in person, solely on the evidence of photographs, letters from clients, and his strong resume. "If it is not asking too much, I would appreciate your helping me, old man, and if I can return the favor at any time I will be glad to do so."[6]

Part of Atlee's interest in California was as a source of some of the materials required to lend a distinctively "Spanish" style to the houses he was designing. When he was in California, he visited showrooms in search of unique tiles, both as ornament and as finish materials for floors and roofs. He also wrote many letters of enquiry to companies that produced and sold tiles. In 1924, Ayres wrote George Washington Smith, Santa Barbara's celebrated exponent of Spanish style, to introduce a San Antonio client, Mrs. Thomas B. Hogg, who was interested in tile for her new Ayres-designed house.[7] Also in 1924, he wrote Robert Rossman Company in New York, "When I was in California in September I saw some very attractive handmade tile about 8 x 8 and 12 x 12 octagon. This large handmade tile is about what my client would like to use: she would want it in a dark reddish brown or mahogany colored tile with a 4" or 6" base on walls." In this letter, Ayres also referred to a circular stairway where he intended to use slate treads with Spanish design, colored tile risers, motifs that he saw and photographed extensively when he was in California.

Atlee was in California in September, 1923. He drove around, took photographs and met Myron Hunt and Elmer Grey, both prominent practitioners in the Spanish and Mediterranean styles in Los Angeles. The itch to move to California grew stronger: "I will tell you frankly, Harry, if I could secure a license to practice architecture without having to come out there and undergo an examination, I believe I would move out to California myself, as I am very much in love with it. Life is such a short proposition that I would much rather live there with all the beautiful surroundings than here as there is no comparison with the opportunities that are around there."[8] In another letter to Mr. Tom Legan, Atlee reiterated, "I would be very glad to move out to California any time I thought we could make a go of it. That country looks wonderful to me and is just the place I would like to live, providing business conditions were all right."

But moving to California at age fifty, and starting a new office after twenty-six years of practice in San Antonio was more easily contemplated than done. Atlee expressed his complex and ambivalent feelings about a California move in a letter to Roy Seldon Price.

Since my trip to California [September, 1923] I have always had a yearning to come back there and locate. After going around and seeing the unusual type of architecture that is carried out, more especially the type of work you did on the Ince home, it certainly makes me feel that I want to get into some of it myself. I can't help but feel that the class of people that come to California are more receptive to original ideas and modes of treatment than elsewhere in the country. It requires a great deal of exertion here in San Antonio to get people to abandon the ordinary way of doing things. I am very fond of color and of trying to carry out things in an original way and I think that I could really accomplish something and make life more interesting, if I could locate there and secure some work. However, I know that there are a great number of other men in our line of work who feel the same way and who are continually coming out to California, thereby creating very keen competition among the Architects.

Atlee went on to worry about the difficulty of getting jobs, securing good fees, and reported that he understood that property values and rents had dropped materially. On the other hand, he had heard reports that rental values were still holding their own and that there was a great deal of building going on. In a rather supplicating tone for a fifty-one-year-old, successful architect, Ayres continued, "Now I realize that you are busy but I certainly would appreciate it if you could spare the time to write and let me know what you think my chances would be if I moved out there and opened an office."

Atlee went on to describe his practice and resources and his son Robert's background and association with the firm. He wrote, rather disingenuously, that Robert, like himself, was very much taken with California and had been the one to suggest that Atlee write and ask Price's advice. "Not considering myself, I feel that I should come out to California for my son's sake. …There is one thing sure we are going to have to do something as business conditions here are very discouraging."[9] At last, after persistent efforts to acquire registration without taking examinations in California, but solely on the strength of his already substantial experience in practice, Atlee received the right to practice there in 1926—California State Certificate No. 1440.

Atlee's interest in California continued. In February, 1928, he wrote to Mr. Windsor Soule in Santa Barbara. "I was in Santa Barbara summer before last. I think Santa Barbara is a wonderful section of the country and I am very much sold on California, to such an extent that I have a license to practice there." During the time that Atlee and his wife were abroad in Spain in the summer of 1928, his son Robert and family were in Santa Barbara for August. They had found a bungalow court cottage but stayed instead at the Mirimar. Atlee planned to join them after he returned from Europe. The next year in October, Atlee wrote a revealing letter to John Byers in Santa Monica that not only confirmed that he was there recently, but which also alluded to the length and depth of his attraction to California and the Spanish style.

My wife and I returned from California several weeks ago and while there spent about ten days at Santa Monica. One Saturday afternoon I don't remember the date, I drove by your office and as I found everything locked up, I put my card in the door. I was very sorry not to have met you as I am quite an admirer of your work having seen it published in the various magazines and also recognized quite a little of it in driving around out there. Your office is very unique and I want to compliment you very much on its quaint design, it certainly gives a true Spanish atmosphere.

Last summer I took a car from here and drove through Spain from one end to the other and had quite an interesting trip. I am very fond of the Spanish style and the work that is done in California is of such excellent design that I thoroughly enjoy every trip that I make out there. In fact, I fell in love with California to such an extent several years ago that I took out a license to practice Architecture out there, and intended moving there, but my son, who is in business with me did not want to leave San Antonio, so I changed my mind.[10]

Nine years after his enthusiastic reply to Atlee's initial California probe, Atlee's old friend Hugh Knight, then out of work, wrote seeking help, but in a still encouraging postscript added, "Surely you will retire and come to California and enjoy life. Why not?" However, Atlee remained in San Antonio and did not retire from practice until shortly before his death forty-one years later.

On his visits to California, Ayres photographed copiously and rather promiscuously. There still exist 945 nitrate negatives of photographs that he took on those trips.[11] Although none of the photographs were identified, a few contained clues to particular places, for instance, in the signage on buildings such as a Daly City bank, a San Clemente grocery, a Beverley Professional Building, and the Santa Barbara Seed Company. Other dating clues were a banner, presumably of 1932, for a "Roosevelt for President" Club on a building in El Encanto, and an advertisement for the Series 24 Studebaker. Street and building signs indicated that Ayres was in the southern California towns of Coronado, Hollywood, and Pasadena, and, further south to La Jolla and San Diego. For Atlee, southern California was a goldmine of the Spanish style that suffused the majority of recent buildings there in the 1920s— not only the houses but also the entire commercial and civic environment. Atlee's photographs are those of a tourist motoring through California, a mode of travel that Atlee loved. Indeed he was celebrated for his fine cars. On his 1928 trip to Spain, he took his own new Ford sedan on the ship with him. A large majority of Atlee's California photographs of houses were clearly shot from public sidewalks and streets. Taken without a telephoto lens, they were mainly views of a single house with a bit of yard; they conveyed little sense of the context of the neighborhood or the larger landscape on the one hand, nor, on the other hand, of small, close-up details. The houses ranged from sizable upper-middle-class dwellings to rather modest single-family houses and apartments. Nearly as numerous as the photographs of houses were those of the commercial buildings of a booming Southern California in love with the automobile. Atlee photographed many places related to his automobile travel: service stations with arches and decoratively patterned domes, two-story, Monterey style motels with long, second-story balconies, and drive-up commercial strips with their florist shops and photography studios, ice cream shops, and tea rooms. Most of these had stucco walls, tile roofs and parapets, round, elliptical and horseshoe arches, metal and wooden grills, balconies, graceful exterior stairs, triple-arched, star-shaped, and scalloped windows, trellises and gates, and a profusion of Moorish tiles (fig. 6). In sum, these represented a rich lexicon of the elements that made up "Spanish style." In Atlee's photographs, there were also grand movie palaces, hospitals, town halls, and towered fire stations in more elaborate Spanish Baroque Churrigueresque dress, likely inspired by Bertram Goodhue's exotic, Hispanic buildings for the 1915 Panama California International Exposition in San Diego, which had kindled the enthusiasm for Spanish style in California and which were still standing when Atlee was there.

Most of Ayres's photographs appeared to be of subjects hastily selected and taken with a casual concern for composition. Moreover, most of the buildings Atlee photographed were archi-

tecturally undistinguished, often awkward in composition, with arbitrary and often excessive ornament, sometimes flamboyantly theatrical like the "Chicken Olas Grandes Inn," but in each one there was probably something that had caught his eye, something he could use later with more discretion and taste. He seemed to be particularly attracted to round and octagonal, tile-roofed towers, which became a leitmotif of several of his major houses including the Thomas Hogg and the Atkinson-McNay Houses (fig. 7). He did photograph a few non-Spanish buildings, a few "French farmhouses" with high pitched roofs and imitation thatch, and one bizarre "Hansel and Gretel" melange of steep gables and turrets. After all, this was "Hollywood."

It is curious that Atlee's own photographs did not include the houses of well-known California contemporaries. He was acquainted in one way or another with a number of prominent California architects—Myron Hunt, Elmer Grey, Roy Seldon Price, John Byers, George Washington Smith, and Winsor Soule—all of whom worked in part in the Spanish style.

However, that Ayres was interested in the work of his contemporaries in California was evident in the large collection of magazine clippings that he had made for his office files in San Antonio, which contained a preponderance of examples of the work of California architects including Wallace Neff, Gordon Kaufman, Reginald Johnson, Roland Coate, Marston, Van Pelt & Maybury, and George Washington Smith. Of the architects whom Atlee knew or had corresponded with, he collected Roy Seldon Price's work from the February, 1930, issue of *The Architect and Engineer,* which also in January, 1930, carried the D. K. Lawyer House in Palos Verdes by John Byers. Ayres had more examples of Byers work, including a selection by Rexford Newcomb of Byers's houses in *The Western Architect* (January, 1929, issue) that featured the interiors of a living room and a dining room with beamed and coffered ceilings and sparse Spanish furniture.

Fig. 6. View of a patio in California, a photograph that Atlee took on one of his several trips between 1919 and 1929. The Alexander Architectural Archive, UT–Austin

Atlee also had a picture of a Spanish well by Byers in *California Homeowner,* (vol. 7, no. 4, March, 1929) and from the *Pacific Coast Architect* (vol. 15), which devoted a whole issue to Byers's houses. The Rexford Newcomb 1929 issue of *The Western Architect* also included houses by Reginald Johnson, Roland Coate, Myron Hunt, and Bertram Goodhue's Dater House. A collection of Southern California architects had appeared in the May, 1927, *The Architect and Engineer* (vol. 89, no. 2), from which Atlee had extracted pictures of two houses by George Washington Smith, two by John Byers, and one each by Gordon Kaufmann, Myron Hunt, and Marston, Van Pelt & Maybury. The frontispiece was the Colonel J. C. Jackling House in Woodside by George Washington Smith. Smith was celebrated for his skill in adapting Spanish, Italian, and Moorish

architecture for the houses he designed mainly in Santa Barbara and Montecito from his arrival in 1915 until his death in 1932. The simple white-walled volumes, few well-placed openings and tile roofs of his houses emanated a charm that was to bring him many clients in a city that, after the violent earthquake of 1926, was the first city in America to mandate a building style, a Hispanic one with strict aesthetic guidelines. In addition to Smith's oft-published Heberton House, Atlee found pictures of his Mrs. Willard P. Lindley House, with its curious little solid stair arching past a pointed chimney to an open loggia, deeply recessed round window and little iron lamp, which was published in *The Architectural Forum,* August, 1921, and in *The House Beautiful,* January, 1922. Smith's forecourt and fountain on the terrace of the residence of Mr. and Mrs.

Fig. 7. Front exterior of a house with round turret, one of the many photographs taken by Atlee on his several trips to southern California between 1919 and 1929. The Alexander Architectural Archive, UT–Austin

Henry Kern of Beverley Hills came from *The Architect,* August, 1928, and the gateway of the Parshall House in Montecito from the same magazine in February, 1924. It is possible that Atlee may have seen some of these houses on his 1923 and 1926 trips, during the years when his passion for Spanish style was at its height. He may have been fortunate to see one of Smith's best houses, the Steedmans' "Casa del Herrero" just finished in 1925, before it disappeared from public view in its luxuriant extensive gardens. There was much to be learned from the double arches opening from the loggia to the garden, and the series of six little arches in the porch above, lessons that could have been useful in the designing of the loggias of the Atkinson-McNay House in 1927. Moreover, Atlee could have seen many public buildings: George Washington Smith's decoratively tiled dome of the little octagonal chapel at the Santa Barbara Cemetery (1924–25), his Lobrero Theater (1922–24), and the intimate Meridian Court (1923). There was also the house that Smith's associate Lutah Maria Riggs had built for herself in 1926, and the buildings of other local exponents of the Spanish style, Reginald Johnson and Carleton M. Winslow, Sr., whose 1924–25 Santa Barbara Museum of Natural History had a handsome entrance portal flanked by twisted columns similar to those Ayres would later use by the entrance to the McNay House. He could have seen many anonymous smaller houses, apartments, and motor courts—all more modest and often adolescent exercises in Spanish style.[12]

Atlee collected many photographs of the houses of architect Wallace Neff, whom Atlee claimed to have met. Neff was a highly successful architect in Los Angeles and Pasadena. When Atlee visited in 1923, Neff had $250,000 worth of work on the boards, mostly houses in the $15,000 to $30,000 range, and mainly in Spanish or Italian style. His work was much published in the major national and regional architectural journals and in the home magazines as well. His designs were sometimes judged to be theatric, but, as the noted architectural historian of Southern California, David Gebhard, observed,

> It has often been argued that all buildings are a stage set, but in this case "theatric" and "stage settings" have to do with the finished building's cultivated lack of reality (and if one considers the place and time, the atmosphere of the silent films of Hollywood). A recurring element in the history of architecture has been the frequently played game between conveying a sense of the reality of the moment, or of the past, and the sense of a dreamlike quality of the improbable and the unreal. In the twenties and thirties this architectural game was looked upon as an open, much-relished sport by architects (and also of course by their clients) who skillfully manipulated a wide variety of traditional images.

Neff's Italian Tuscan and Andalusian Spanish designs had a highly original, romantic painterly quality and charm, but as Henry Humphrey, Jr., wrote in 1926 in *Country Life:* "It has been said that there are no houses in Spain so Spanish as those that are built in America." Ayres clipped the photographs of one of Neff's loveliest houses, that for Arthur K. Bourne in Pasadena, which—along with Neff's own house in San Marino—

had been published in *The Architect and Engineer* in April, 1926, just before Atlee was to begin the design of his Atkinson-McNay House in San Antonio. From *Pacific Coast Architect,* Ayres culled shots of the grounds and large swimming pool of Neff's Thomson House in Beverly Hills and of the William Goetz House in Brentwood. From the same magazine, he had pictures of the house that Myron Hunt had done for the famous landscape designer Frederick Law Olmstead in Palos Verdes. Ayres had excerpts from the *Palos Verdes Bulletin* with many illustrations of the residential and civic buildings following the mandatory restrictions requiring Mediterranean style.[13]

Though principally interested in the southern California work, Atlee did not ignore his old classmate from New York days at the Metropolitan School, George W. Kelham, who had a successful practice in San Francisco. Atlee collected Kelham's design for wrought-iron window grills for International House at the University of California at Berkeley from *The Architect and Engineer,* February, 1931. Nor did Atlee ignore work done elsewhere in the country in Spanish style, such as the house on the grounds of the Westchester-Biltmore Club in Rye, New York, which was published in the June, 1930, *Arts and Decoration* with the comment that "Spanish and Italian homes are taking possession of many fine stretches of northern landscape and are convincing that this terrain is inherently harmonious as background for the stucco walls, the colorful tiles, the delicate ironwork, the clean lights and shadows of these architectural types."[14]

California continued to attract Atlee, who traveled there nearly yearly in the 1950s, and frequently throughout the remainder of his life, though more for relaxation than for architectural inspiration, the vogue for Spanish style long gone.

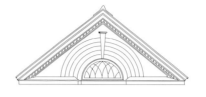

CHAPTER 5

Florida

Though Atlee looked longingly west to California, he was also aware of the flowering of Mediterranean styles in Florida in the 1920s. In October, 1925, he received a letter from architect E. P. Behles that indicated that Ayres had made an auto tour through Florida that year. Behles wrote that Miami was booming and urged Atlee to relocate there. Behles was also anxious to acquire books on Spanish architecture, which had become all the rage in Florida. As he put it, "We want to put the Spanish atmosphere in our designs." A few months later, in February, 1926, Ayres received a letter sent from West Palm Beach by J. J. Maessen, a well-known San Antonio developer, for whom Atlee had designed a house published in the May, 1925, *Pacific Coast Architect* (vol. 29). Having seen the new Addison Mizner–designed hotel, the Alba, Maessen urged Ayres to consider the development of San Antonio as a winter resort, capitalizing on its historic Spanish missions. Soon after, in May, Ayres received a letter from *The Western Architect* in Chicago informing him of their publication of Spanish architectural types with examples of the Florida work of Addison Mizner and Marion Sims Wyeth.[1]

In 1925, Florida was approaching the maximum of a frenzied land speculation bubble that was to burst the next year. It was one of the earliest events of the collapse of an overheated economy countrywide that would see the stock market crash, the closing of the banks, and the long Great Depression of the 1930s. But in 1925 Atlee could still have seen extraordinary sights of prosperity, especially the elegant and fanciful Mediterranean style houses of Palm Beach, and, in particular, the creations of the architect Addison Mizner. Mizner had arrived from New York in 1918 as the guest of sewing machine heir Paris Singer, who sought the salubrious winter climate, and who had the intention of building a convalescent home and hospital for the servicemen of World War I. After the end of the war in January, 1919, the buildings Mizner had designed were transformed into the Everglades Club: an opulent, formal, limited-membership club ruled by Paris Singer. Within a year, Mizner began receiving the commissions for private houses that were to make his reputation as the most fashionable architect in Palm Beach.

Mizner, born in 1872, was only two years older than Atlee Ayres, but by age forty-five, he had led a much more exotic life, having lived with his parents in Guatemala, Nicaragua, Costa Rica, and Honduras. He had seen great Mayan pyramids in the jungles. He had sketched Spanish Colonial houses, patios, and churches. In 1890, he studied in Spain for a year at the University of Salamanca, following mainly a humanities curriculum that was even less a professional architectural course than that which Ayres was to pursue two years later in New York. In 1892, Mizner went to work in the small office of the San Francisco architect Willis Polk who was influenced by the Spanish Colonial missions in California. In addition to professional practice, Mizner had the opportunity to develop skills as cabinet maker, plasterer, electrician, plumber— a practical education that was to stand him in good stead when he pioneered sophisticated buildings in a rather primitive Florida twenty-five years later. After four years, Mizner left on an odyssey of rather swashbuckling and largely unsuccessful—even dangerous—adventures in Hawaii, Manila, Siam, India, Shanghai, Australia, Alaska, and Canada. Returning to Guatemala on an expedition to buy cheaply, treasures from old churches, he acquired carved and gilded altars, vestments, and vessels to sell in the United States. In 1905 Mizner settled in New York City where

he developed a respectable, fashionable practice in large country houses. Though proficient in many styles, including a half-timbered Norman manor, and a Japanese tea house, Mizner's past gave him a special feeling for Spanish architecture. Not surprisingly, a number of his houses on Long Island and in the surrounding counties had a Mediterranean flavor—with tiled roofs, loggias, trellised pergolas and fountains, beamed and paneled ceilings, and tile floors.

It is unlikely that when he first went to Palm Beach in 1918 he imagined that his life would change radically, or that he would live there for fifteen years until his death in 1933. But it was to be the beginning of a spectacular career as architect to a group of rich and socially prominent clients initially from Philadelphia and New York, but soon after from other cities in the Midwest and elsewhere. With the arrival of Ernest Flagler's railroad and the opening of his hotels, the Royal Ponciana in 1894, and the Breakers two years later, Palm Beach was already a fashionable winter resort.[2] It became even more so during the First World War years, especially for the rich who were prevented by the war from going to the south of France or Italy. However, by 1918, some of the winter residents were ready to abandon Flagler's large, old-fashioned, wooden hotels in favor of membership in Singer's new Everglades Club, and wanted to have houses of their own for guests and lavish entertaining. Addison Mizner was their man. Socially adept, a raconteur and talented gossip, a bit flamboyant, Addison had captivating dreams for what were, after all, to be elaborate playhouses. The Moorish tower, loggias, and palm-shaded, fountained courts of the Everglades Club on Lake Worth emerged from his romantic, eclectic vision of "a nunnery, with a chapel built into the lake. . . . A mixture built by a nun from Venice, added onto by one from Gerona, with a bit of New Spain of the tropics."[3]

The first of Mizner's Palm Beach houses to rise in 1919 along Ocean Boulevard was El Mirasol for Edward Stotesbury, a senior partner of the Philadelphia banking firm of Drexel and Company and a senior partner of J. P. Morgan and Company. The Stotesburys had already had Horace Trumbauer design their six-story, 154-four-room mansion in Chestnut Hill. The Palm Beach house was nearly as grand and a great deal more exotic. From the living room, which could seat 175 people, guests could drift through French doors onto the balmy ocean terrace or into the perfumed loggia and patio. Richly paneled and furnished, and illuminated by chandeliers from an old Spanish castle, the rooms, according to one former ambassador to Spain "far surpassed anything in Spain with the exception of the Royal Castle of the King and Queen."[4] Mizner built four more large houses that year and went on to build thirty-five more by the time of Ayres's visit two years later. Mizner's bonanza year was 1923 with twelve houses, as well as several additions and remodelings. In that year he completed six

of his greatest mansions, including the Villa Flora for Edward Shearson (fig. 8), Anthony J. Drexel Biddle's El Sarimento, the Mesker's La Fontana, and the largest of all Mizner's houses—Playa Riente, built for Joshua Cosden, a former Baltimore streetcar conductor who had made $50 million in Oklahoma oil. Playa Riente's great hall may have been Mizner's masterpiece, a great stony room 60' long, its rib-vaulted ceiling springing from twisted, two-story columns, a double flight of stairs climbing grandly to an ornate doorway where Mrs. Cosden could invite her guests up into the living room with its loggia and belvedere, to the dining room, the morning loggia and bar, and the 70' ballroom overlooking the sea. "The size of Playa Riente, and the Cosdens' demand that it be completed for the next season, caused Mizner to depend more heavily on his collection of postcards and photographs for design sources than he usually did for his Palm Beach houses. Although he simplified and adapted

Fig. 8. Villa Flora, Palm Beach, Florida. 1923, Addison Mizner, architect, front exterior view reproduced from Ayres Clippings Files. The Alexander Architectural Archive, UT–Austin

the originals to meet his design needs, the great hall and much of the window tracery clearly derived from the Casa Longa in Valencia and the double stairs from the Cathedral of Burgos."[5]

Mizner's special brand of Mediterranean style, though rooted in his Spanish background, was in fact his own invention specifically designed for Florida, and particularly for Palm Beach—for its tropical, waterborne existence, its coral stone and pecky cypress that Mizner used liberally. Palm Beach suggested to Mizner the lagoon and canals of Venice, the reflections of pastel-tinted palaces in the waters, the dazzling skies and soft breezes. He used many Venetian details: windows surmounted by scalloped and pointed medieval arches, doors embroidered with delicate Romanesque moldings. Inside were deep-coffered, Moorish ceilings and marble railings. Yet Palm Beach was not Venice. It was brand new. There were not enough fragments of the Old World available, even to enormous American fortunes, to reproduce Venice. Mizner's project was to be an elegant fringe on a largely still undeveloped state with little industry and untrained construction workers. Undaunted, Mizner taught them techniques of building with hollow tile and stucco, tile roofs, and the trades that he had learned through his own experience. He produced his own building materials, decorative elements, and furniture. In 1923, he established Las Manos Potteries to make handcrafted roof tiles whose subtly varied colors and textures belied their commercial production. This was the first division of what would become Mizner Industries. He went on to manufacture a cast stone and a faux-wood named "Woodite" a cast composite material that could be treated like real wood to make convincing and less-expensive substitutes. He established workshops for "antique" and "new" furniture. Mizner regularly went to Europe to replenish his supplies of Spanish antiques, which he used as models for his new pieces. Although he was an expert at "distressing," creating new wormholes, chips, and scratches to

capture the look of the old, he was scrupulous about authenticity. His workshops also produced wrought-iron grills, gates, lanterns, andirons, and hardware. Mizner, like many eclectic architects, including Atlee Ayres, used his extensive library of architectural photographs and sketches for inspiration, through rarely directly copying. The pleasure was in the invention, not in academic accuracy. Mizner's dream world ended abruptly with the collapse of the land market that thwarted his schemes for development of a large new resort community at Boca Raton and ruined him financially. The devastating hurricanes of 1926 and 1928, the increasing financial difficulties of the whole country—the collapse of the banks and the dark years of the Great Depression—radically altered and limited Mizner's career until his death in 1933.

Most likely Atlee's principal experience of Mizner's houses was from driving along Ocean Boulevard and looking through the gates and across the manicured grounds of palms to the mansions on the low ridge above the beach and sparkling sea. Most of the houses were spread out, one-room thick to invite the cooling breezes. For this purpose, unlike real Spanish houses traditionally built around fully enclosed patios, Mizner's houses used semi-enclosed garden courts and loggias and terraces open to the sea. Ayres was to use similar elongated plans and open gardens to capture the prevailing breezes in San Antonio. Most importantly, unlike seeing black and white photographs in the books and magazines of his day, Atlee could see the houses in real color. To mitigate the glare from the brilliant sunlight, Mizner painted his houses in subtle pastel shades: yellows, pinks, and pale orange. The Cosden House was colored cream, which "became shaded with the rising and setting of the sun, reflecting the brilliant white light in a delicate amber, pink, saffron, and old wine." More subtly, "The Mesker house is finished in a sober color that defies classification. At certain perspectives it assumes the aspect of a mottled purple. At others it will be a decided grey color, with a tinge of indigo in it."[6] While there is no evidence that Atlee gained access to any of the great houses, he could have visited the offices of Mizner Industries, the shops in Mizner's shopping streets—Via Mizner and Via Parigi—and perhaps the Everglades Club.

During Atlee's visit in 1925, in addition to viewing Mizner's houses, he might well have seen similar Spanish style houses by Mizner's rivals. Marion Sims Wyeth and Bruce Paxton Kitchell had opened their office in 1919 and built their share of large houses. Wyeth was associated with the New York architect Joseph Urban on Mar-a-lago, the vast Moorish fantasy for Marjorie Merriweather Post. In 1925, Fatio and Treanor opened their office, and a year later John Volk his. As many of these other architects used the products of Mizner Industries, it was often difficult to distinguish their houses from Mizner's own. But few of them had the refinement of composition, detail, and color, the sequence of evocative spaces, the perfect placement of the marble panel—all of which made Mizner's houses exceptional.

In 1925, there were other great Mediterranean style houses further down the east coast of Florida and on the Gulf Coast as well. Behles's letter indicated that Ayres may have driven down to Miami, where one of Florida's greatest Mediterranean winter estates had been built by the International Harvester magnate James Deering in 1916. Deering transformed 130 acres of tangled trees, vines, and black marsh undergrowth on the edge of Biscayne Bay, with a three hundred-foot-long seawall, a canal and lake, miles of roads and paths, hamlets of farm and service buildings, ten acres of formal Italian baroque gardens, and—as the jewel in the crown—a seventy-room mansion that evoked the seventeenth-century Italian Villa Rezzonico. The arched loggia and Palladian window of its noble façade flanked by twin three-story towers could be seen mirrored in the opalescent waters of Biscayne Bay. Forming a

breakwater in front of the villa, a sculptured marble boat recalled the Dowager Empress Tzu Hsi's marble barge indulgence in the Kun Ming Lake of the Imperial Garden of Ease and Harmony in Peking. One of Deering's guests recalled, "The house was not for show. . . . Mr. Deering had no exhibitionism in him at all. And it really wasn't for entertaining, although he did entertain some. I think he built it solely for the joy of creating Vizcaya."[7] Notwithstanding, it was undeniably a vast absorbing creation. Surrounding the central court, the rooms of the villa followed a conceit invented by Deering and his architect Paul Chalfin, that Vizcaya was a villa that had grown over time, succeeding generations adding, modifying, decorating, and furnishing the rooms with their accumulating treasures. The interiors were rich and subtly eclectic examples of Italian, French, and English styles of many periods, all of the highest quality. "Chalfin provided at Vizcaya a superb text for a different way of looking at the decorative past, the art of *melange:* the subtle, complex, and very risky practice of composing authentic objects from different eras into a coherent unity."[8]

A few miles apart from the magnificent Vizcaya, there was a rash of speculative houses hastily thrown up in the frenzy of land development, many "Spanish" houses, cheaply and poorly built with thin walls nothing more than rough stucco slathered over light frames and chicken wire, wobbly arches and coarse details, a fringe of tile to embellish a roof parapet. The obvious cheapness and fragility of the houses left some of those who fled Florida with a permanent distaste for the Spanish style altogether. It was not that beautiful small houses could not be built in Spanish style. Indeed Mizner himself constructed a section of Boca Raton named "Floresta," with single-story houses of only 625 square feet, which were published as "Bungalows in the Spanish Manner" in *The Ladies Home Journal* in 1927. Though small, their plain façades were distinguished, "simplicity being always dominant in the best of Spanish architecture."[9] The living rooms had fireplaces with cast-stone mantles, tile floors, wrought-iron fixtures, and ornamental work by Mizner Industries. The ceilings, doors, and exterior trim were the same pecky cypress he used in his mansions. The houses were well oriented, with multiple exposures in many rooms, full-length casement windows for maximum ventilation, and arcaded porches.

In addition to his traveling in Florida, Atlee culled the magazines for residential work being done there, especially in Palm Beach by Addison Mizner, Marion Sims Wyeth, Fatio and Treanor, and others. Though clearly not as extensive as the range of California architects on his list of architects whose work was to be clipped, the Florida architects were represented by work in *Vogue,* which carried Mizner's addition to the Cosden House after it had been sold to Mrs. Horace Dodge, and the patio of her new house in Grosse Pointe. *Vogue* also published three interiors of another Mizner house in its January, 1926, issue. Photographs of Mizner's early Stotesbury and William Gray Warden Houses were collected in Ayres's clippings files, along with houses by Marion Sims Wyeth published in *Southern Architect and Building News* in June, 1929. The files also included an elaborate "Romanesque" doorway by Fatio and Treanor and the vaulted ceiling of the loggia of the Codman House.[10]

Whatever conjectures may be made about Atlee's experience of the Mediterranean styles in Florida, it is reasonable to assume that Florida would have seemed to him a foreign, even exotic and theatrical world, springing so suddenly and so extravagantly from the sandy hummocks and swamps along the sparkling sea. It was quite unlike San Antonio. It was more tropical, with a different heat—more damp, insistently humid. There were large-leafed plants, palms that could withstand the winter more easily, palmetto and vines, bougainvillea, and orchids, not the mesquite and small-leafed huisache and retama that endured the barren hills where Atlee's houses rose in San Antonio's new suburbs. San Antonio was not a Venice, not even blessed with a sizable river or lake, though fortunate to have a large aquifer under the limestone hills and an enterprising group of citizens that by 1941 had seen to the transformation of a bend of the San Antonio River into a charming canal and riverwalk. It was furthermore an old city, with real Spanish ancestry, lovely crumbling Missions rivaling those of California, quite unlike the newly minted, theatrical resort coast of Florida. Only San Augustine in northern Florida still retained a little evidence of its original Spanish heritage. And unlike Palm Beach and Miami, San Antonio was not a winter playground made fashionable by a handful of the rich and parvenu from elsewhere, escaping the rigors of winter in the cities of the upper East Coast and Middle West—people who brought their notions of society to create the cachet of this new world in Florida. San Antonio by contrast was a small, conservative city, where society was led by established families who lived and entertained with elegance and gusto but rarely with the flamboyant extravagance of Palm Beach's society hostesses nor the magnificence of Deering in his villa-palazzo. The scale was different. So too were the financial resources, which while ample, even abundant—from ranching, lumber, banking, and later from oil—rarely matched the income of a senior partner of J. P. Morgan or Drexel, or International Harvester. When seeking a second home, those in San Antonio were more likely to spend their money on a sizable ranch or house in the cool highlands of New Mexico, Colorado, or the seaside of Martha's Vineyard or Bar Harbor. Nevertheless, Florida provided Atlee with more inspiration for his own eclecticism.

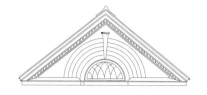

CHAPTER 6
Ayres's Library

In the first decades of his professional practice, Ayres concentrated on assembling a substantial library as a source of inspiration and scholarly acquaintance with the architecture of other times and places. Especially for one with his relatively untraveled, limited formal architectural education, a fine library would enhance his professional respectability and social cachet. In 1925, he could write with confidence to a prospective client, "As you know, we have quite a large library and can work out whatever character of design you may want, whether it be Georgian, Italian, Spanish, or English."[1] In 1926 Ayres claimed—well, perhaps boasted—that he had "the best library in the State of Texas," and that he was "continually adding to same"[2] (fig. 9).

Ayres was not unusual in the importance he attached to a good architectural library, which was deemed essential for an early-twentieth-century architect to aspire to the high levels of authenticity and quality heretofore apparent in the work of only a small number of Beaux-Arts–trained and well-traveled practitioners. Charles Follen McKim, of the celebrated firm of McKim, Mead and White, was remembered as spending "hours and hours looking up data, particularly in *Letarouilly* which was a kind of office bible"; also, "Like all American architects now, he filled his office from the start with the great German folios of Italian work."[3]

However important a library may have been to the inspiration and scholarly credentials of the architect, it was perhaps even more important to the actual production of the architect. The possibility of practical application was presented in Ayres's 1926 copy of *The Smaller Houses*

& Gardens of Versailles 1680–1815, in which the authors made clear in the introduction that the buildings described therein provided examples "from which we of today may draw a very direct useful lesson. . . . Modest in size . . . elegant though simple in all their appointments, . . . the type is the embodiment of sophisticated simplicity and it is applicable, with but little modification, to the present requirements of a large and growing portion of the American public." The authors further contended that "the house of moderate size is a matter of far more general interest than the pretentious dwelling of vast extent." Furthermore, they were designed for the requirements of a simplified, though elegant, mode of housekeeping that minimized the num-

ber of servants necessary for proper maintenance. A good architectural library could thus be used to contemporary purposes, in the new circumstances of economics and social conditions after World War I, which, in fact, did require smaller houses for servantless living.

The importance Ayres placed in his library was evident in the efforts he made to assemble it. In San Antonio in the first decades of the century, Ayres's local access to books on architecture was extremely limited. The nearest architectural library of substance was at the University of Texas eighty miles away in Austin. In San Antonio, no bookstore carrying quality architectural books existed until Rosengrens opened in 1935. Thereafter, representatives of major publishers came to

Fig. 9. Library in Office of Ayres and Ayres, Architects, 1929. The UT Institute of Texan Cultures, No. 83-711, courtesy Florence Collett Ayres

the city three or four times a year with samples. But compared to the resources available to architects in New York City, such as Columbia University's Avery Library, the New York Public Library, major publishers, and numerous bookstores, San Antonio provided meager selections for Atlee. Thus his collecting was principally done long distance—involving much correspondence and shipping back and forth of works on approval. His office correspondence was peppered with letters and telegrams to publishers and sellers of architectural books. He enquired of Scribner's Sons for illustrated books on Italian architecture in 1919, and again the next year for books on Robert Adam, and the English Renaissance and Gothic. That same year he wrote to Mr. Ernst Wasmuth in Berlin: "I am particularly fond of the Italian and Spanish style. . . . Have you any new publications on Italian or Spanish wrought Iron work?" (This was the same publisher of the early work of Frank Lloyd Wright.) To fuel his growing special interest, Atlee wrote to J. B. Millet, Publisher, in Boston on November 24, 1923, regarding publications on Spanish architecture. This was the same year that he started the earliest of his houses in the "Italian-Spanish" style, the Thomas Hogg House on Bushnell. Ayres continued to pursue books germane to his current work such as *Masterpieces of Spanish Architecture,* which he requested on approval from The Pencil Points Press in May of 1926.[4]

Although in most cases it is difficult to know when many of Ayres's books came into his possession, the dates of their publication give some idea of the possibilities of the time of their acquisition and of their potential influence on his buildings. The earliest publication date of a volume in the Ayres Collection was 1862: *Specimens of Medieval Architecture Chiefly Selected from Examples of the Twelfth and Thirteenth Centuries in France and Italy.* Published in London, it consisted largely of lithographs of cathedrals drawn by W. Eden Nesfield. Thereafter, *Suggestions in Brickwork* of 1895 contained illustrations of the archi-

tecture of Italy, together with a catalogue of bricks made by the Hydraulic-Press Brick Company of Philadelphia, which published it. Next in time, released in 1903, was a publication in German on ornament and, from the next year, another in German on the work of the Viennese Succession architect Joseph Olbrich. These two large folios, emphasizing Olbrich's work at the Turin Exposition of 1903, contained photographs and drawings of exteriors and interiors, as well as designs for lighting fixtures, mirrors, plates and silverware, and jewelry in pearls, gold, and sapphires. Concurrently, published in 1909 and 1910, there were more books on contemporary Viennese work, including the 1905, 1906, and 1908 folios of *Der Architekt.* Their elegant plates of ink-line drawings with striking flat areas of bright green, gold, and black, and geometric decorative motifs—not unlike those of Frank Lloyd Wright at the time—illustrated projects of Otto Wagner and Josef Hoffman, as well as a fantasy for a gate to the pleasure garden of Harum al Raschid. At this stage in Ayres's early years of practice, he also evidenced interest in the work of the English Arts and Crafts Movement, in the work of M. H. Baillie Scott whose book *Houses and Gardens* was published in 1906, and he collected special issues in 1908, 1909, 1910, and 1911 of *The Architectural Review* on recent English Domestic Architecture.

Some of the books in the Ayres Collection published in those early decades were curiously exotic, such as *The People of India* of 1910, and the earlier *Indian Domestic Architecture,* an 1885 collection of photographs by Lockwood de Forest of the intricate wood and stone carving of the façades, doorways, balconies, and window lattices and grills of Hindu houses in Bombay, and Mohammedan influence in Rajaputana and Northern India.

To the extent that one can infer a chronology of Ayres's interests from the dates of publication of the books that he acquired, it would seem that although he had some interest in the Arts and

Crafts Movement and some of the innovative new architecture in Europe and America, his major tastes followed more traditional historic examples both at home and abroad. He made a serious effort through his books to be more knowledgeable about the tradition of Western European architecture. As expected, Ayres owned Sir Banister Fletcher's synoptic *A History of Architecture on the Comparative Method,* the 1908 edition, which included an illustrated Tree of Architecture bearing the charming warning that it "must be taken as suggestive only, for minor influences cannot be indicated on a diagram of this kind."

As the prevailing taste of some of those who commissioned private houses in San Antonio in the first two decades of the twentieth century tended strongly to the old buildings of England, especially picturesque medieval manor houses and smaller residential buildings, it is not surprising to find volumes such as *The Domestic Architecture of England during The Tudor Period, Volume Two,* by Thomas Garner and Arthur Stratton—a series of photographs and measured drawings of country mansions, manor houses, and smaller buildings, with historical and descriptive text. A more extensive and opulent resource were the seven volumes of 1922 titled *English Homes,* which ranged from the Norman and Plantagenet periods of the eleventh through fifteenth centuries, through sixteenth- and seventeenth-century Early and Late Tudor and Stuart periods, to the eighteenth-century Early and Late Georgian styles. Ayres's *The Architecture, Decoration, and Furniture of Robert and James Adam* had illustrations photolithographed from the originals of 1778–82. Ayres acquired from London volumes two, three, and five of *The Architectural Association Sketch-Book,* dating from 1896 to 1908. These contained freehand drawings of diverse subjects in ink, pencil, and wash, reproduced by photolithograph. They included views of the Alhambra, buildings in Verona and Venice, and a study of a 16' x 13' Flemish tapestry, "The Triumph of Pru-

dence—The Part Shewing the Dragons Drawing the Cart." The *Sketch-Books* also contained intricate measured drawings of molding profiles of a Northamptonshire medieval church, of the newel-post of the oak stair at The Hall, Glastonbury, Somerset, and of a bay window of the garden front of St. John's College, Oxford, whose elevations and profiles of cornice, architrave, string course, corbel course, and base course illustrated over sixty elements at scales as large as three inches equals one foot. Other books owned by Ayres on English architecture included *The Smaller English House of the Later Renaissance 1660–1783,* published in 1925 by William Helburn, Inc., of New York (who was to publish Ayres's own book on Mexican architecture the following year). The range of Atlee's eclecticism, and an indication of the avenues of his interests both practical and aesthetic, was represented by other titles published toward the second decade of the century and likely acquired by Ayres in those years. For example, the 1909 *The Art of the Plasterer,* was an account of the decorative development of that craft chiefly in England from the sixteenth to the eighteenth century, with a further chapter on the stucco of the classic period and of the Italian Renaissance. These may have been useful, or at least inspirational, in the design of the 1923 Tudor Revival style house for J. D. Oppenheimer and the 1922 Italian Renaissance style David Straus House, which may also have benefited from Ayres's 1907 volume *Brickwork in Italy.*

Over and above any practical use to which these volumes could be put, it seems likely that one with Atlee's aesthetic sensibilities and perfectionist temperament would find some of his large and handsome volumes irresistible as precious objects, as works of art. He was justifiably proud of the quality of many of his volumes, perhaps of the very weight and size of his 12⅞" x 18⅓" *Hotels et Maison de la Renaissance Francaise,* of its red, blue, and yellow marbleized cover, tomato red spine and corners, its golden ribbons, published by the Librarie Central des Beaux-Arts, in French. He might well have savored his *Art of the Garden Design in Italy* for its 73 photographic plates reproduced in expensive collotype, twenty-seven plans and numerous sketches and plates delicately protected by thin tissues, from Longmans, Green, and Co. in London. Some were large and sumptuous portfolios of plates. The oldest, published in 1884 in Stuttgart was *Denkmaler Der Kunst.* The thick portfolio—measuring 14⅞" x 18⅛" and weighing more than fifteen pounds—held 193 exquisitely delineated and rendered plates crowded with plans, sections, perspectives, details, paintings and sculpture of Assyrian palaces, Greek temples, Gothic cathedrals, Renaissance palaces and churches, and examples from into the nineteenth century, a staggering compendium. It was rivaled by the even larger (14½" x 19½") and weightier (nearly twenty pounds) *The Domestic Architecture of England During the Tudor Period,* Batsford, London, 1911, by Thomas Garner and Arthur Stratton. Other large books included "Volume III—Gothic in Italy, France and Northern Europe" of A. L. Frothingham's 1915 *A History of Architecture,* and the portfolio of photographs of stern, stone churches in *Architettura e Scultura Mediovale nelle Puglie,* published in Turin. From Berlin in 1903 came the 70 plates of fine, ink-measured drawings of details, rendered elevations, and photographs of Venetian palaces in *Palast Architektur von Oberitalien und Toscana,* one of several portfolios for buildings in Tuscany, Siena, Pistoia, San Gimignano, Montepulciano, Lucca, Verona, Mantova, and many other Italian cities. Ayres's Italian resources included a Mixed Folio *Arte Italiana #9 1908–1910* (a monthly periodical of decorative and industrial art). One of the most impressive of his Italian volumes is the 1910 collection of original sketches and drawings of *Brick and Terra-cotta Work during the Middle Ages and the Renaissance in Italy.* The elegant drawings showed every brick of the façades, voissiors and arches, string courses, cornices, every individual roof tile,

all manner of detail, every egg and dart, dentil, rosette, and guilloche, with lovely three-dimensional effects of shadings.

There was also a French connection. Sumptuous volumes illustrated the Louis XIV, XV, and XVI styles in buildings, decoration, and furniture. But perhaps of more immediate usefulness was his collection of books from the École des Beaux-Arts in Paris. Though not himself a graduate of the École, Ayres clearly sought the examples of projects done there. His library included volumes one through five of *Grands Prix de Rome Architecture,* volumes one–three, from 1850–1904, and volumes four and five, 1905–10. He also possessed a number of volumes of *Concours,* competition projects that were required for the diploma from the École. *Les Medailles des Concourse d'Architecture de l'École Nationale des Beaux-Arts a Paris 1904–1905* included "A Center of Mutual Assistance," which featured a "Place de la Solidarite" and a "Mansion for a French Ambassador Abroad," replete with multiple axes and oval rooms. Other projects were for a department store with iron structure (artfully concealed above allegorical ceilings and elaborate moldings), a library, and a military barracks. In the elaborately rendered projects, Ayres could study the celebrated principles of planning, spatial organization, and character of movement *(marche)*—the products of studious archeology and reverence for history reinterpreted for the present. He could also savor the beautiful presentation drawings themselves, marvels of graphic technique, of subtly gradated ink and watercolor washes, and exquisite colors. Imagine Ayres bending over his large portfolio with its worn, red faux-leather cover and faded gold title *Fragments d'Architecture Antique,* perusing the thick plates of engravings of restorations of antique buildings by pensionniers of the French Academy in Rome.

As all architects who approach architecture from an aesthetic point of view—who see architecture as something more than building—

Atlee was aware that the difference required a heightening by ornament, an element that went beyond necessity. Ornament lay at the heart of the eclectic architect's research both in his mining of the past and in the possibilities of the present. It is not surprising therefore to find a number of volumes in Ayres's library that dealt with ornament. Ayres would likely have taken special interest in perusing the 120 plates in color, gold, and silver in Racinet's *L'Ornement Polychrome,* a folio containing ancient and Asiatic art—Egyptian, Chinese, Moorish, Ottoman, Russian, Armenian, Celtic, and Byzantine examples—with full pages of text preceding the brilliant chromolithographic illustrations. He also owned Alexander Speltz's translation from the second German edition of *Styles of Ornament,* whose four hundred full pages of illustrations with illustrated descriptive text were ambitiously intended to be "A Handbook for Architects, Designers, Painters, Sculptors, Wood-Carvers, Chasers, Modellers, Cabinet-Makers and Artistic Locksmiths as well, as also for Technical Schools, Libraries and Private Study." *An Encyclopaedia of Ironwork* of 1927 provided Atlee with examples of Spanish, German, French, and Italian ironwork from the Middle Ages to the eighteenth century. Interior and exterior decorative sculpture could then be ordered through the catalogue of Fischer and Jirouch of Cleveland, Ohio.

Ayres's library included the work of some of his most prominent contemporaries. He had two large portfolios of *A Monograph of the Work of McKim, Mead and White 1879–1915,* which contained 176 plates of plans, sections, elevations, and excellent black and white photographs. There were similarly impressive volumes of the work of Charles Platt, Mellor, Meigs, and Howe, and Dwight James Baum, whose 1927 folio included buildings in Colonial, Formal Georgian, Italian, English, and Dutch Colonial styles. Also directly useful were the 18 large plates of measured details from the buildings of other well-known architects. They included Adamesque details from Warren and Wetmore's Ritz Carlton Hotel and from a residence by Albro and Lindeberg, who was to design several houses in Houston; Georgian detail by Aymar Embury, who complied several collections of American country houses; and an Old English doorway by Frank Forster. Ayres—who maintained friendships with several Houston architects, most notably Birdsall Briscoe—may well have seen a house in Houston that Forster designed. *House and Garden's Book of Houses,* published by Conde Nast in 1919, contained over three hundred illustrations of large and small houses, service quarters and garages, plans and such necessary architectural detail as doorways, fireplaces, windows, floors, walls, ceilings, closets, stairs, chimneys, etc.—all of which would have kept Ayres abreast of current work in many parts of the United States.

It is surprising that Ayres's library contained so few books on Spanish style. It did include *Californian Architecture in Santa Barbara,* with preface by Charles H. Cheney, AIA. As it was a published in 1929, it could only have reinforced Ayres's interest in and knowledge of the Spanish style, but it could not have been of influence on what was his major work in the Spanish style, the Atkinson-McNay House, which was designed beginning in 1927 and had finished construction in 1929. Nevertheless, the book was very interesting as it actually defined "California Architecture" as a distinctive style, "deriving its chief inspiration directly or indirectly from Latin types which developed under similar climatic conditions along the Mediterranean, or at points in Mexico and California." It further specified that "Color is generally light in tone" and that "Materials used are plaster, adobe or stucco exterior wall surfaces of durable construction, or of concrete, stone, or artificial stone." It required that "Roofs are low pitched, seldom steeper than thirty degrees, with thirty-five degrees maximum, usually of tile laid random, but sometimes in the galleried Monterey type, using shakes or shingles, often with thick butts." This was part of an effort after the earthquake of 1925 to establish an official style for Santa Barbara whose city council created an architectural board of review and made an effort to discourage the use of the terms "Mission Style" or "Spanish Style" in favor of the chauvinistic "California Architecture." The book included work from the major local practitioners—George Washington Smith, Myron Hunt, Reginald Johnson, and Lutah Maria Riggs—as well as one house by the Easterner Bertram Goodhue, who had introduced the Spanish style at the San Diego Fair of 1915.

Atlee's library also contained an elegant book on *The Florida Architecture of Addison Mizner,* published in 1928 by William Helburn, New York. Within its marbleized cover and end pieces were a short introductory text, plans, and large black and white photographs of thirteen houses—mainly in Palm Beach, with names like Casa Bendita, Lagomar, El Salano, El Mirasol, Sin Cuidado, Villa Flora, and Casa de Leoni. Most of the houses were inspired by the exotic architecture of Venice: gothic pointed arches, delicate marble balconies, and slender columns.

For Atlee, as for many of his eclectic contemporaries, style was not a skin-deep matter. Unlike the stylistically hybrid costumes of Post-Modernism of the 1980s, the eclectic production of Ayres was not only based on extensive acquaintance with the past and scholarly appreciation of its buildings but also on the desire to create buildings of consistent and authentic character. He was as concerned with the interiors and furnishings as with the exterior appearance. It is not surprising to find books such as *The Practical Book of Period Furniture* containing 250 illustrations and text treating of furniture of the English and American Colonial periods. The 1911 *The Practical Book of Oriental Rugs* included ten illustrations in color, seventy-five in doubletone, and sixty-seven designs in line, chart, and map. Later, as

Ayres's growing affection for Spanish style permeated his residential work, he sought artistic nourishment in books such as that published by the Pencil Points Press in 1926, *The Treatment of Interiors,* by Eugene Clute. Atlee could consult the three hundred magnificent pages of the portfolio of volume three of *Spanish Interiors and Furniture* to study its photographs and measured drawings by Arthur Byne and brief text by Mildred Stapley who were corresponding members of the Hispanic Society of America and authors of several well-known books on Spanish architecture, including *Spanish Ironwork, Spanish Architecture of the XVI Century,* and *Decorated Wooden Ceilings of Spain.* In 1924, Byne and Stapley also published in *The Architectural Record* a series of articles on Andalusian gardens and patios that Ayres had cut out of the magazines and bound in handsome leather hardcovers in San Antonio. For further furnishing of the garden, he could refer to the Erkins Studio of New York's catalogue of *Garden and Hall Furniture* for vases, pedestals, fonts, fountains, benches, balustrades, well-heads, gazing globes, and pergolas, in Pompeian stone and marble. For examples from his contemporaries, Ayres could consult the first and third volumes of *Gardens Old and New, The Country House and Its Garden Environment.*

Many of Ayres's books were concerned with the materials and techniques of building. In 1924 and 1925, he subscribed to *Atlantic Terra Cotta,* a collection published by The Atlantic Terra Cotta Company of New York and Atlanta, which claimed to be the largest manufacturer of terracotta in the world. The collection included issues on historical examples in Italy such as the Romanesque Certosa of Pavia, the Renaissance Pazzi Chapel, The Old Sacristy of San Lorenzo, and the work of the sculptor Giovanni della Robbia. One issue was devoted to "Studies in Polychromy—Spanish and Mexican XVII c." and another to "Old Mexico." The 1924 issue number three featured Ayres and Ayres's own Smith-Young Tower in San Antonio, the pacesetting high-rise office building that housed the Ayreses' architectural office. Other issues demonstrated "Atlantic Terra Cotta in Combination" and "Polychrome Terra Cotta." The Ayres library also included a book on *Metal Crafts in Architecture* 1929 dealing with bronze, brass, cast iron, copper, lead, and tin, as well as lighting fixtures, and including specifications. As inspirational as the buildings of the past were to him, Atlee was a man of the present, interested in twentieth-century technology and standards of comfort, and of twentieth-century mass production of the sort described in the 1917 *Details to Which Standard Hardware Can Be Applied*. Important for his larger buildings, such as the Smith-Young Building, were reference books including 1924 data on reinforced concrete buildings from the Kalman Steel Company. The library also contained the 1915 publication from the National Warm Air Heating and Ventilating Association of *Formulas and Rules for Installation of Warm Air Heating,* the Pencil Points Library's *Good Practice in Construction Part Two* of 1925, and the Building Code of the City of Cincinnati of 1933. The meeting of past and present, especially the abrasion of contemporary materials and technology with forms derived from the past, posed for Ayres—as it did for his contemporaries—a serious problem. This was apparent in his effort to create new buildings in a style based on Spanish vernacular buildings that had been created of local building materials and construction techniques, conditions radically different from those in San Antonio in the 1920s.

During the flowering of their traditional eclectic houses, Atlee and his son Robert also successfully developed civic and commercial projects of great variety and richness that in the 1930s and after World War II began to reflect the influence of the various forms of Modernism. As early as 1929, Ayres's library included *The Logic of Modern Architecture,* and *Moderne Bauformen,* published in Stuttgart in 1929 two years after the influential exhibition of the Modern Movement at the Weissenhof Seidlungen. By 1947, the library included a book by the industrial designer Paul Laszlo, and by 1950, others on the great Brazilian modernist Oscar Niemeyer and the celebrated Italian engineer Pier Luigi Nervi. By 1951, it included *A Decade of New Architecture* by Seigfied Giedion, whose canonical history of the Modern Movement *Space, Time, and Architecture* had been published by Harvard in 1941. Ayres showed interest in contemporary American work as well, in The Museum of Modern Art's *Built in USA: Postwar Architecture* edited by Henry-Russell Hitchcock and Arthur Drexler in 1952, and in *Mid-Century Architecture in America,* the Honor Awards of the American Institute of Architects 1949–61. There were books from the 1950s and '60s on the modern church, public school, hotels, motels and restaurants, libraries, the new museum, shops and showrooms, apartments, office planning and design, and on parking and parking structures. There are also books on new materials, aluminum, and curtain-wall construction.

In short, the library became increasingly focused on the present. The past as inspiration and authority, the past as stimulus to memory and reflection, was clouded over by the present during the decades after the end of the Second World War. When the past was "rediscovered" by Post-Modernism after 1965—by Charles Moore and the firm of Robert Venturi and Denise Scott-Brown, and then by Michael Graves—there flourished a variety of eclectic expressions, mostly mannerist, theatrical, sometimes playful, often promiscuous, uses of the past. By the 1990s, the new eclecticism had invented novel interpretations and uses of the Western tradition. It became a frantic, free-wheeling search for the new, akin to the competitive world of fashion. The scholarly exercise of libraries of books, and direct experiences with books, had become supplanted by online images and shallow texts, supplying the designer with graphic warehouses of the past to be plundered and reassembled to new effects, with little understanding of the buildings of the past or their underlying principles. The tactile pleasures afforded by books had alas virtually disappeared as well.

It may be useful to compare Atlee's library with that of another prominent, eclectic Texas architect, Houston's John Staub, eighteen years Atlee's junior, who presented the 127 volumes of his library to the Franzheim Library at the University of Houston in 1978.[5] The two collections were similar but had different strengths. As to be expected from the predominantly English and Colonial styles of most of Staub's houses of the 1920s and '30s, his library was decidedly focused on English and American Colonial styles. Although Staub did only one major Spanish style house in Houston, the William T. Crabbe House of 1935—in the Spanish style that Ayres had explored in the previous decade—their libraries overlapped with Arthur Byne and Mildred Stapley's 1924 *Spanish Gardens and Patios.* Staub's library also included Mack and Gobson's *Architectural Details of Southern Spain,* Helburn, New York, 1928, and *Spanish Farm Houses and Public Buildings,* published in New York in 1924. Another work owned by both Ayres and Staub was John V. Van Pelt's 1925 volume four of *Masterpieces of Spanish Architecture: Romanesque and Allied Styles.* Miss Ima Hogg presented Staub with the gift of

Jose Ortiz Echague's 1954 *España, pueblos y paisajes.* Both Staub and Ayres were interested in the work of their contemporaries, in monographs on Charles Platt, Delano and Aldrich, and Mellor, Meigs, and Howe, as well as collections such as *The House Beautiful Building Annuals 1925 and 1926.*

For the eclectic designer, graphic images were—and still are—the most potent influences, often overriding scholarly, even intellectual interests. Yet, in the essays that accompanied and often introduced the illustrations, one sometimes finds very thoughtful observations about eclecticism itself. In the 1931 introduction to *Colonial Houses of Philadelphia: Pre-Revolutionary Period,* Joseph Hergesheimer critically observed: "The America they formed was created by their honesty of construction and correct proportion. Their honesty and correctness. The houses built now are neither honest in materials nor correct in design. Men, then, were more intelligent about such things; they had less and, for that reason, demanded more." He went on, "I am not referring, sentimentally, to the life and habits, the mere appearance of the past, but to the intrinsic and practically timeless value of line and purpose and mass; I am engaged with the effect they have on the human spirit."

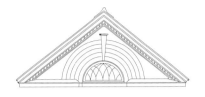

CHAPTER 7

Ayres and the Magazines

The Clippings Files and Publicity

In addition to the books in his library and the many photographs that Atlee collected on his travels, current magazines were a very important resource. They served him in several ways. They were his principal means for keeping up to date on the work of his contemporaries, especially those outside of Texas. They also exposed him to current thinking on the practice of architecture, current developments in the history and theory of architecture, and, not least, trends in popular tastes. Atlee mined his magazines assiduously for images that served to stimulate his own imagination and expand his architectural vocabulary.

Ayres's magazines included national professional architectural journals such as *American Architect, Architectural Record, Architectural Review, Architectural Forum, Architectural Design, Pencil Points,* and the more regionally oriented *Western*

Architect, Pacific Coast Architect, California Home-owner, and *The Southern Architect and Building News.* He also collected magazines that dealt with architecture, interiors, and design for the non-professional public, publications sometimes referred to as the "shelter magazines," such as *House and Garden, Southern Living,* and *Country Life.*

As most of the architectural magazines were unavailable in San Antonio in the first part of the twentieth century, Ayres had a number of subscriptions, including that in 1919 to the national professional magazines *Architecture* and *Architectural Forum* (the latter titled *Brickbuilder* from 1892 to 1910). In 1920, Atlee subscribed to *The AIA Journal,* and to *Pencil Points* (which was to become *Progressive Architecture*). In 1924, with his growing interest in California architecture much stimulated by his trip there in September, 1923,

Atlee wrote to subscribe to *Pacific Coast Architect.* Occasionally he wrote to request a particular issue of interest, such as the March, 1919, issue of *Western Architect,* which had begun a series on "Spanish Colonial Architecture in America" by Rexford Newcomb, a particularly prolific, young assistant professor at the University of Illinois at that time.

What were these magazines like in the 1920s, especially those in which Atlee's work appeared? The established *American Architect,* founded in 1876, which published more of Ayres's work than any other journal, rewards closer study. The January 20, 1928, eleven-page lead article "Architectural Impressions of Southern California" was by Dwight James Baum, architect and gold medalist of the Architectural League of New York. Baum himself had taken the twenty photographs in Pasadena, Beverley Hills, and Hollywood. The publisher's page, in introducing the Baum article, admitted: "Domestic architecture in California has perhaps not always received the appreciation that it deserves," at least not from the East Coast architectural establishment in which Baum was an "eastern practitioner." The Baum article was followed by two pages of pen and ink perspectives of suggestions for a mausoleum and a study for an art museum. The succeeding editorial comment included a potpourri of observations on rooms for music, the set-back forms of tall buildings, the "peculiarly American" style trend of wallpaper and dress silks, and a surprisingly sanguine view of business conditions that conveyed a blind optimism in predicting no falling off of building construction, shortly before the 1929 economic crash.

Next the magazine showed New York's Lombardy Apartment Hotel, whose exterior and interiors were shown in photographs, plans, and measured drawings of scale details. Hard on the heels of the Romanesque arch of the Lombardy's entrance was the Fifth Avenue shopfront of "Delettrez Paris" in the "Modern French Style," an elegant, symmetrical façade of marble, aluminum, and bronze, with characteristic Art Moderne female nudes, decorative lozenges, floral chains, bouquets, and radiating patterns. There were two interiors as well with more nymphs, wreaths, and octagonal medallions. There followed a full page of photographs of the front of the Pythian Temple, Assyrian terraces, and seated pharaohs.

The rich variety of styles continued with the publication of Ayres's English Tudor style Oppenheimer House of 1923, and a "Collegiate Gothic" school in La Grange, Illinois. There were "Notes on Wrought Iron" illustrated with pencil sketches by Samuel Chamberlain, which—after a short introductory text—comprised measured drawings of ninety-four items, including hinges, fanlights, gratings, balconies, grills, gates, locks, knockers, latches, and bolts of Italian, German, Spanish, and English origin. This compendium was followed by a photograph of the model of the modernist prize-winning design for the Shakespeare Memorial Theatre at Stratford-upon-Avon.

American Architect at this time included a section on interior architecture. This issue featured the interiors of the Lombardy Apartment, including the main dining room in Tudor style, with paneled walls, plaster frieze and ceiling, faux-leaded, diamond-pane windows, and iron chandelier. The first-floor corridor, on the other hand, had a richly coffered Italian ceiling and oriental rug. The main lounge was "Georgian," with Chippendale style furniture, classical pilasters, a correct, bolection molding on the chimneybreast, elsewhere egg and dart and richly foliated moldings. The magazine followed the Lombardy with another hotel in Columbus, Ohio, before focusing on the offices of the architecture firm of Walker and Weeks, which occupied the entire top floor of a Cleveland office building. A large two-story drafting room, illuminated by long clerestories, was lined with small offices for the designers, specification writers, and stenographers. There was a commodious library with a fireplace, several conference rooms in English styles, a sample room, and other service rooms. Upstairs, a balcony overlooking the drafting room had a grand piano. Accessed from a private elevator was a dining room and Walker's office and studio in the homey style of the English Arts and Crafts architect Baillie Scott, brick fireplace and all. Next in the magazine, probably of particular interest to Ayres, were exterior and interior photographs and plans of two Los Angeles houses in Spanish style.

American Architect was not entirely about styles and decoration. One of its regular sections was on engineering and construction. The 1928 volume 133 continued with information on sound-insulating materials and partitions; the bearing power of soils; a new shower and bath fixture catalogue; the three hundred-foot-high, first skyscraper in Rio de Janeiro, Brazil; non-slip-floor data; Lupton's steel windows; and the move to standardization and reduction in building costs. A "Group of Buildings of Moderate Cost" included two cottage houses in Southern California, a laboratory building, a Sioux Falls, South Dakota, grade school in a style recalling the Viennese Otto Wagner, and Americans Frank Lloyd Wright and Louis Sullivan. A fraternity chapter house at the University of Illinois, Champaign, clearly owed much to the seventeenth-century English architect Sir Christopher Wren. In sum, the magazine mainly supported a wide spectrum of historically based eclectic styles, but there were also faint murmurs of the growing argument between the advocates of traditional eclecticism and modernism, which was to become a major issue in professional architecture within a few years in the 1930s.

The architectural magazines also helped Ayres pursue his personal design interests such as his focus on Mediterranean styles. The magazines carried examples of houses in the Spanish style and opinions about the style itself. *Pacific Coast Architect,* published in San Francisco, carried an article in 1926 titled "Spanish Atmosphere,"

which praised the work of the Santa Barbara architect George Washington Smith, one of the most celebrated of the architects designing in the Spanish style. The author, Harris Allen, AIA, wrote, "size has nothing to do with it; substance does; but it must have that intangible quality we call 'atmosphere' and to create atmosphere one must be an artist. Mr. Smith is an artist." Allen went on to discuss Smith's houses in terms of intuitive sense, the relationship of mass and detail, sun and shadow, color, texture, materials, and craft. Yet in 1927 when Atlee was just hitting his stride in the Spanish style, he may have been affronted with an article in *The Southern Architect and Building News* of February, 1927 (vol. 53, no. 2), in which Howard Major, AIA, testily commented that "it is evident that much foreign influence has crept into the architecture of the South. . . . [W]hat can be more inappropriate than a Southerner in a Spanish House. Ridiculous today is the 'hysteria' for things Spanish. This travesty of Spanish architecture in our Southern States is a rank fad sponsored first by California, then Florida." Still, the magazine published a house in Spanish style in Houston by Charles W. Oliver and three others in Dallas including that of the Dallas architect H. B. Thomson—both contemporaries of Ayres.

The "shelter magazines," on the other hand, dealt less with building structure, material, construction, and professional practice, and concerned themselves more with residential style and taste, focusing on the decoration and furnishing of interiors, and on landscaping and gardening. Ayres collected plates from *The House Beautiful* and *California Homeowner,* as well as from national arbiters of style such as *Vogue, Town and Country,* and *Country Life.* One of the leading magazines of this ilk and one that was to publish Ayres's Atkinson-McNay House—one of his finest—was the Conde Nast Publications, Inc., *House and Garden.* The flavor of this publication may be sensed from perusal of its August, 1929, issue, which, although it opened with advertisements for insulation by Celotex and for "Manufactured Weather" by Carrier—a new heating system that heated, humidified, cleaned, and distributed air under pressure, replacing old-fashioned furnaces and boilers and gravity systems—continued with a directory of decoration and fine arts with advertisements for a nineteenth-century Directoire daybed, a Queen Anne secretary, a Colonial bedroom group displayed in a "fine old paneled pine room," The Chintz Shop, and The Florentine Craftsmen purveying iron gates. The advertisements continued with "Plans for Fine Houses" by Henry T. Child, architect, and "Stucco Houses" in English, French, Italian, and Spanish styles. The news section noted an exhibit of "Harmonized Rooms" at the New York City Art Center, including work of Europeans Bruno Paul and Paul Poiret, and new storage systems. Page thirty-one displayed "delightfully different maid's uniforms." (Two months later the stock market would crash, radically altering the lifestyle portrayed in the magazine.) Lastly, preceding the title page and list of contents, came two pages of the Dog Mart, presented as guardians and companions.

Beginning the main bulk of the issue was the Bulletin Board's essay "Modernist Ramblings," which opined that "the heavens will probably fall on the day when one school of Modernists shall be heard to say good of another school. Those who go in for extreme simplicity and those who make rooms and furniture of strange materials and those who faintly follow traditional lines all seem at loggerheads. Perhaps we might call a `Disarmament Conference for Modernists.'" It went further with the imperative to "Start inside. It cannot be too often repeated that the way to design a house is to start inside. Start with the plan. After that, the style of architecture can be fitted onto the skeleton." It was in this climate of threatening modernism versus eclectic tradition that Ayres, along with most other architects of the late 1920s, made his way.

There followed a full-page plate, captioned

"setting a distinguished standard." It showed a New York dining room with an English Georgian mantel, Waterford glass wall sconces, and flower-filled porcelain figurines. Following that, gender stereotypes unblushingly characterized Richardson Wright's article "The Fascination of Gadgets" in which he advised the reader to "receive the wife's display of her new furniture and everything nice, with all the glowing appreciation you can give, but save a little for that journey into the less decorative parts of the house where the husband will show off his gadgets and machines."

Swaying from side to side with editorial impartiality between Traditional styles and Modernism, the magazine juxtaposed the beautifully detailed Georgian paneling, broken pediments, and fluted columns of the prominent Atlanta firm of Hentz, Adler and Shutze with "House and Gardens Modern House Series," "over which efficiency rules." It featured a sleek, chrome and rubber tile kitchen designed by the celebrated modernist architect and industrial designer Donald Deskey, who wrote: "Strongly as one may object to the term 'Machine Age' when applied to modern architecture, there can be no doubt of its fitness when considering the kitchen. We may cling tenaciously to words like 'liveable' and 'traditional' in a description of a living room, but the kitchen is best thought of in terms of the machine."

The pendulum then swung to a scholarly essay by Sir Lawrence Weaver, editor of the distinguished English periodical *Country Life*. His article focused on a major figure of the English Arts and Crafts Movement, Ernest Gimson, whom he discussed as of the tradition of William Morris, Webb, Lethaby, The Art Workers Guild (1884), and the Arts and Crafts Exhibitions of 1888 and 1890. Gimson's furniture celebrated the beauty of solid wood. There was no question of veneering. This article was immediately followed by "Rooms in the colors of Louis XV and XVI," before the magazine moved on to the essentials of closet planning—showing efficient arrangements of the linen closet—and then to gardens and meadows of iris. Plaster ornaments for collectors were presented as American antiques, which were "to the poor and middle class what Staffordshire pieces were to the rich and well-to-do."

In 1929, after a study of brick textures in home interiors, illustrating color, shadows, joints, and bonds of brick, *House and Garden* presented "A House of Distinction in San Antonio—Atlee B. & Robert M. Ayres, Architects." This was the Carl Newton House, captioned "In A Restrained Andalusian Design" and described with stern admiration as a distinguished expression of Spanish motifs. "Colorful, yet restrained, it avoids the picturesque excesses generally committed in the name of Iberian architecture." Two full pages showed two elevations, a close-up of an entrance door, and first- and second-floor plans. The Ayreses' house was followed by one by John Staub, inspired by the old Absinthe House in New Orleans, which Staub found suitable to the Louisianan climate of Houston. The architecture section of the magazine continued its survey of southern houses with a new adobe house in Santa Fe.

Eclectic interiors required knowledge of a wide range of finish materials, furniture, and furnishings. One page included chromite wall tiles, sterling silver in Adam, Stickley, Early American seventeenth-century reproductions, imported Old World fabrics, and Wedgwood dinnerware. There followed pages advertising Frigidaires, incinerators, trunk lifts, hardware of Spanish origin, toilet seats in "lovely sea-pearl tints," period moldings in Flamproof [*sic*] wood, health foods, and Della Robbia Mints. The prevailing Euro-snobbery emerged in the French Line advertisement that addressed itself to "People who have been everywhere. . . But don't talk about it. . . . People who couldn't bore you. . . wouldn't be bothered impressing you. . . . Casual, amusing, lightly critical, recognizing their own kind at a

glance." The issue ended in a flurry of advice for tree and lawn care, flowers, bulbs, fertilizers, grass seed, and deterrents to fleas and lice.

Atlee mined his magazines assiduously. He had his employees cut out pages that contained material that particularly interested him. His cache of plates was useful to him for design inspiration. He would also show selections to clients in the early stages of design in order to stimulate and flush out their desires, preferences, inclinations, and tastes. These in turn would help Ayres in deciding the appropriate style for the client's house. The plates, augmented by photographs taken by Ayres on his travels, became an extended library that served not only as a rich source of images and expansion of his design vocabulary but also that of his clients. Style became a common language and bond for working together. Not least in importance to Ayres, the magazines provided him the publicity, the valuable exposure of his own projects and articles as they were published in both professional architectural journals and in the popular press.

The plates and articles that Ayres had cut out of the magazines were carefully filed in specially designed storage cabinets in the penthouse office he occupied from 1929 in the Smith-Young Tower in San Antonio. As described by Ayres in his article titled "Efficiency Rules in the Pent-House Office" in *The American Architect* April, 1935, volume 146, the specially built storage system comprised a 14' x 8' filing cabinet protected by paneled doors. It was divided into two sections: an upper cabinet that contained nearly 5,000 mounted, classified, and indexed photographs of architectural subjects. The lower section contained 134 open-fronted drawers, 5" x 11" x 15", which held flat architectural plates trimmed to a uniform size and numbered to correspond to a drawer number. These were filed about every four months, according to an index covering two hundred classifications. The index sheets to the various trays were mounted on the rear of the doors. Text matter was indexed according to classification and filed in a steel cabinet. Judging from the irritable tone of Ayres's letters to magazines when issues failed to arrive on time or arrived in poor condition, it seems that the plates were clearly of great importance to him. In fact, to facilitate this operation, he suggested in a letter to Scribner's Sons that the plates have perforated edges. Scribner's tactfully replied that it was a good idea but not permitted by the U.S. Postal Service.

Even a small random sampling of the hundreds of items in Ayres's clippings files gives an idea of the sort of material that Ayres had culled from the magazines.[1] Although as a good eclectic, he cast his net wide, including projects of the proponents of the anti-historical, modernist International style—Walter Gropius, Richard Schindler, Richard Neutra, and Philip Johnson—Ayres mainly collected material on American houses in the Mediterranean, especially the Spanish style, and on those architects who were well known for their Spanish style projects. Most of those were in Southern California. From *Architectural Record,* Ayres culled a picture of the patio

of the Arthur Vincent House by George Washington Smith, one of the most famous exponents of the Spanish style. From *The Architectural Forum* came pictures of more Smith houses: his 1916 Heberton House, the first house of the simple, rural, Andalusian type built in California; and Mrs. Willard P. Lindley's house with its curious little exterior stair arching up to an open loggia by a pointed chimney, with its deeply recessed door and round window and little iron lamp. In *Pacific Coast Architect,* Ayres found houses by the most well-known Los Angeles architects: the Eisner House by Gordon Kaufmann and the shining sweep of the long stucco façade of the Arthur Bourne House by E. Wallace Neff (fig. 10), architect to many of the Hollywood elite. Not immune to celebrities, Ayres saved pictures of the Spanish style Falcon Lair, the estate of Rudolph Valentino in Beverley Hills, and the fireplace in Buster Keaton's house (fig. 11). In *The Western Architect,* a house by the Santa Monica architect John Byers was illustrated by interiors of the living room and dining room, whose beamed and coffered ceilings, and sparse and lean furniture

Fig. 10. Arthur K. Bourne House, San Marino, California, 1925, Wallace Neff, architect, front exterior view reproduced from Ayres Clippings Files. The Alexander Architectural Archive, UT–Austin

were in the purest Spanish style. Another Byers house featured a charming outdoor fireplace under a wood Monterrey balcony, similar to that at Ayres's Atkinson-McNay House. Ayres also collected plans and aerial views, and pictures of the streets and buildings of Palos Verdes, a Mediterranean style, Los Angeles suburb planned by Frederick Law Olmstead. Ayres's files included the Dater House by Bertram Goodhue, whose baroque Churrigueresque style buildings at the 1925 San Diego Pan-American Exposition contributed significantly to the popularity of Spanish styles. Atlee also saved the May, 1927, issue of *The Architect and Engineer,* which had a collection of seven Spanish style houses by leading Southern California architects such as Marston, Van Pelt, Maybury, and others.

One of the most charming items in the clippings file is a large, fancy booklet, titled "Santa Barbara Biltmore Souvenir," published in May, 1927. The cover was a steel chromatic etching in three colors. The luxurious inn was described as "an approach to a Don's estate." Further praise included: "Barcelona might look like this, but here the air is perfumed. . . . The footman in a Spanish officer's uniform lends the proper atmosphere for this bit of Andalusia." Of course, there were bullfight posters. The brochure contained a photograph of a debonair Reginald Johnson, the properly pedigreed architect, son of the bishop of the Episcopal Church of Southern California. He graduated from the Massachusetts Institute of Technology and then studied architecture in Paris and traveled abroad for several years. Recipient of the 1921 gold medal from the American Institute of Architects, Johnson might well have been someone for Ayres to emulate. And well he might have wanted his own houses to be described like the Biltmore: "Its lines are elegant, its appearance immaculate, it portrays gentility and culture, and its red tile roof rests gracefully on it like the brilliant cloaks gathered about the bodies of proud old 'Señors.'" There was also much to be learned from the

lengthy text, which, in the days before color photography, described in detail the colors of the materials of the exteriors and furnishings of the interiors.

Not all the houses in Mediterranean and Spanish styles were from California. Indeed, the clippings files reveal that Atlee was very much interested in the work being done in Florida, particularly in Palm Beach, and especially the houses that Addison Mizner was designing for the very rich winter crowd. In 1926, *Vogue* remarked on the "new castles in Spain that are rising on the shores of Florida." Atlee had pictures of the vaulted loggia ceiling of Mizner's Codman House, and Mr. and Mrs. Hugh Dillman's patio— a lacy, trefoiled, cross-vaulted, gothic cloister paved in a large herringbone, with a Romanesque

Fig. 11. Buster Keaton Cast Stone Fireplace, reproduced from Ayres Clippings Files. The Alexander Architectural Archive, UT–Austin

fountain, high Italian chairs, and lilies in pots. While much of the material Ayres culled from magazines focused on the views of the whole house, many photographs studied picturesque parts of the exterior: a corner of the patio, an exterior stairway, a doorway or window, a fountain, a gate. Nor did Atlee's collection neglect the palatial Mizner living rooms with their tapestries, stiff chairs, draped piano, lecterns, and iron candleholders.

While the preponderance of the examples in Ayres's clippings files came from California and Florida, where Mediterranean style buildings dominated the 1920s scene, some were of houses elsewhere in the country. The April, 1919, *Architecture* provided Ayres with a picture of an "Italian" loggia of a house in Andover, New Jersey. The *Architectural Forum* of February, 1926, had the Villa Maria on the dunes of Southampton, New York, and in February, 1932, a Spanish style house in East Hampton. The prominent Chicago architect David Adler was represented by an Italianate interior of vaulted plaster and terrazzo floor, culled from the October, 1922, issue of *Architectural Record,* and by his Dillingham House in Honolulu, which was based on the Medici villa in Fiesole. The clippings files contained examples of Italian and Spanish style houses from climates as different as those of Denver, Colorado, and Dublin, New Hampshire, the latter with an arcaded cloister as well as ten fireplaces. One of the most opulent period interiors was that of the English architect Alfred C. Bossom in New York. The plates of the article, captioned "A Sumptuous New York Spanish Interior," showed Bossom's drawing room and exhibition-reception room offices. Under the ponderous antique wood beams, the rooms were crammed with heavy Italian and Spanish pieces, Savanarola and high-backed, velvet-covered, gold-fringed chairs, elaborate, tall torchères of electrified candles on floors covered with rare oriental rugs. On the stenciled plaster walls hung large antique tapestries of gods and heroes and classical landscapes.

Ayres also had a description of the Malcolm Whitmanses' New York apartment, "On both sides of the fireplace, executed after the old Italian style, are rare sixteenth century Genovese tapestries of red velvet." The back of the blue damask sofa was a piece of rare Sicilian lace. An 1928 advertisement of A. Kimbel & Son—a New York firm dealing in antiques, fabrics, interior decoration, and reproductions—showed a photograph of an "Early Italian Study" with finely leaded windows, on which someone had penciled in "Dining Room-Windows," perhaps for use on an Ayres project? While Ayres concentrated on Italian and Spanish styles in the 1920s, his earlier focus had been on English and American Colonial styles and those practitioners who were especially skilled in them. His clippings files contained *The Architect* detail series of measured drawings of Georgian doorways (fig. 12), the *Brickbuilders* collection of Early American architectural details, pictures of the Hammond Harwood House in Annapolis, and the work of John Russell Pope.

To augment the photographs he had collected on his travels in Italy and Spain, Ayres extracted from the magazines further examples of authentic Mediterranean architecture. The clippings files contain pictures of the Villa d'Este at Tivoli near Rome, the Villa Frullini near Florence, and the fourteenth-century Palazzo Contarini-Fasan in Venice with its lacy marbled balconies and embroidered windows. There were also pictures of Moorish architecture: the Alhambra in Granada, a fountain and tiled arches from Tangier, and a portfolio of sketches of patios in Spain.

As a practicing architect, Ayres was naturally interested in building materials, especially those that were essential to Italian and Spanish styles. He saved an article from *Arts and Decoration,* July, 1929, that advised: "No Spanish home is complete without balconies and window grills. In fact, these appear to be inevitable features of the homes in every land where women are—or have been—held as glorified prisoners. At any rate, one

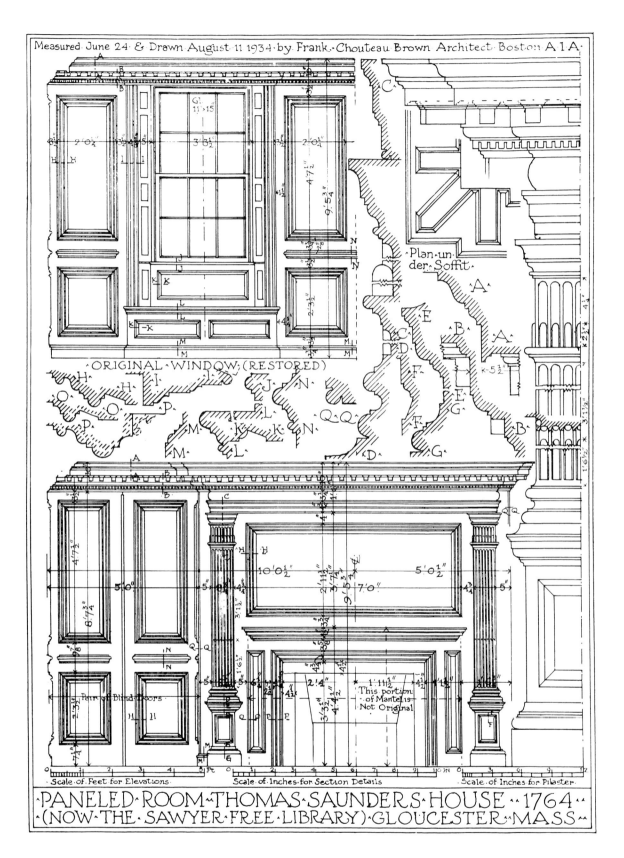

ORIGINAL WINDOW (RESTORED)

Plan under Soffit

Pair of Blind Doors

This portion of Mantel is Not Original

Scale of Feet for Elevations

Scale of Inches for Section Details

Scale of Inches for Pilaster

PANELED ROOM THOMAS SAUNDERS HOUSE 1764
(NOW THE SAWYER FREE LIBRARY) GLOUCESTER MASS

Fig. 12. Paneled Room, Measured Drawing, Pencil Points, 1934, reproduced from Ayres Clipping Files. The Alexander Architectural Archive, UT–Austin

may be grateful for conditions which inspired these grilles for the effect is always picturesque." He found examples in *House and Garden, American Architect,* which had details from northern Italy, *Metalcraft* and *The Metal Arts.* Andirons in wrought iron (boiled in oil) were available from William H. Jackson in New York City. Evident in his clippings file—as well as from his office correspondence—was his interest in tiles, decorative wall tiles, paving tiles, and the barrel-shaped roof tiles that were so characteristic of the Mediterranean styles. The files contained a color catalogue from Casa Gonzales containing "ceramica artistica, azulejos de relievo" from Seville, Cordova, and Madrid. From *Arts and Decoration* Ayres had a photograph of the Zuloaga Potteries in Segovia (fig. 13), from which in April, 1925, he bought a tile panel marked "madrid." He had another catalogue of Puebla talavera, handpainted Mexican ceramic tiles shown on stair risers, countertops, pool copings, and oven fronts, as well as terra-cotta floor pavers. William H. Jackson Company's catalogue provided a photograph

of Number 4060, Verona Marble Well Head and Base.

In addition to providing inspiration for Ayres and illustrations for his clients, the magazines played a major role in the Ayres practice as vehicles for publicizing the firm's projects as well as his ideas, opinions, and theories about architecture. The Avery Index lists twenty-three entries for Ayres and Ayres.[2] Ayres persistently sought publicity in magazines, and newspapers as well. He allowed—and on more than one occasion solicited—publication of the firm's buildings in the major architectural journals. In 1920, he received a letter from *Country Homes Magazine* requesting photographs of work and offering to have it photographed. During the late summer or fall of 1921, Scribner's wanted photographs and professed themselves pleased to find a place for publication of an Ayres house. The principal journal that published Ayres work was *The American Architect.* In July, 1923 (vol. 124, no. 2423, p. 46), it published two Ayres houses: the Colonial style Kray House and the Italian style house for Dr. Garret C. Robertson. In the same issue, in an article captioned "Modern American Interiors and Their Correct Furnishing," the author Morris King wrote, "We have lost the grand manner. Our civilization is too raucous, restless, and meticulous to admit of the austerity, dignity, and stateliness of classic times or the Renaissance. . . . Work is often furtive and undecided, proportions are ungracious and walls apt to be overcharged with ornament. . . . In the less costly homes, it is unusually difficult to make any attempt at architectural treatment, as the money has been expended on the building proper, and rooms are merely 'decorated' and furnished."

In the May issue of 1924, *American Architect* published Atlee's own house on Belknap. The photographs of the house, a remodeling of his original 1909 Arts and Crafts style house, showed a pleasant mixture of faintly English Tudor gables with half-timbering and stucco on the upper story above a ground story of random ashlar stone. The two-page spread showed a close-up of the front façade and both floor plans. The coverage of Atlee's own Anglicized house was followed by official notification from the Beaux-Arts Institute of Design of awards for a preliminary competition for the seventeenth Paris Prize. The issue also carried the sad obituary of one of America's most original architects, Louis Henry Sullivan, who had been Frank Lloyd Wright's early employer and mentor. Later, in the August, 1924, issue, *The American Architect* used Atlee's illustrated article "The Earliest Missions of San Antonio."

Southern Architect solicited Ayres's "best" houses plus other photographs suitable for the Annual Country House Number, which was "to contain both large and small houses of all styles." In January, 1924, Atlee subscribed to *Pacific Coast Architect*—indicative of his growing interest in Southern California. The next year, in May, 1925, the same magazine published ten Ayres houses, those for Dr. Garret C. Robertson, W. C. Rigsby, Hiram Partee, Wallace Newton, Dr. F. T. Maessen,

Dr. G. A. Pagenstrecher, David Straus, M. Schreiner, and his own house—all in San Antonio—plus the W. M. Abbey House in Del Rio. This was the first, and as it turned out, the only, published compendium of Ayres's houses, though more individual houses appeared in the succeeding years. The Hiram Partee House was also published in *American Architect* in November of that same year.

In December, 1926, Atlee Ayres attempted to publish the new house of his son and partner, Robert, in several magazines including *Pacific Coast Architect, House and Garden,* and *Country Life,* whose editor replied, "I think that the little Spanish house that your son has just completed is one of the most charming I have seen for a great many months. Will use, send photos, in our July issue which is to be the 'Spanish Renaissance.'" The house was published in *Pacific Coast Architect* in their December issue as well as in the January *Country Life.*

In December, 1927, *The American Architect* published two pages of photographs and plan, without text, of the William M. Abbey House in Del Rio, Texas. The front and rear elevations showed a rather plain rectangular block with a pitched tile roof and stucco façades with faintly Spanish touches. The plan revealed Ayres's continuing dependence on symmetry even as he leaned away from Beaux-Arts principles on the asymmetrical façade.

In January, 1928, *American Architect* published the English Tudor style Oppenheimer House in a single photograph without text. However, later that year on August 20, 1928 (page 237), they published more extensively the 1924 Thomas E. Hogg House, which was really the first of Ayres's houses in an amply realized, Spanish style. There were plans of both floors, showing the use of tile floors in the loggia and morning room, tiled baths, and outside, a brick entrance terrace, and flagstones on the rear terrace, which had a lily pond. There were two close-up details, one of the elaborate entrance with serried moldings of floral motifs arching over the deeply recessed front door, and the other of the rear loggia arches embellished with colonettes and spiral moldings. Photographs of the front and rear façades clearly showed the thick, rather crinkled stucco walls, the rounded corners of deeply recessed windows and doors, the round stair turret, and decorative elements such as the low-relief baronial shield and grilled library windows. Perhaps encouraged by the fine coverage of the Hogg House, Ayres sent photographs of the Carl Newton House to *House and Garden,* which published it in August of 1929.

The Spanish style P. L. Mannen House was first published in November, 1927, in San Francisco in *The Architect and Engineer,* but it received much more lavish coverage in the January issue of *American Architect* under the caption "Old Spanish Ideas Adapted to the Design of a House in San Antonio, Texas." The six pages had photographs of the entire front elevation, of part of that elevation, the front door, and the loggia. There were plans of both the first and second floors and a short introductory and quite laudatory text. It noted, "Much of the architecture in this country today, as during the last twenty-five or fifty years, is designated as an adaptation of one or other of the old periods or styles. . . . These reproductions of certain old forms are lacking almost entirely in evidence of creative ability." However, the Mannen House was judged to be *not* merely a reproduction but rather to be "appropriate to the climate of Texas, and, while it bears marked evidence of Spanish influence, it may be said to be truly a modern American home." The close-ups emphasized the light on the uneven stucco walls, the arches of the loggia arcade, the trellis of rough cedar limbs, the tiled fountain, the iron window gratings, and the second-story wood balcony.

The qualities of Ayres's by now full-blown Spanish style were evident in the group of pen and ink sketches—by Atlee and Robert for the Terrell Hills Development Company—published in *American Architect* in July, 1929. These were perspective views of asymmetrical houses romantically nestled in deep foliage and dark shadows, houses with thick buttresses of stuccoed hollow tile, fat chimneys, low arches, tile grills, and solid board shutters, with evocative descriptions of brown trusses and oak floors in the interiors and blue exterior wood trim.

After publication of the Carl Newton House in *Architecture* and *House and Garden* in August, 1929, as "A House of Distinction," Ayres received letters of inquiry from San Francisco, Havana, and Quincy, Massachusetts. Following the July, 1923, issue of *House and Home,* he received a letter, in August, 1924, from an admirer in Long Island City: "I can frankly say your pictured home is as 'friendly' a one as ever seen and as I contemplate building, this is what I aim to strike." There is no evidence that this bore fruit.

House and Garden, in June, 1930, published Atlee's major San Antonio house in the Spanish style—the Atkinson-McNay House—with major captions, "Mediterranean Architecture Inspires The Design of a San Antonio House" and "Nature and Man Combine to Produce the Romantic Atmosphere of Old Spain." The article used three, half-page views of the exterior and the lushly planted tropical courtyard, and four smaller shots of the elaborate arched front door, the ornamental glazed tiled stairs to the roof terrace, and details for the courtyard pool and fountains. There were also plans of all three floors. The emphasis was on the relationship of the rooms to the courtyard garden, via arcades and loggias. The text suggested, "Wherever Nature decrees a zone of perpetual summer, men turn toward the florid, ornate forms in architecture and introduce strong colors in every possible place. While the temperate northern sections of this country derive most of their architectural forms from England and France, the southern parts follow the precedents of Spain and Italy—countries whose climatic conditions are the nearest approach to their own." This was an argument that, in part, Atlee himself used in defense of the Spanish style for San Antonio, though he would have disagreed that either florid forms or strong colors were appropriate. Indeed he preferred the plain white walls and subdued trim colors typical of rural Spanish buildings to the brighter, often garish colors of neighboring Mexico. The text also identified the essential elements of the Spanish style: the decorative wrought iron, ceramic and terra-cotta tiles. The courtyard of the Atkinson-McNay House was published again by Yale University Press much later in 1990, in Mark Alan Hewitt's *The Architect and the American Country House,* along with a view of the Italian-Spanish style house he designed for Dr. and Mrs. Sam Roberts in Kansas City, Missouri. The book included both Atlee and Robert Ayres in a section on architects' biographies.

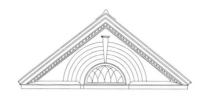

CHAPTER 8

Ayres Houses: Eclectic Experiments, 1898–1923

Colonial Revival, Mission, Prairie, Tudor Revival, Arts and Crafts Styles

Atlee Ayres's search for architectural distinction proceeded through a succession of styles that possessed outward and visible signs by which each one was recognized and identified. Many architects and architectural historians will be familiar with historic styles and most of the terms used to describe Ayres's houses. For others, a number of easily available sources would be very helpful either as a preparation for enjoying the following studies of thirty-six houses in the design of which Atlee had a hand—either alone or with his early partner C. A. Coughlin or for the majority of his career with his son and partner Robert M. Ayres. As the houses were done in a number of styles, a knowledge of the vocabularies of the styles should make the houses more accessible to all. Of course, many other approaches could be made to the houses, ap-

proaches that focus on their cultural, social, and economic dimensions, or on technological matters of construction and materials, all of which were undoubtedly important to Ayres himself as a practicing architect. But it was the aesthetic dimension of architecture that elevated Ayres's work above that of many others and which is best understood in terms of style.

One form of the history of architecture can be written in terms of styles. One of the most comprehensive presentations of stylistic detail is Banister Fletcher's *History of Architecture on the Comparative Method,* first published in London in 1896. The title page, "The Tree of Architecture," illustrated the growth of architecture from prehistoric times to the present, the major loci of its development, and the principal influences that shaped it. Although a net would be a more effective image to illustrate the myriad interconnections across space and time that have actually formed architectural style, Fletcher's linear tree is still a useful introduction to the identification of architectural styles. His large volume is an excellent reference source for their characteristics and was an excellent resource for Atlee and the other architects of his generation who felt a responsibility to be well acquainted with the styles of the past.

Although acquaintanceship with the European and English styles of the past that influenced American architecture is very helpful, Ayres's houses are better enjoyed by those who possess a knowledge of the styles of American architecture itself, from its Colonial beginnings in the seventeenth and eighteenth centuries, through its eclectic transformations in the nineteenth century. For the identification of residential styles and their characteristics, it would be very helpful to be acquainted with Virginia and Lee

McAllester's *A Field Guide to American Houses,* Rachel Carley's *The Visual Dictionary of American Domestic Architecture,* and John Milnes Baker's *American House Styles: A Concise Guide.* There are beautiful color photographs and style notes in *House Styles in America,* by James C. Massey and Shirley Maxwell. For the larger picture of all categories of American building, refer to Alan Gowans's *Styles and Types of North American Architecture: Social Function and Cultural Expression.*

Especially useful in the descriptions and analyses of Ayres's houses was Dora Ware and Maureen Staffords's *An Illustrated Dictionary of Ornament.* Banister Fletcher's *History* also contains a glossary of architectural terms that includes a graphic illustration of comparative arches. Many of the chapters of Fletcher contain excellent illustrations of elements of architectural style, such as the Greek and Roman Orders of columns and capitals, essential for understanding and describing classical architecture, whose influence has continued

Fig. 14. Aerial View of Monte Vista, San Antonio, 1927. The UT Institute of Texan Cultures, no. 83-1069, Atlee B. Ayres Collection

through American Colonial architecture to the present day. For assistance with architectural terms, a glossary of those used in the chapters on the houses is provided at the end of the book.

The author has seen, at least from the outside, all of the extant San Antonio houses presented in this book, and an especially fine Ayres house in Kansas City, Kansas. However, it was thorough study of the extensive original working drawings and specifications—in the Alexander Architectural Archive, in the Battle Hall Library of the University of Texas in Austin—that provided much of the data used in the descriptive analysis of each house. The Alexander Archive also contains historic photographs of most of the houses shortly after their completion. As most of the houses have been changed over the years—some of them radically so—the book focuses on them as they were designed and originally built. However, new photographs of some of the best-preserved houses have been taken for this book by W. Eugene George.

Atlee Ayres's early career was nurtured by the timely flourishing of new residential suburbs in San Antonio. By the 1890s, the city—by then with a population of nearly 38,000—was outgrowing the old city of plazas, wandering streets, and the early residential blocks of the King William District, the first planned subdivision established in the 1870s. Later in the nineteenth century, attention turned to the area north of downtown, where the land rose gradually. Rocky, dry, and barren hills sustained only mesquite brush, cat claws, chaparral, and wild mountain laurel. But the location offered more salubrious air, quiet, and the possibility of gardens and lawns. In the 1890s the area known as Tobin Hill began to attract San Antonio's affluent. On French Place, Judge Leroy Denman built a stately classical mansion, and the Woodhulls built a sprawling, verandahed house overlooking sweeping lawns. It was in this area that Ayres—together with his first partner, C. A. Coughlin—designed his first houses, mainly in the popular Colonial Revival style.

The residential suburbs continued to grow up the hill with the development of Laurel Heights (fig. 14), whose original seventy-five acres were bounded by Summit and McCullough, south to Woodlawn, west to San Pedro, and back to Howard at Magnolia. Early advertisements extolled its virtues: "It is 100 feet above the city, above the mud and the mosquitoes, has the finest views, the healthiest location with the purest air, best shade, the best ocean breezes, widest streets and avenues." Thanks to San Antonio's underground water resources, the barren hills began to support new planting, palm trees along the streets, and landscaped lawns extending to the front property lines. Many of the residents supported a public campaign against fences and participated in annual contests for "the most beautiful yards," inaugurated in 1911. From the beginning, Laurel Heights was seen as a high-class suburban property, with ample restrictions to ensure the quality of the houses and their residents. Residents of Summit Place agreed to the following 1906 restrictions: "the said premises shall be used for residence purposes only, and no part thereof shall be used for business purposes. . . . Only . . . a first class private residence with the customary outbuildings, including private stables, garage and servant house" was permitted. It was also stipulated that "such residence shall cost and be fairly worth not less than Twenty Thousand Dollars." (By 1926 the minimum cost had been raised to $30,000.)

By 1907, Laurel Heights was San Antonio's premier residential location: "a dream of loveliness and architectural beauty." In this choice and salubrious area, Ayres's practice multiplied, producing designs for many of the houses in Laurel Heights in a variety of eclectic styles. Some showed influences from American Colonial and English Tudor precedents, from the Spanish missions, the work of Louis Sullivan, Frank Lloyd Wright and the Midwestern Prairie School, as well as from foreign examples of the Viennese Succession and the English Arts and Crafts

Movement. Ayres's wide-ranging eclecticism was not a matter of youthful uncertainty or lack of principle. More likely, it was a matter of youthful experimentation. In the first decade of the twentieth century, diversity was much admired. A reporter noted in 1912 that "One of the elements of San Antonio's picturesqueness is found in the variety of styles represented in her residences."

Growth continued north of Laurel Heights with the development of Summit Place and Laurel Heights Terrace in 1910. Advertisements pointedly claimed that "this is not a district of inexpensive bungalows, but of stately mansions, of homes that represent the culture and wealth of San Antonio's most exclusive, aristocratic circles." Residential construction did not falter during the First World War. Next to be developed were the ninety-four acres of Monte Vista stretching between McCullough and San Pedro from Kings Highway, with further additions to Hildebrandt, and the addition of Oakmont—proclaimed to offer a "mountain view stretching north to the hills of Blanco and Bandera," and (even more exaggeratedly) a view "veiled in a lazy purplish haze," stretching "to the foothills of the Rockies." It was to be a neighborhood of "culture, refinement and good breeding," with fifteen homes from $40,000 to $62,000 in 1923. As for style—

In the home under construction in San Antonio at the present time it is safe to say that the Colonial entrance is the most popular. This probably comes from the way homebuilders in the United States are adopting the Colonial type of architecture. But it is also safe to say that the Colonial entrance is one of the most beautiful. It immediately bespeaks the hospitality of the home. It offers the visitor a cordial welcome. People are finding this out and as the doorway is now receiving a greater part of the attention of the homebuilder, it is estimated that every tenth house

erected recently is either entirely colonial or has windows, doors and mantels in that style . . . . There are modified Spanish types of architecture and the extreme Spanish types of architecture and the extreme Spanish lines. During the recent years Italian designs have been mixed with Spanish and Moorish and the result, so far as the entrance is concerned, is pleasing to the eye. There are only a few doorways in San Antonio alike. The same is true of people. A neighbor's house is hardly ever copied, nor are any part of its architectural designs duplicated in the grounds or outhouses.[1]

It was for those rapidly expanding suburbs that Atlee and his partner, C. A. Coughlin, designed their early houses. Beginning in 1898, they soon had a thriving practice, building large houses for San Antonio's elite. One of their earliest was the 1900 J. Bruce Martindale House at the northeast corner of West Magnolia and Belknap (figs. 15 and 16). Like most of Ayres's houses built in the first decade of practice, the house was an elusive mixture of motifs applied to a simple, two-story, brick block. The house was capped with a high, green-tiled, pitched roof with deep overhangs ornamented by pairs of large brackets and rows of exposed purlins. In the attic's gable, there was a large Palladian window keeping company with one of the several tall, narrow chimneys. The front slope of the pitched roof had two large dormer windows, each with its own heavy projecting gable and dwarf balustrade. These, together with a corresponding pair of large bay windows in the second floor, lent the house a semblance of symmetrical balance. However, the symmetry was violated on the ground floor by a long, deep porch that extended beyond the house to form a *porte cochere* beside the asymmetrically placed front door. Brick piers flanked by rectangular brick columns with Corinthian capitals supported a flat roof deck with a continuous wood balustrade. On the south side, a two-story,

Fig. 15. James Bruce Martindale House, 1900, front exterior view. The UT Institute of Texan Cultures, no. 83-787, courtesy Florence Collett Ayres

classical flat-roofed sleeping porch supported by wood, circular, fluted columns would catch the prevailing breezes. The miscellany of window sizes and placements further diluted the gestures of classical Colonial elements, which, in the end, appear as curiosities rather than an integral part of consistent style—an effect not without charm. This was true of the interiors as well. Despite the classical plaque over the fireplace, they retained a *fin de siecle,* even Victorian, atmosphere of high, dark wood wainscoting, cornice, ceiling beams, and square columns with Art Nouveau capitals. Strikingly similar to the Bruce Martindale House was the house Ayres designed at about the same time (1903) for John W. Furnish at 515 Belknap Place. A pair of similar gabled dormers emerged from the steep-sloped gabled roof, but—unlike the Martindale House—there were pairs of small Doric columns and no dwarf balconies. The similarly asymmetrical front porch and *porte cochere* were again more elaborate: two stories, the upper story supported by slender paired columns that also supported the *porte cochere.* The main supporting piers of the lower porch were faced

with pilasters supported on triangular brick corbels. Two of these had narrow arched recesses. Two more supported intricate Corinthian half capitals at the entrance bay, which was distinguished by a curved pediment. Railings of closely spaced, slender balusters ran between the columns and piers. The presence of classical elements, though used with singular innovation and lack of integrated consistency, would have been accepted as what would have been called Colonial, though not at all like authentic seventeenth- or eighteenth-century American Colonial houses. The side of the house was an even more eccentric collection of gables, of corbelled, arched pediments and a balconied, Serlian window in the attic. Overall, the house presented a sturdy, compact, dignified block with some rather pretty ornamental architectural details that were scented faintly with classicism.

This caused some confusion of terminology in its day and still does. Freely applied classical elements—used previously in Colonial America sparingly and with at least an attempt at accurate reproduction of precedents in England—characterized most of the houses that Ayres designed in the early years of Laurel Heights for prominent clients (Dalkowit, Silliman, Sam Harris, C. T. Priest, Judge Winchester Kelso, J. O. Terrell, the Lang brothers, and H. P. Drought). The presence of recognizably Colonial elements, no matter where or how used, was sufficient for a house to be labeled as "Colonial." This nomenclature, somewhat inaccurate but entirely intelligible in its day—and not only in San Antonio—persisted in the press of the day. Ayres's 1903 Jarratt House at 238 West Craig was described in the local newspaper as "Neo-Georgian Revival" or "Colonial in every detail." Ayres himself in 1906 declared that "the Colonial style seems to be the most popular at present."[2]

However, quite early, in the William Negley House—built 1901–1903 (plan 2) at 421 Howard in Tobin Hill—Ayres looked with a more scholarly eye at the American Colonial houses of the

Fig. 16. James Bruce Martindale House, 1900, interior view of entrance hall. The UT Institute of Texan Cultures, no. 83-790, courtesy Florence Collett Ayres

East Coast (color plate 1). Perhaps it was that his client came from Maryland and was familiar with the quintessential center hall plan, and the perfect symmetry of façade—the nobility of portico of the pure eighteenth-century American Colonial houses. In any case, the Negley House was a dignified brick block with a hipped, tin roof crowned by a decorative, turned balustrade. The majestic, two-story, pedimented portico had four, stately, fluted columns of cypress, 20" in diameter at the base and 17" at the top. They were crowned with elegant capitals—a mixture of Ionic and Corinthian orders—labeled "composition" on the working drawings of the house. Ayres took liberties by spacing the columns wide in pairs, probably to show off the Palladian, fan-lighted front door and the iron-railed balcony above it. Otherwise

the house presented a dignified, ordered classical façade of two stories, with balanced windows and side porches. The detailing was conservative and more or less "correct," with narrow stone quoins at the corners, stone lintels with keystones, and stone sills at the windows (in the original drawings shown correctly without shutters), the correct pitch of the pediment and gabled roof, the crowning balustrade. These conspired to make a fine piece of academic eclecticism, at least from the front. The symmetry began to dissolve on the sides, as the internal requirements for light began to take precedence. It disappeared entirely at the back of the house, which frankly revealed the diversity of the spaces behind it. The stair landing was illuminated by pairs of semicircular-headed windows with leaded glass and diagonal wood muntin bars. The Colonial multiple-paned, double-hung windows of the living room gave way on the rear wall to three high, leaded glass windows and a flower shelf in a curious shallow bay with a little shingle roof. Behind the kitchen was a two-story, latticed service porch.

Inside, Ayres was also true to tradition. The stair rose from a 15' x 32' center hall with Ionic columns. The hall gave onto a library on one side and a dining room on the other, all with 11' ceilings—spacious, balanced rooms with each wall symmetrically arranged. Upstairs, under 10' ceilings, there were four bedrooms, a bathroom, and a servant's room. The strict formal relations, so carefully manipulated on the ground floor, were less easily managed in the many upstairs rooms, which were generously sized and pleasantly proportioned, but full of little awkwardnesses where functional convenience decided the placement of doors or the ad hoc installation of a triangular closet. But even with the more complicated requirements of the early twentieth century, the overall character of the house was clearly and relatively authentic Colonial.

Ayres was again relatively true to authentic eighteenth-century Colonial buildings in the 1911 John W. Kokernot House (color plate 2) at 119 East Kings Highway—at least from the outside. Tall fluted columns, 22" in diameter at the base, with "staff" capitals, supported the triangular pediment of the dignified portico. The symmetrical façade—the white, turned balustrades and little classical urns, the corner quoins, the dentils, the egg and dart moldings lining the eaves of the roof—all lent an air of true Colonial architecture. Inside, it was less convincingly so. Though arranged around a traditional central stair hall flanked by the living room on one side and the dining room on the other, the interior lacked the simplicity and lightness of Colonial interiors. Instead, one found heavy beams crossing the ceilings of the rooms, a fireplace with a semicircular arch lined with rows of brick voussoirs and flanked by leaded, plate-glass cabinet

fronts reminiscent of Louis Sullivan or of some Arts and Crafts master. *The San Antonio Express* described the house: "The general style is colonial and Atlee. B. Ayres, the architect, has taken advantage of the commanding site, with its view over the entire city, and erected a truly beautiful house."[3] The article's admiration was not reserved only for the traditional style but also noted, "As an indicator of the up-to-dateness in every respect, in this twentieth century home, a vacuum system of cleaning has been installed, something which the housekeeper is beginning to demand in San Antonio, and it is safe to say the great majority of the new homes in the future will have these labor-saving systems." The house also had garages capable of storing two cars and three carriages. Atlee, as most eclectic architects of the early twentieth century, saw no schism between the traditions of the past and the inventions of the present.

The early years of Ayres's practice were not entirely focused on the Colonial Revival. In fact, they were better described as a time for experimenting. For in 1909—at the same time that the Colonial Revival John W. Furnish House rose on Belknap—another very different Ayres house was completed in the neighborhood west of Monte Vista known as Beacon Hill. Apparently built speculatively by D. K. Furnish and his partners, it is now known only from drawings as the Nicholson/Furnish/Smith House (fig. 17; plan 1). It was one of a number of Ayres's houses of the first decade that eschewed Colonial references and defied clear stylistic attribution. It still intrigues and challenges analysis by the diversity and ambiguity of its architectural elements, a kind of eclectic hybrid.

The house, located at 1015 West Woodlawn, was a standard, solid, Victorian four-square, two-story-plus attic block. This substantial mass was wrapped on the front and one side with a broad porch, designated a "gallery." In these respects, it was similar to the Colonial Revival houses. But, unlike them, it was nearly devoid of the elements

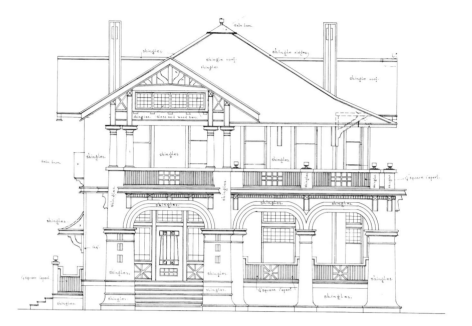

FRONT ELEVATION.
SCALE ¼"-0.'

Fig. 17.
Nicholson/
Furnish/Smith
House, 1908,
drawing of front
elevation, repro-
duced from origi-
nal working
drawings, n.d.
The Alexander
Architectural
Archive, UT–
Austin

of the classical vocabulary: the classical orders, the Greek and Roman motifs, or the English Palladian or Adamesque neoclassical elements that were essential parts of Colonial style. Only the plain Doric dwarf columns of the upstairs porch over the entrance, and the balustrade of the front porch, where square, Roman, wooden grills alternated between the posts, sounded brief classical notes. Unclassically, the house was neither of brick nor stone, but, except for its tall stuccoed chimneys, was completely clad in wood shingles that went all the way from the ground to the high, hipped roof crowned with a galvanized iron ridge. The shingles also sheathed the slightly battered piers of the porch. The shingles recalled the earlier work of H. H. Richardson.[4] They may also have come to Ayres's attention in the current architectural journal coverage of contemporary English country houses, including the early country houses of Edwin Lutyens, which reflected the Edwardian nostalgia for the timber structures of medieval and Elizabethan

English buildings.[5] In the Nicholson/Furnish/Smith House this was mingled with the decorative structural exhibitionism of the American Arts and Crafts Movement in the gables of the attic where multipaned, "belly" windows were screened by elaborated compositions of brackets and beams and cosmetic half-timbering. The picture was made even more elusive by the strange, broad, flattened arches of the porch and the front door itself, vaguely recalling the Art Nouveau work of Ayres's Scottish contemporary, Charles Rennie Mackintosh.[6] Ayres's striving for effect can be seen in his ingenious design for the windows, which were complicated combinations of large, clear panes and small, rectangular panes below the transom bar, and multipaned segment above. Despite appearances, the windows were simple, with a single-hung sash, whose lower two-thirds slid up into concealed pockets in the wall above, a meeting of English style with the need for ventilation in the hot climate of San Antonio.

The house was arranged very conventionally for its time, with a generous reception room leading through double sliding pocket doors into a parlor, which in turn connected through similar doors into the dining room. The dark-beamed reception room had a built-in seat under a low arch that screened the stair, a little *mise en scène,* strongly suggestive of the rooms of the Viennese Succession, which Atlee could see in his books, in the magazines, and on his travels.[7] He was sufficiently fond of this arrangement to use it again, in virtual duplicate, in the Alex Halff House in 1908. The stairs were a typical combination of front stairs and back service stairs that joined at a mid-landing. The second floor held four bedrooms and a bathroom. The design of this house seems to reveal Ayres's desire to experiment, especially to extend the turn-of-the-century four-square house with an interesting variety of influences, of motifs and materials—some perhaps from England and Europe, some from the Shingle style and the emerging Chicago School, others from the American Arts and Crafts tradition, and what one local newspaper called the "California style." His taste for simplicity, even formality—perhaps the lingering effects of his Beaux-Arts training in New York—appeared in his obvious efforts to resolve the eccentric complexities of the bedrooms, to simplify and regularize the shapes of the rooms, by accommodating the jogs of the plan behind arches, creating subspaces instead of complicating the main volume of the room. What at first glance appeared to be a conventionally complicated Victorian interior, was instead a set of carefully ordered, well-proportioned, tailored rooms. It was this attention to the finer possibilities of design that formed part of Ayres's early reputation that blossomed in the first decades of the century.

It was in this same vein of imaginative hybrid eclecticism that Atlee designed in 1907 the Armand and Hattie Halff House (plan 1) at 105 Madison (fig. 18). It was another substantial four-square building with a shingled hipped roof and projecting lateral gables in the attic. Above the stone base and wide steps, there were giant, two-story columns with capitals of "Exterior Composition" similar to Number 315 in Atlee's copy of the Decorators Supply Company's catalogue. These were all edged with classical egg and dart moldings, and dentils in galvanized iron. But there was little else classical, or "Colonial," about it. The shingled gabled ends of the attic had unusual, low, arched windows and dwarf balconies. The house was entered through an asymmetrical entrance under a low-springing depressed arch, an early example of Ayres's many experiments with arched forms. Beyond, there were beveled glass panes and leaded glass sidelights in the front door. The windows had large single panes of plate glass below and leaded, beveled, plate glass transoms, ashlar stone sills and lintels. The effect was still vaguely Queen Anne, but simplified—perhaps by winds from the Chicago School, from Sullivan or even Wright?[8]

Within, the picture became even more variegated. The plan was very similar to that of the Nicholson/Furnish/Smith House, but reversed: consisting of a generous entrance reception room and stair on the right front corner; the parlor on the other; the dining room behind the parlor; and the service areas behind the front stair hall. It was an arrangement well suited to the requirements of family living and entertaining with the help of servants who could operate unseen by the back stairs. The principal stair rose behind a seat and arch with turned spindles in the dark paneled and beamed reception hall. The atmosphere was vaguely European, like some turn-of-the-century bourgeois town house, but also vaguely English, though perhaps a little too tidy for the Victorian taste. It was a generous house, 12'6" from ground floor to second floor. There were fireplaces in the reception, parlor, and dining room. The dining room had large, triple windows of plate glass and a transom of diamond-paned, cast-iron ornament. Evidence of Atlee's Beaux-Arts training was in the use of linear axes to align

FRONT ELEVATION
SCALE ¼"-1'0"

ATLEE B. AYRES.
ARCHITECT

Fig. 18. Armand and Hattie Halff House, 1907, drawing of front elevation, reproduced from original working drawings, n.d. The Alexander Architectural Archive, UT–Austin

the rooms and the many local symmetries formally. Even in the four large bedrooms upstairs, Ayres was careful to shape each room clearly and simply, relegating odd necessities to a set of subspaces.

At that point, in 1909, Atlee, by then well established, built a house for himself, his wife, and his two young sons at 201 Belknap (fig. 19; plan 3, 1909). The house was identifiably in the currently fashionable Craftsman style, featuring twin, high-peaked gables and a similarly pitched, tall dormer in the attic roof; heavy, dark, applied half-timbering above the rubble stone of the first floor; and large glass panes of the thickly framed and divided windows. The style also permeated the interiors, especially the dark wood paneled

living room with its deep raised inglenook where cozy banquettes flanked the heavy wood chimneypiece (figs. 20 and 21). Sturdy, simple wood chairs and tables completed the classically Craftsman picture. The room had some of the qualities so admired by Herman Muthesius in *The English House* published at the turn of the century, qualities that attracted many architects interested in the Arts and Crafts in Germany and Austria. The upstairs was similarly compact and well planned. The three bedrooms, sitting room, and even the two baths all reflected Ayres's lingering concern for symmetry, axes, and balance—carefully placed windows and doors, and pleasant proportions. Large porches on the east and south sides of the ground floor and sleeping

Fig. 19. Atlee B. Ayres House, front view of 1909 exterior. The UT Institute of Texan Cultures, no. 83-488, courtesy Florence Collett Ayres

porches above responded to the warm climate and prevailing breezes from the southeast. The house was a little ahead of its time, and a little "foreign."

In the early 1920s, Atlee extensively remodeled his 1909 house, transforming it to a more clearly defined English Tudor style (fig. 22). He removed the prominent gabled dormer in the attic. He lightened the scale of the dark half-timbering and replaced the windows with generous banks of small-paned windows. He simplified and unified the front façade with a continuous band of half-timbering. The house became more properly English on the outside. Inside (plan 3, 1922), Atlee transformed the dark, wood-paneled living room (fig. 23). He eliminated the projecting inglenook and added instead a shallow bay window. He replaced the heavy wood paneling with pale, mottled plaster that lent an antique flavor. The fireplace was repositioned symmetrically on one wall and a new, cast-stone chimneypiece bore figures in decorative niches with trefoiled arches, so authentic in appearance as to suggest that it might actually have been excised from a late

medieval Tudor manor house. (It was in fact virtually identical to a chimneypiece in the opulent New York apartment of the architect Alfred Bossom.) On the wall above, Atlee placed a small circular plaque in the style of the Renaissance Italian sculptor Luca della Robbia. With richly carved chairs, tables draped with tasseled cloths, and the floor covered with a large oriental rug, the room had acquired a European elegance and a semblance of historical pedigree. In fact, the interiors of Atlee's house had a distinctively European flavor—similar in simplicity to some of Adolf Loos's Viennese interiors—especially in the breakfast room, which had a beamed and slightly arched ceiling from which was hung a wrought-iron chandelier with candle-like bulbs, and walls of stained Flemish oak. A long seat with a pile of pillows was built in under a high bank of windows in a low-arched niche. French doors led to a tiled, open-air dining terrace.

After completing his original house in 1909, Atlee's interest soon turned to influences from the Midwest, from Louis Sullivan, Frank Lloyd Wright, and the Prairie style, which gave subtle inflections to the large houses he continued to build in Monte Vista.[9] The 1911 Roy Hearne House (fig. 24) was a light-cream-colored, brick volume under a spreading, hipped roof of glazed green, Mission tile, which sheltered vast porches and terraces on the second level above the equally spacious porches of the first floor. A smaller terrace opened off the attic ballroom/billiard room and was sheltered by its own projecting, tiled roof and Mission style, Alamoesque pediment. Thus, the house formed something of a pyramid rising in three tiers of porches from a smooth, cream limestone base. The house was entered either through a broad, stone-trimmed, segmental arch or from the side *porte cochere.* Both the arch and the Romanesque decorative frieze within the front porch were similar to the work of the famous Chicago architect Louis B. Sullivan.[10] There was a bit of the Craftsman style in the wide overhangs and rows of exposed beam ends. Yet there

Fig. 20. Atlee B.
Ayres House,
interior view of
the 1909 living
room. The UT
Institute of Texan
Cultures, courtesy
Florence Collett
Ayres

Fig. 21. Atlee B.
Ayres House,
interior view of the
1909 dining room.
The Alexander
Architectural
Archive, UT–
Austin

Fig. 23. Atlee B. Ayres House, interior view of 1920s living room. The UT Institute of Texan Cultures, no. 83-494, courtesy Florence Collett Ayres

was also a simplified classicism in the plain, square columns and capitals that supported the upper porch and that clustered there supporting the third-floor deck. And there were faint echoes of Colonial architecture in the continuous, wood balustrades and little classical finials of the upper terraces and the long rows of dentils that embroidered the porches. Through the beveled glass doors, the rooms still bespoke a Victorian, heavy richness of dark woods: the dining room in mahogany, the living room in early English oak, the hall in birch. The wide stair rose to a landing illuminated by a noble Palladian window, albeit with stained glass. Heavy beams crisscrossed the dining room ceiling. The parlor spoke more in light French tones. The conservatory delighted guests with its coved ornamental ceiling with concealed electric lighting effect. Illuminated by large dormer windows, the ample attic under the high-hipped roof might well have seen much play, perhaps dancing too.

By 1913, Atlee's eclectic experiments began to move away from traditional styles, either American or foreign, and to focus on some of the same issues that were generating the houses of the so-called "Progressives" who were trying to respond to the "genius loci" (that is, the nature of the place—the climate, the landscape, the local traditions). They were most active in the upper Middle West, where a new type of house appeared, a horizontal house, with low-spreading hipped or gabled roofs, long banks of windows, horizontal courses of brick, scant ornament of abstracted geometry—the so-called "Prairie" style. Atlee's interest in the Prairie style may well have been stimulated by the presence in his office of George Willis, a Texan who had been head draftsman in Frank Lloyd Wright's studio from 1898 to 1902.

Atlee's response to this influence could be detected slightly in the 1914 Marshall Terrell House (fig. 25) at 213 West Agarita. The open-ness of its broad porches on two floors supported only by widely spaced piers and columns made it seem exceptionally open to the outdoors. However, the large roof and strangely shaped, pent gables, the exaggerated brackets and wood siding gave it an air of an Arts and Crafts Swiss chalet, a style not uncommon as a cladding for the popular bungalows of the time.[11] More clearly related to the Prairie School were two houses from 1909 and 1914. The earlier John J. Kuntz House (Frank Winerich House) (fig. 26; plan 4) at 118 Kings Highway was obviously inspired by some of the houses of Frank Lloyd Wright—and of those associated with him such as Walter Burley Griffin and Marion Mahoney. Like Wright's Robie House of 1906–1908, the Kuntz House spread wide its shallow, shingled, hipped roof wings with big overhanging eaves,

Fig. 24. Roy Hearne House 1910, front exterior view. The Alexander Architectural Archives, UT–Austin

sheltering a large verandah on one side and a *porte cochere* on the other, giving access to an asymmetrically placed entrance hall. Conspiring to emphasize the horizontal flow were the squat chimneys, the stone copings and base of the long walls, and the sills and transom bars of the windows with their big panes of clear glass. Ayres cleverly designed the windows to disappear entirely into concealed pockets in the walls above, in order to increase the ventilation. Inside, the scale of the rooms was set by a heavy horizontal line at door height, below which were rectangular panels of plaster framed in simple flat wood moldings. Above this human-scale datum line, a plaster frieze went up to the 10' ceiling. This may be compared to the 12' ceilings of his earlier houses. The living room had a low horizontal brick fireplace, surrounded by a 5' curly birch mantel. Upstairs, under low, 9'6" ceilings, the six bedrooms and three bathrooms were lined up along a skylighted hall. They opened into a long, screened sleeping porch oriented to the southeast breezes.

Fig. 25. Marshall Terrell House, 1914, front exterior view. The Alexander Architectural Archives, UT–Austin

The 1914 Lonnie Wright House, at Wilkins and Roosevelt off South Saint Mary's, was even more low and spread out over only one story, wrapped around a long, narrow, trellised patio ending in a gazebo with small seats. The shingled, hipped roof sheltered stucco walls up to a continuous band of windows with horizontal panes of plate glass. Under the eaves there ran a continuous ornamental band at the top of the walls. The house was more interesting inside, surprisingly rich in the architectural treatment of the rooms. Past the beveled, plate-glass front door, the reception room was partly separated from the living room by bookcases and an unusual beam that served also as a kind of lantern. The living room walls were paneled only up to 7', where horizontal moldings returned up the frieze and across the ceiling, a device used by Frank Lloyd Wright and others of the Prairie School. At the far end of the living room, a fireplace faced in small tile squares was illuminated by corner windows of art glass in the geometric designs favored by Wright.[12] The slightly curved plaster ceiling and the paneled and mirrored buffet of the dining room continued Atlee's extensive attention to interior architectural detail, in what from outside seemed to be a relentlessly low and plain house.

Coming on the heels of his Prairie style houses, Ayres did four houses in several South Texas towns: the 1914 L. E. Cartwright House in Uvalde; the Graham Hamilton House and the Alex Hamilton House in Cuero (both in 1915); and the 1916 J. A. Browne House in Brownsville. They presented a wide range of styles, so wide as to indicate an unfocused eclecticism, even momentarily out of control. One of the houses was modestly Prairie style; another, in the Mediterranean manner that was to become Atlee's passion. Another was an imposing neoclassical mansion, and the last, a hybrid that defied precise identification.

The Cartwright House continued Atlee's investigation of the Prairie style, with low, hipped, shingled roofs juxtaposed at right angles. Cement

Fig. 26. John J. Kuntz (Frank Winerich) House, 1913, front exterior view. The UT Institute of Texan Cultures, no. 84-785, courtesy Ann Russell

base and belt courses, and copings at the top of the low chimneys emphasized the horizontal. The house was entered by a Sullivanesque semicircular arch with brick vousiors and through an entrance door with beveled plate glass. To the left of the entrance hall, an axis ran through the living room and its large bay to a porch and verandah. To the rear of the living room was an inglenook with a tiled fireplace and windows of colored art glass. To the right of the entrance hall, the axis of the dining room ran toward the street through another bay window with built-in flower boxes. Again, Ayres used the device of double hung windows that slid up into concealed pockets. The detailing throughout—the flat 8" base, the simple square balusters on the stair, the trim of the interior stucco panels—was severely plain, totally unclassical.

Ayres's two houses in Cuero of 1915 presented an extraordinary contrast. The Graham Hamilton House was possibly his first attempt at a small house in a Spanish influenced style. The two-story stucco house with a simple, pitched, wood shingle roof had a number of features that characterized Spanish vernacular buildings: stucco balconies (metal alternatives were shown on the working

drawings); window grills of turned-wood spools and spindles; round-ended, exposed rafters; a stucco cove under the eaves; and an exterior tile fountain on the end of the living room. The front door was adorned with stepped, concentric, semicircular arches of stucco. Oddly, there were sketches for more classical, pedimented alternative versions. Although the house had very unMediterranean double-hung windows and solid, paneled, exterior shutters, the overall effect was distinctly Spanish—in surprising contrast to the Alexander Hamilton House (fig. 27) of the same year, also in Cuero, which was an imposing, neoclassical mansion. Its strictly symmetrical façade was dominated by a monumental entrance porch with clusters of giant, fluted columns 24" in diameter, crowned by large Ionic composite capitals. These supported a flat balustraded roof deck accessed by an attic dormer with a fanlight. Classical dentils were used everywhere under the cornices. The stucco house stood on a 36" plinth of spacious terraces that curved around to the matching side porch and *porte cochere,* each with their own clusters of smaller 14" classical columns. The front door itself was an elaborate composition, with a fanlight and flanking panels, whose

Fig. 27. Alexander
Hamilton House,
Cuero, 1915, front
exterior view.
The UT Institute
of Texan Cultures,
courtesy Robert
Oliver

lead glazing bars were in neoclassical patterns of the sort used by the late-eighteenth-century English architect Robert Adam. The door was flanked by a pair of 7" diameter columns and a pair of pilasters supporting a balcony above. The classical theme continued in the full-blown Palladian windows in the end of the attic gables. The windows were double hung with a single plate of clear glass below and nine panes above.

Although the exterior was convincingly and expensively neoclassical, the interior was even more elaborately considered. The plan was of great formality, though somewhat unusual. From the imposing portico, one entered directly into a transverse living room that occupied the entire front of the house, and opened through elegant French doors to flanking verandahs. While not especially large (15' x 33' with a 10'6" ceiling), it was a room of distinguished quality in its detailing. The fireplace had handsome paneling and a mantel shelf supported by brackets of finely carved acanthus leaves. The interior trim around doors and windows was a handsome combination of classical molding profiles: cyma recta, cyma reversa, and many fillets, all painted a bright

white enamel. In the hall behind the living room was a stair with a delicately turned, spiral newel post, surmounted by a little classical urn. The birch handrail led up over slender tapered balusters. Similar attention to the neoclassical character and refined detailing of the interior was evident in the paneled wainscot of the dining room and the continuous picture moldings. Despite all the attention to detail, to authentic classical vocabulary, the house would have benefited from more generous dimensions, especially the vertical ones. Ceiling heights of only 10'5" and French door heights of only 6'10", even with a 1'4" transom, lacked the stately scale of their English and European models. This smallness of dimension would continue to distinguish Ayres's and most of his American contemporaries' eclectic houses from their original models. This became even more evident as Atlee's eclecticism focused on Italian Renaissance models after 1918.

One more South Texas house was built in the next year, 1916, for J. A. Browne in Brownsville. This strange amalgam of elements and stylistic motifs still defies precise categorization. The façade had projecting symmetrical two-story brick gables, with ornamental brick and cement stone panels on the lower story and herringbone brick panels edged with a soldier course of brick on the upper story. The lower portion of the projecting wings were open porches flanked by piers with cement stone capitals of abstracted geometry. Inserted awkwardly between the two gabled wings, a shingled shed roof protected a terrace with a solid brick railing, pierced decoratively and topped by a brick soldier course. The actual entry was through the right-hand porch and a door with plate glass and sidelights. The south side of the house presented another, dis-connected picture, dominated by one, large, gabled, symmetrical screened porch with brick piers. Inside, there were more anomalies: 12" fluted, Doric columns between the reception and living rooms; elaborate, wide ceiling trays and Colonial ceiling and base moldings; and other fancy details. Overall, the Browne House was a peculiar hybrid, to be understood best as a continuation of Atlee's search at the time for a uniquely American style. After the war, he was to turn from his "Progressive" innovations to the traditional eclectic styles that seemed to be his natural aesthetic medium.

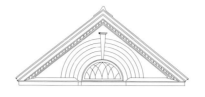

CHAPTER 9

Mediterranean Style I, 1918–31:
Italian Renaissance Style

In the first twenty years of his practice, Atlee had produced houses in a wide spectrum of styles: Colonial dressings on four-square, Late Victorian houses, Mission style, Prairie style, American and British Arts and Crafts, his own house's essay in English Tudor Revival, and Central European Modernism. The quartet of houses in South Texas of 1914–16 were of such wildly diverse and hybrid styles as to suggest that Atlee may have begun to be concerned that his highly experimental eclecticism needed a more substantial footing, some clear principles, or at least some clear focus. Where better to find this than in the authority of the long-established tradition of Western European architecture, especially that of the Mediterranean countries, which seemed to be more appropriate to the landscape, climate, and history of Texas than even American Colonial

architecture—so derivative of the English Georgian and neoclassical tradition. Atlee looked first to Italy as the next step in his eclectic odyssey. His interest there lay in both the historical Renaissance precedents of the fifteenth, sixteenth, and seventeenth centuries, and also in the vernacular villas and farmhouses that existed in his own day, which were of a size and expense more applicable to his own practice.[1]

American interest in the architecture of the Italian Renaissance began on the East Coast, in 1883, with the landmark Villard Houses in New York by McKim, Mead and White. That stately mansion, strictly modeled on Italian Renaissance precedents—in particular the imposing Roman Palazzo Cancelleria—reflected a desire on the part of architects and clients alike to escape the uneducated, free-wheeling, even promiscuous, eclecticism of Victorian building, and to pursue an informed eclecticism based on careful study of historical examples through direct observation on their travels and by scholarly study of drawings and photographs in books and journals. As McKim pored over his copy of *Letrouilly,* Atlee perused his handsome volumes of Italian buildings. This approach was distinctly different from the mid-nineteenth-century Italianate style, which had been part of a romantic reaction to formal classical ideals in architecture and thus looked with a less scholarly eye to formal Renaissance models and more to pattern books of elements that were used with little discipline or understanding of the original buildings. Like the earlier Italianate houses, the twentieth-century Italian Renaissance Revival house had simple massing, symmetry, and clarity of proportions of the whole and the parts. Its low-hipped, tiled roof with broad overhangs cast emphatic terminal shadows on the stucco walls. In distinct contrast to Late Victorian frills and furbelows, and the spindles and polychromed patterns of the Queen Anne style, the Italian Renaissance style spoke of educated and traveled sophistication in its restrained and accurate use of historical ornament.

Atlee's shift to Mediterranean inspiration was first to be seen in the 1918 trio of houses on West Mulberry that presaged his handsome Italian Renaissance houses to come. Local newspapers noted:

> Mulberry Street is acquiring a number of handsome homes these days. The new home of Ira Havins . . . is built of tile and finished in cream, white, and cement stucco with dark red metal roof. . . . Jack W. Neal's residence stands at Mulberry Street and Belknap Place. An Italian motif is carried out in the architecture, the outside walls being of white limestone and the roof in dark red earthen tile. . . . The residence of Atlee B. Ayres, Jr. [Atlee's elder son] . . . contains six rooms and has outside walls of hollow tile and is finished on the outside with white cement stucco. The roof is of dark metal shingle and painted green.[2]

This third house was actually a small one-story house with a chastely Georgian front door.

Those houses of white stucco with red or green tile roofs were Atlee's stepping stones to the next stage, which was centered on interpreting the buildings of Renaissance Italy and the myriad villas of their descendants. He had seen some Italian buildings on his 1911 trip to Europe that had begun with northern Italy— Genoa, Turin, Como, and Venice, then down to Florence and Pisa, Rome, Naples, Pompeii, Capri, Amalfi, and across to Brindisi. On the Ayreses' trip around the world in 1914, they only sped by train through Italy en route to sail to Egypt from Naples. It was not until 1921 that Ayres made another extensive trip that focused mainly on two months in Spain, with another month spent in Italy and France. However, beginning in 1919 with the Hiram Partee House, Atlee produced a series of houses of assured scholarly eclecticism that demonstrated his understanding of the historic Italian models and his ability to adapt them with credible authenticity to contemporary San Antonio. The Partee House was followed by houses for W. G. Rigsby in 1920, Dr. F. L. Thomson in 1921, and the David J. Straus and Garret P. Robertson Houses in 1922.

The Hiram Partee House at 695 Belknap had most of the characteristic elements of the American Italian Renaissance style. It was a single, simple, well-proportioned block with a low, hipped, tile roof, generous overhangs, and a many-bracketed soffit that cast deep shadows terminating the elevations and lending the house a dignified, assured Italian presence. There was a tiled terrace that led to the broad front door, deeply recessed within a solid, square portico with a pair of Tuscan columns. Flowers lined the metal railing above and the window boxes of the four upper windows that flanked the triple windows of the balcony. The simple façade was ornamented only by shallow blind arches over the downstairs windows. These typical elements of the American Italian Renaissance style continued around the side porch, which had a totally glazed, upper sleeping porch that appeared to be a garden room capped by a bracketed wood trellis. At least from the front and the one side, the house appeared perfectly balanced, calm and dignified, and clearly of Italian extraction. On the other side and rear, the volumes became more complicated, giving way to interior requirements that could not be fitted into the single, simple volume, and that, in a real Italian villa, would likely have been accommodated within the ground floor of the main block, or in separate dependencies or outbuildings. Also, in Italy the principal rooms were usually located on the second floor, or *piano nobile*. The Partee plan was classically, neatly, and logically organized in three parts. A central stair hall, which terminated in the breakfast room, gave access to a long living room to one side and dining room to the other—they were linked axially through pairs of sliding doors. Behind the dining room lay the kitchen, rear porch, and service stair. On the second floor, the four bedrooms and three baths were similarly disposed symmetrically about the main stair hall. The careful attention to formal order, simple massing, and a few passably Italian motifs, such as the Tuscan columns, gave the house a sense of authenticity and dignity beyond its size. However, Atlee's persistent use of six-over-six, double-hung windows, instead of the typical Italian pairs of inswinging casements with exterior shutters, the relatively thin, exterior walls and interior partitions, and the large ratio of window opening relative to solid wall, revealed contemporary American building materials and technology and denied the house a truly Italian presence.

Although Atlee was to do three more Italian style houses afterward, he completed the largest and most elaborate of his strictly Italian style houses in 1920. This was the W. G. Rigsby House (fig. 28) on an entire block in Alamo Heights between Grove Place and Arcadia.[3] The house dominated a site that sloped steeply to Broadway, the main street north from downtown. The S-curve of the entrance drive passed below the terraces and formal façade of the west front and continued behind the house to a turnaround and arbored terrace, which appeared to be the most-used entrance. Garages and other separate buildings occupied the rear of the property toward Cleveland Street. The lawns, the commanding position of the house, its large balustraded terraces, arcaded loggia and symmetrical side porches, the sheer size of the main house—with over 7,000 square feet plus 900 square feet of porches and loggia—and the several outbuildings, created the impression of a small estate rather than a house on a suburban lot.

In the rosy light of the western sun, the stately façade was perfectly symmetrical, amply scaled, and classically proportioned. The façade rose from a 97' wide, tiled terrace with a cement-stone border, base, and low balustrade. On the central axis, an antique mask spouted water into a glass-mosaic-lined basin, which was surrounded by a lower pool into which nine small frogs, mounting electric light bulbs, contributed their own jets of water. One could sit on flanking, imitation stone benches to enjoy the cool, pretty sight and enjoy the view down over Broadway.

The terrace led through five semicircular arches, with round marble plaques, evoking memories of Lucca della Robbia's roundels in Brunelleschi's Hospital of the Innocents in Florence. With a loggia connecting two-story, projecting wings, the exterior composition reflected perfectly the internal organization of the house where a central reception hall connected the living room on one side and the dining room on the other. Although the loggia had a plain, sturdy, wood-beamed ceiling, it led to a front door that grandly announced the richness of the architecture. A pair of 8' glass doors were covered with an elaborate diamond pattern of wrought iron. These were surrounded by a wide band of

*Fig. 28. W. G.
Rigsby House,
1920, rear exterior
view. The
Alexander
Architectural
Archive,
UT–Austin*

antiqued cement-stone and surmounted by a scrolled pediment with an oval shield (cartouche) displaying the owner's initial "R."

Beyond the impressive introduction to the quality of the house within, there was a small vestibule sumptuously floored in black marble and roofed with a high, crossvaulted ceiling outlined with cement-plaster ribs of bundled reeds and a central rosette. Beyond, aligned on the central axis, lay the principal glories of the house: the reception hall (35' wide and 19'6" deep), and an oval stair hall (16' wide and 13' deep). These rooms were among Atlee's most intricate and richly detailed. The architectural frame of the reception hall was organized with fourteen fluted, plaster pilasters (8' high and 11" wide), with 12" Composite capitals, a variation on the Corinthian order. They supported an elaborate 22" frieze and complex series of moldings that made the transition to the ceiling, which was 11'8" above the black and white, diamond patterns of the marble floor. The succession of motifs

in the serried bands of moldings demonstrated Ayres's scholarship in the classical Renaissance vocabulary, as well as the ample resources of his clients. The moldings and decorative rosettes were not carved on the site but were all specified by number from the catalogue of the Architecture Decorators Supply Company, in Chicago.[4] All the dentils, eggs and dart, entwined ropes, gouges, strigils, and Greek keys, were prefabricated in plaster. Some of the larger rosettes called for models to be submitted.[5] Atlee's art lay in their selection and arrangement, which replaced the art of the craftsman in most twentieth-century American buildings.

Beyond the reception hall, through a pair of 8' plaster columns that matched the pilasters of the hall, a black marble stair ascended in a graceful curve within a tall, oval chamber of plaster-faced concrete walls. The curving stringer and fascia of the oval well of the second floor were faced in imitation Caen stone with a Greek wave pattern. Along the wall there was an elegant, silk rope rail held by stock bronze rings. The balustrade alternated slender, twisted wrought-iron balusters with ones containing decorative cast-iron pieces. The richness continued in the upper stair hall, whose oval was ornamented with 7' flat pilasters and 12" capitals. There was a complex frieze of small arches and anthemion, and a series of moldings from which rose a gently domed ceiling 11' above the floor. Certainly the most elaborate and richly detailed of Ayres's Italianate interiors—and the most academically informed if not really a "correct" reproduction of a historical style—this sequence of rooms set a standard that would prove difficult to maintain. For a number of reasons economic and artistic, Atlee's odyssey led him to favor Spanish precedents over the Italian Renaissance. Still Ayres would follow the Rigsby House with three more important houses in the Italian style in the next two years, and was to include Italian motifs in other major houses until 1931; however, none were to be as purely and elaborately accomplished in this eclectic mode.[6]

In addition to the tour de force of the reception hall and the stair, the main floor of the Rigsby House contained only a few other large rooms: a 42'6" x 19' living room that led to a east-facing sun room, a 28' x 19' dining room, a smaller breakfast room, a pantry, kitchen, and back stair. All the principal rooms were carefully arranged in the best Beaux-Arts traditions of symmetry, of proportions, and of careful detail. This was particularly difficult to accomplish given the number of openings to be accommodated: two windows to the front, two pairs of French doors to the porch on the south, doors into the sun parlor on the east, and large double doors and flanking sidelights to the reception hall on the north. Each opening was flanked by a transom and pilasters with Composite capitals. Between the openings, the living room walls were organized in plaster panels trimmed with plaster moldings, with a wood wainscot and base. The room had a herringbone pattern oak floor and a

ceiling divided into fifteen, deeply coffered, 6' square panels with a series of moldings and 2' diameter central rosettes. Although the many radiators of the central heating system were present behind bronze grills in the wainscot, the main feature of the room was an appropriately large-scaled fireplace, 5' to the top of the stone mantel, and 9'3" to the top of the slanting chimneybreast. Capitals (3'3" high) and consoles supported a mantel adorned with a shield, again selected from the catalogue of the Architecture Decorators Supply Company.

On the other side of the reception hall, the dining room continued the architectonic preoccupations of the Italian Renaissance style. From a cornice of Greek key and other moldings, there rose a shallow barrel-vaulted ceiling divided by 3'-wide plaster bands that reiterated similar wall panels. Rosettes ornamented the bands, as well as the transom overdoors. The openings of the dining room were flanked by slender, wood engaged columns (3" in diameter) with plaster capitals. As expected, there was another stately fireplace with stone consoles. The adjoining breakfast room was even more elaborate, somewhat more theatrical with a crossvault and ribs rising to a central rosette 11'3" above the floor. (The working drawings showed a deer head mounted on the north wall, perhaps banished from the more formal rooms.) Beyond, adjoining the service stair, lay the pantry and its copper-lined sink and countertop, the well-lighted kitchen with its high tiled wainscot, marble countertop and backsplash, roll-out bread board, and 42-square-foot refrigerator room. A pretty, latticed service porch completed a well-planned and totally logical ground-floor arrangement that demonstrated Atlee's understanding of the major elements of a Beaux-Arts plan of clarity and disposition of elements, as well as his scholarly knowledge of the complex vocabulary of classical ornament. Nevertheless, the Rigsby House, although large for San Antonio, seemed overloaded with small versions of classical detail, all those 2" moldings, 3" colonettes, those tiny rosettes and dentils, all perfectly scaled to each other and the house, but compared to the scale of the rooms and ornament of the originals in Italy—or even to the much larger mansions on the East Coast, the Villard Houses, for example—the Rigsby interiors seem somewhat pretentious miniatures. Alas, the Rigsby House was allowed to fall into disrepair and finally demolished.

Ayres continued to explore the Italian style in the Dr. F. L. Thomson House (color plate 3) of 1921, at the corner of West Mulberry and Belknap. It was built for the president of the Grayburg Oil Company for approximately $100,000. It was smaller than the Rigsby House and more compact under a hipped roof of green barrel tiles. The Italian flavor was distilled in the triple semicircular arches, Tuscan columns, and Composite capitals of the entrance loggia, and in the balustraded terrace that elevated the house above the small front lawn. Apart from modest elaboration of the frames around the windows and some plain ironwork for the second-story balconies, the house had a simplicity and a larger ratio of bare wall to openings that made it more true to authentic Italian villas.

In 1922, the David J. Straus House (color plate 4; plan 5) at 315 West Lynwood, Ayres reiterated many of the ideas of the Rigsby House: volumetric composition and plan arrangement, although on a smaller scale at a little more than 5,000 square feet enclosed. It continued Ayres's Italian theme and architectural vocabulary, with a low-sloped, hipped, terra-cotta tile roof, wide overhangs with projecting false rafter ends, chimneys with little tiled hipped roofs, stucco walls, and a long brick paved terrace with elegant cast stone balustrade and French doors. Affirming the symmetrical balance of the front façade, twin wings containing the living room and dining room projected symmetrically on either side of the central portion, which was dominated by a front door with serried ranks of richly ornamented, semicircular arches. Above, windows

flanked by twisted, cast-stone colonettes overlooked a substantial stone balcony. The remaining second-story windows had wrought-iron balconies designed to hold flowers in pots.

As in the Rigsby House, the principal feature of the interior of the Straus House was a large transverse entrance hall (fig. 29). There Ayres made a serious attempt at Renaissance grandeur, for upon entering on a striking pavement of large black and white diamonds, one was in a classically proportioned room, whose walls were of imitation Caen stone in courses varying from 8½" to 10½". As in the reception hall at the Rigsby House, the walls were decorated with flat pilasters, arranged in pairs and in clusters. The pilasters had full height inset panels of a truly Renaissance collection of classical motifs, arabesques, swags and foliate tendrils sprouting from a succession of urns. They had Composite capitals that supported a beautiful frieze of classical anthemion, and delicate rows of egg-and-tongue and fillet moldings. Above, the ceiling followed a gentle plaster vault to 11' high. Beyond the rich gallery, the marble floor and base continued into the rear vestibule and stair hall, similarly ornamented with pilasters and a vaulted ceiling. A stair of black marble treads and risers rose to the second floor. This stair hall was in fact the principal everyday entrance to the house from a driveway and circular turnaround on the north side of the house, with the ceremonial formal façade and terrace facing south. Still, the rear elevation was sufficiently imposing with triple, arched casement windows reiterated in seven arches of a cast-stone balcony railing and supporting brackets. One end of the gallery led into the 31' x 17', oak-floored living room that was further elongated by a sun parlor with a tile floor, cast-stone and decorative tile wainscot and fountain, and a wood frieze suggesting an outdoor trellis. As in many Ayres houses, the sun parlor and the sleeping porch above were oriented to enjoy the prevailing southeastern breeze. Beyond the living room through French doors decorated

*Fig. 29. David J.
Straus House,
1922, view of en-
trance hall. The
Alexander Archi-
tectural Archive,
UT–Austin*

with Adamesque urns was an open loggia with a tile floor. The other end of the gallery led to an oak-floored, dining room, matching exactly the size of the living room: 22' x 17'. In the dining room, Ayres took pains with the plaster paneling and ceiling moldings. Early photographs of the gallery showed rich furnishings, a pair of high-backed, Renaissance style chairs of leather or velvet, profusely studded, and a pair of tall, baroque ecclesiastical *torchères* electrified with clusters of pointed bulbs. Oriental rugs were arranged on the marble floor.

Although the main façade faced Lynwood to the south, the house was ordinarily entered from a driveway from Belknap to a circle and rear entrance through the stair hall. Perhaps, as at Rigsby, Ayres preferred not to clutter the principal façade with automobiles. Above a low balustraded terrace, there was a handsome façade, a rather broad and low two stories with shallow, hipped, terra-cotta tile roofs. Quite plain except for the richly elaborated front door, flanking French doors in the reception hall, and a filigreed, cast-stone balcony above, the startlingly white stucco struck a Mediterranean note. The rear elevation was not as rigorously controlled. Protruding from the back of the living room was a semicircular palm room with a fountain. Its ceiling was to be arched and the walls treated with latticework, the floor of tile in color designs. On the other side of the house, the kitchen wing and service porch extended even farther. Even though the staff quarters were placed over the three-car garage in a separate building, the casualness of the rear façade adulterated the volumetric simplicity of the main house in a way that service wings and outbuildings of a real Italian villa would not.

The illusion was almost convincing, and yet one could never mistake this, nor any of Ayres's Italian houses, for the real thing in Italy. It was not only the newness, the freshness of their stucco walls and tiled roofs that lacked the carefully cultivated and prized patina of age—the worn and mottled surfaces of wall and roof of old Italian villas and farmhouses. That could come in time, although American culture usually destroys it by a penchant for eternal newness. But there were major telltale differences in the original design itself. The principal one was Ayres's persistent use of double-hung windows, completely unknown throughout Italy and the Mediterranean, where pairs of inswinging casements with a few horizontal glazing bars were traditionally preferred. Atlee's choice is particularly puzzling because one hundred percent ventilation was to be greatly desired in San Antonio before air-conditioning. Indeed, he did use casements on the Straus sleeping porch of the master bedroom and had devised, for the son's sleeping porch, sliphead windows that slid completely up into pockets in the wall above, of the sort he had used on several houses previously. In addition, traditional Italian buildings did not have screens on the windows, though they would certainly be as useful there as they were in San Antonio. Still, even if those differences had been resolved, Ayres's Italian Renaissance houses lacked the sheer size and scale of their Italian exemplars. Though the David J. Straus House was substantial in America—nearly 6,000 square feet including loggia and porches—it was small compared to even minor Italian villas, not only in its plan dimensions, but even more so in its vertical dimensions. In Italy, villas and even large manors and farmhouses often contained three or more stories of vast, high-ceiling rooms, with heights of 14' or 16' not uncommon, much higher than the hall and living room of the Straus House. Correspondingly, Italian windows were larger but

consumed less of the extensive exterior wall surfaces, a ratio of solid to void noticeably different from that of American houses. The solid masonry walls of the Italian villa were much thicker, giving the buildings a weight and tectonic gravity much greater than any of Ayres's Italian houses of stucco over hollow clay tile. Inside, apart from the rich materials and Renaissance detail in the gallery and stair, the Ayres rooms lacked the majestic austerity of most Italian rooms, where ornament was limited to an imposing, carved stone chimneypiece, or severe door surround, or beamed ceiling—that was all. Atlee's decoration was drawn from the richly carved, gilded and polychromed details of opulent rooms of vast palaces and translated into a plethora of smaller moldings and decorative details, largely chosen by number from catalogues.

Atlee's persistent efforts in achieving an "Italian" character were evident in his office correspondence, which was peppered with inquiries and requests for materials and architectural elements appropriate to the Italian style.[7] But how to adapt to the American smaller dimensions of rooms and ceiling heights, the greater desire for comfort and convenience and more openness to the outside, the difference in building materials and methods of construction, the absence of skilled decorative artists for frescos, carving, gilding? It may have become clear to Atlee that in scale and character, in construction and craftsmanship, the authentic Italian model was not suitable for contemporary houses in San Antonio. It may be that Atlee realized the difficulty and expense of making a suburban San Antonio house, however grand, a truly Renaissance villa. Soon he began to look more to a corollary prototype of more manageable scale, less demanding composition, less strict vocabulary of ornament, and more related to San Antonio's past and present character, landscape, and climate. He began to look to the smaller vernacular houses of southern Spain for inspiration.

However, there was no doubt in the minds of

the owners and children of the Dr. Sam Roberts House, completed in 1930 in Mission Hills, a new exclusive residential enclave of Kansas City, Kansas, that their house was "Italian." Sam and Ada Roberts had fallen in love with each other and Old Europe as students in Vienna in 1912, he studying medicine and she music. One of their daughters reminisced that when they moved into the house in August, 1930,

> Inside the finished house there were thick rugs with sculptured borders, pictures and paintings new to us children and Renaissance furniture some of which, mother told us, was very old and had to be treated with care. The walls of the living room and dining room were gold-leafed and even the ceilings in those rooms were breathtaking. The large oval center hall was floored with black and white squares of marble and the walls were Travertine marble. Instead of the old banister we

could slide down, the new one was covered with red velvet and definitely not for dirty hands. We were now living in Kansas City's Country Club District in a beautiful Italian villa overlooking a sunken garden and a reflecting pool.[8]

Her mother tried to be faithful to the Italian image. On her trip to New York where she "browsed" for Italian furniture and interiors at Sloans and Tiffany Studios: "We educated ourselves into some sort of idea of just how far we want to go into Italian effect. We found at the New York Galleries wonderful reproduction of a dining room—different pieces assembled—all hand carved walnut—some after some old pieces. We feel we want that and I think a glazed plaster wall—and beamed ceiling—and a red velvet valence hanging around the ceiling." On the way back she wrote from the Golden State Limited that she had bought some interesting seven-

Fig. 30. Dr. Sam Roberts House, 1929, view of dining room. The Alexander Architectural Archive, UT–Austin

teenth-century Italian furniture for the dining room and living room (fig. 30). She was especially intent on being "Italian" rather than "Spanish." "The arch doorway, so beautiful, set me wondering. I know it is essentially Italian, but seems Spanish to me the arches being so cheaply overdone here. Another reason this Spanish house right back from us has the same doorway—blackstone and all. Will you submit another tower front plan with balcony" (fig. 31). She was intent on her house being distinctly unlike those of others in her circle. Mrs. Roberts admitted to Atlee

This problem of keeping up with Lizzie. The LeRoy Snyders are to build an Italian house spent one year in Italy. Purchased car loads. Much beautiful wrought iron. Everybody raving through our crowd. . . . Got them for a song. Mrs. Snyder wants me to let her order, she has all addresses. You know, I wouldn't dare the delays, misfits, etc. But, I sometimes get "cold feet" on my iron order there [San Antonio]. But, you are there, your knowledge of his work and first of all contact with the real stuff in Italy, etc. will not let you accept for me anything but best. I want it far from commercial flavor as possible, or as I can afford.

Fig. 31. Dr. Sam Roberts House, 1929, view of entrance door. The Alexander Architectural Archive, UT–Austin

Mrs. Roberts also wanted the house to be substantial. "Instead of wood stairway and wrought iron which is in every English house and new cheap apartment house up here, now, a stone stairway, stone steps, stone balustrade." She was worried that she had seen the same designs for iron on the stair in an ironwork book and in a local shop designed by another architect. "Do we care? Do we want our own individual design or an Italian palace copy better?" Atlee's typically diplomatic reply: "In answer to your letter of the 6th regarding the wrought iron balustrade, will say that after you left we took one of our Italian wrought iron books from the bookcase and found the same design as the one you had se-

lected, in a house built in this country and pictured in the book. You mentioned in your letter that. . . an architect there had also used the same one for a house in your city, so I think perhaps, we might revise ours a bit. In other words, maintain the same general feeling but change the scrolls." Mrs. Roberts's complicated ambivalence continued: "I've changed my mind about the oval hall. Upon my return from New York. I have studied hours on the plans and I see the oval hall is the 'cleverest' arrangement we could have and will be very *distinctive* without being *eccentric*. . . ." Her concern extended to small details. "Would like to avoid the standing downspouts on front corners of the house. Is that Italian to stand out?"

Even for the travertine grills concealing the radiators in the reception hall, she wondered, "is Grecian key out of keeping?" and sent one of many sketches to illustrate her point. At the same time she wrote, "I am at the end—making changes at $100 a whack." But, fortunately, she wasn't. For the exterior, Mrs. Roberts sought a "very Italian atmosphere. Could you look over the elevations and sketch one a little novel something for 'here and there.'" As for exterior ornament, "Have never been very keen on 'animal trimmings.' Couldn't you kill those. The more the shields obscure the lions' legs the better I like it. I mean I do not like the design too obvious such as 'the house with the two lions.'" The effort to maintain the Italian theme extended to selection of the style and color of the exterior awnings. Mrs. Roberts wondered whether they should be henna or brick color, plain or scalloped, with blue bands stitched on, the blue shaded into green as under the eaves, box awnings for upstairs and spear awnings on the tower and third floor. Atlee's reply specified plain awnings to be taken down in the winter. "The henna colored awning is the proper color for an Italian house, in fact they use this color in Italy entirely." Mrs. Roberts usually deferred to Atlee's judgment. In a letter to his son, just as construction was beginning, "Of course, Robert, you know I began this arrangement with your father. He and I have corresponded mostly. His book he was writing on Italian and Spanish architecture made us feel him an authority and won our decision." On the other hand, she was persistent in many matters of design. Contrary to Atlee's design to keep the main floor all on one level, Mrs. Roberts wanted the living room to be down several steps from the reception hall, so that the upper level could be used as a stage, curtained off for tableaux effects. She also thought that the heavy beams of a higher living room ceiling would be more effective. Atlee was concerned that the exterior elevations would lose symmetry and balance, to which Mrs. Roberts replied that she liked the

"touch of informality. . . . I feel it might break the 'a la museum' look it might have." Atlee himself consistently fought for architecture of the "plain, simple, true, Italian type."

The resulting house had a three-story central tower flanked by long two-story wings with shallow, hipped tile roofs. One of the wings was turned back at a slight angle, following the contours of the corner site. Despite the break in the façade, the departure from frontal massing, the house nevertheless gave the impression of formal bilateral symmetry. The wings appeared to be the same length; the windows and French doors of matching sizes were symmetrically placed; and the long balustraded terrace tied the parts together in one composition. The three-story central tower provided an impressive focus. The entrance was through a recessed porch screened by a pair of round columns and flanked by a pair of square pilasters, all with finely detailed Ionic capitals done to Mrs. Roberts's specifications. She wrote rather hastily, "I made them make 4 capitals over . . . I had expected 'handsome' stone. . . . These ionic scrolls? Seem so little and flat and I thought they would detail and scale out sharply—one cannot see them 50' away hardly." Large, Italian wrought-iron lamps were mounted on the faces of the pilasters. Through the massive and elaborately scrolled wrought-iron gates, a glass door provided a preview of the marble-floored reception hall. Above the recessed porch was a stone balcony supported on heavy consoles, its balustrade a series of small round columns with pretty, small capitals. This balcony had been a victory for Mrs. Roberts who had argued for the replacement of the original high arched doorway proposed by Ayres with a balcony where Dr. Roberts could step out through the triple arches from his tower study to view the pond below, which had been a stop on the Oregon and Santa Fe Trail. The Ludiwici tile roof was a mixture of reds and salmon toning off into browny orange without looking spotted. Atlee wanted the shutters to be orange stained a browny red tone, the window sash a rich, red brown. The exterior stucco that he preferred over stone for its "much freer feeling," was originally off-white, which Atlee wanted for photographs that emphasized the house against a dark sky. The color in 1998 was a soft, grayed salmon with pale tan for the raised surrounds of the French doors and windows with their very dark brown, steel sash. The effect is still striking amidst the luxuriant green of the tall trees, mature shrubbery, and sweeping lawns that mantle the hill dominated by the villa.

The floor plan was arranged logically and simply, with the two major rooms—the large living room and dining room—opening off opposite sides of the central reception hall and stair hall beyond. Beyond the living room through iron gates was a garden room with a large window on the axis of a long, narrow reflecting pool. Past the dining room, there was a breakfast room and trellised arbor, the service rooms, the pantry, the kitchen, and the back stairs to the second floor. Such a bald description belies the real opulence of the interior—of the black and white diamonds of the marble floor of the reception hall, the 11" x 23" blocks of imitation travertine walls, the pilasters of rich Renaissance ornamental floral scrolls and urns, the composition Ionic capitals, supporting a deep frieze of acanthus leaves and moldings of egg and dart and multiple fillets, and the gracefully low plaster vaults of the ceiling—all motifs direct copies of those in the earlier Ayres David Straus House in San Antonio, a photograph of which Ayres had sent the Roberts to illustrate his intentions. However, the similarity ended in the shape of the hall, which in the Roberts House was an elongated oval leading to a vaulted stair hall with similar ornament. In the corner, above circular velvet-topped benches, niches held terra-cotta statues. Down two steps, the 12' ceiling had deep, darkly stained wooden beams with painted decoration. The massive chimneypiece was a seventeenth-century copy of a fourteenth-century Italian original. The

room was often filled with music. Lily Pons sang there. Off the reception hall, through heavy tapestries, glowed the real gold-leaf walls of the dining room and the pale reds, blues, and golds of its coffered ceiling. Up the marble stairs, on the landing overlooking the reception hall, was a red Roman sofa. The second floor consisted of five bedrooms and four baths, dressing rooms, sleeping porches, and a walnut-paneled study with a fireplace in the central tower. As in all Ayres houses, the bedrooms were pleasantly sized and proportioned, and mostly oriented to the south for light and ventilation, thoroughly detailed, and functionally well planned down to the smallest detail of storage. Mrs. Roberts's dressing room was a mirage of mirrors. Her adjacent bathroom had triple arches of rose-pink marble over a lavatory and mirrored niches for many bottles. The pink tiled tub was set in its own vaulted niche. Throughout the house, for the first time, and at the insistence of the Robertses, Ayres used outswinging casement windows that provided the full ventilation that would have been so useful in San Antonio as well. The steel sash was manufactured by Crittall in Detroit and came with interior roll-down copper screens.

In addition to the two main living floors, the house had a third floor in the central tower where there was a room for the upstairs maid who also supervised the three daughters of the family. In the basement was a room for the gardener-houseman-chauffeur, along with the laundry and drying rooms, a trunk room, fruit storage, and the boiler room. In addition, there was a cook and housekeeper who did not live in and "a woman who came two and one half days each week doing the laundry and ironing, and sewing lady who came with some regularity to mend and make over clothing." It was, after all, the midst of the Great Depression. "As the Depression deepened, so did my doubts about that great presence in our lives, the house. I never forgot that I was lucky, but I would much rather have been a little less lucky and lived in a more modest

Cape Cod style home like that of a friend." Still there were many good times, especially in the vast basement recreation room, dubbed "the casbah" with its white linoleum floor and caricatures on the walls, where Dr. Roberts entertained his doctors' poker group, even though, as one of his daughters recalled of the days as the Great Depression darkened, "My parents were understandably worried, especially my father. Living through that time meant you didn't know how long hard times would last or how deeply they would cut." They did not have to worry that their house would not last, with its sturdy interlocking hollow tile and concrete slab ground floor. It is fortunate to have present owners who respect and cherish it.

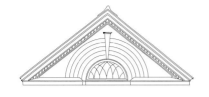

CHAPTER 10

English Interlude, 1923

Immersed as Atlee was in Mediterranean styles—first the formal Italian Renaissance style houses of 1918 to 1923 and then the more picturesque Spanish style houses that would dominate his residential design after 1923—quite unexpectedly, in 1925, he produced a distinguished house in a style not at all Mediterranean, but instead clearly derived from the traditions of English architecture. The Jessie D. Oppenheimer House was in Terrell Hills. Only recently incorporated in 1922, unlike the older suburbs of Monte Vista to the west of Broadway where Ayres's houses were on rectangular lots along the orthogonal grid of streets, Terrell Hills was designed with winding, circuitous roads, producing irregular lots that suggested more irregular plans in more countrified settings. The fourteen-acre site of the Oppenheimer House, on the corner of Burr

Duval and Arcadia, was designed as a small English estate of trees and rolling lawns and luxuriant plantings. A curving drive led to the north façade of the dark brick mansion with its tall, pointed, asymmetrical gables, slate roofs with little gabled dormer windows, and 19' twisted chimneys, all distinctly reminiscent of the sort of houses that had appeared in the suburbs of English cities in the late nineteenth and early twentieth centuries, houses designed by well-known English architects such as Philip Webb, Richard Norman Shaw, Eden Nesfield, John Sedding, F. A. Voysey, and M. H. Baillie Scott, among others.[1] In an effort to correct the promiscuous excesses of Victorian taste and what they considered to be the dehumanizing influence of the Industrial Revolution, they had looked to their own past, to the gabled brick, stone, and half-timbered manors and village houses of thirteenth- through sixteenth-century medieval and Elizabethan England.[2] Their influence appeared in many houses, principally, but not exclusively, along the Northeast Coast of America, at first in the 1880s Shingle style houses of H. H. Richardson and, later in early twentieth century, eclectic houses such as John Russell Pope's 1912 Bonniecrest—an archeological, but homey, Tudor house.[3] They were published in the American architectural journals to which Atlee subscribed. He may well have drawn inspiration from his copy of Muthesius's *The English House,* which illustrated the curved half timbering by Baillie Scott, and the many-mullioned bay windows and soaring, twisted chimneys of Richard Norman Shaw's Leys Wood. Poorly adapted to the hot Texas climate, the English style was surprisingly popular in Texas—especially for large

houses in Houston and Dallas and, to a lesser extent, in San Antonio—and for stylistic touches on smaller houses with their curved-gabled, front doors, leaded glass windows, and miniature "great halls" with dark-stained false beams.[4]

The front of the Oppenheimer House had two, projecting, gabled wings of unequal length, and a smaller gable over the centrally placed front vestibule. Framing the front door, the porch had the characteristic low, pointed, Tudor, ogival arch. It was trimmed with ashlar stone and surmounted by an ornamentally carved-stone transom and typical drip molding, all very properly English. The drip molding was used also over the large banks of 9'6", narrow casement windows with transoms, which helped to create the desired English character. Above the ground floor, the façade became stucco and false half-timbering, with diagonal, leaded-glass windows in the

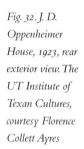

Fig. 32. J. D. Oppenheimer House, 1923, rear exterior view. The UT Institute of Texan Cultures, courtesy Florence Collett Ayres

heavily ornamented gables. Only on a small wing to the east side were there actually vestigial fortifications in the crenellations. The charming irregularity continued around the west façade where a little gabled porch sheltered a low, wood-paneled side door. Further along, there were the arched casement windows of the sun room and a large projecting bay window in one of the second-floor bedrooms, all facing west. In England this was a favored orientation that welcomed the rosy late afternoon light. It was perhaps not as welcome in the heat of the Texas summer.

While the entrance and side façades were convincingly in the asymmetrical tradition of English manor houses that eschewed formal composition and reflected ad hoc changes over time, the rear of the house was surprisingly symmetrically composed (fig. 32). The architectural vocabulary remained English, but the arrangement of the principal room and the exterior elevation were decidedly classical. A large central living room was entered axially from the front hall. The flanking dining room and sun room were lined up axially across the rear of the house. From outside, the rear—or south—façade reflected this formal, Beaux-Arts organization, with equal projecting gabled bays flanking the central chimney of the living room fireplace. With its long terrace, a fountain 7' in diameter, and steps that led to the spacious lawns through brick piers capped with stone flower pots, the south side of the house was a rather Italian house in English clothing. Still, the tall gables were decorated with very English applied, curved, and wood-pegged half-timbering and capped with carved-wood terminals. The second floor was framed in wood with herringbone brick panels that projected slightly over the ground floor. As in many of the great Elizabethan houses—like Hardwick Hall, described as "more glass than wall"—the south façade of the Oppenheimer House had very wide, leaded glass windows and doors 10' high, with diagonal glazing bars in the dining room, living room, and sun room, and long banks of

Fig. 33. J. D. Oppenheimer House, 1923, entrance hall from living room, photo taken after completion in 1923. The UT Institute of Texan Cultures, no. 83-782, courtesy Florence Collett Ayres

casement windows that admitted the prevailing southeast breezes to the row of bedrooms on the second floor.

Beyond the tile-floored vaulted vestibule, a long, elliptically vaulted, transverse hall of white marble (fig. 33) with black inserts gave access to all the major rooms, to the wide oak stairs to the second floor, and to the service areas on the east side of the house, beyond which spread a series of courtyards, quarters for the maids and chauffeur, and garages. Straight ahead and down two steps, across the marble-floored 32' living room was a baronial fireplace with a typical Tudor pointed arch and herringbone brick fireback. The walls were paneled in wood and topped by a premolded plaster, Jacobean cornice, specified by number from a catalogue. The shallow, vaulted and paneled ceiling had catalogue plaster ornament "similar to old English ceiling from Haddon Hall"[5] (one of England's finest medieval country houses). The dining room was similarly richly developed with a wood wainscot 2' high, wood moldings around rectangular plaster panels, and an ornamental stained glass coat of arms in the transoms.

The Oppenheimer House demonstrated Atlee's ability—like that of the best eclectic architects—to work knowledgeably in many styles, even ones not among his personal favorites at the time. The house also represented his desire to be true to the spirit and the vocabulary of its source of inspiration without direct reproduction of the past. However, in his few essays in English style, he never managed to depart completely from his taste for classicism. For Atlee, English style was a byway on his eclectic odyssey.

1. William Negley House, 1903, east façade

2. John W. Kokernot House, 1911, south façade

3. F. L. Thomson House, 1921, entrance loggia

4. David J. Straus House, 1922, entrance

5. *Garret P. Robertson House, 1922, entrance*

6. P. L. Mannen House, 1926, south façade

7. Atkinson-McNay House, 1929, view from southwest

8. Atkinson-McNay House, 1929, patio stairway

9. Atkinson-McNay House, 1929, patio door

10. Ward Kelley House, 1928, northwest façade

11. H. L. Blackstock House, 1937, east façade

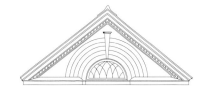

CHAPTER II

Mediterranean Style II, 1924–31: Spanish Style

Whereas the Italian Renaissance style had emanated from the East Coast, the twentieth-century Spanish style flourished in California, Arizona, Texas, and Florida, all formerly Spanish colonies where remnants of Spanish Colonial architecture still existed in the missions and old domestic buildings. At first, from the 1880s on, these influences were reflected in amalgams of motifs of the Mission style, recognizable by curved parapets, bell towers, arches, and quatrefoil windows. Later, in 1915, Bertram Grosvenor Goodhue's buildings for the San Diego Panama-Pacific Exposition demonstrated a wider palette of styles found in Spain itself and its colonies in Central and South America, especially the florid decoration of the sixteenth-century Plateresque and the baroque exuberance of the seventeenth-century Churrigueresque.[1] Stimulated by the success of the Panama-Pacific Exposition, architects and clients looked to the deep architectural traditions of Spain and North Africa themselves, where there were Byzantine, Gothic, and Renaissance buildings and the Islamic Alhambra, mosques, and madrasas.[2]

American twentieth-century Spanish style houses were a blend of many elements: "The threads that weave themselves into that architectural fabric which we call 'Spanish,' colorful Oriental threads of the North African Moor, the staunch monk's cloth of the Burgundian Cluniac, curved gables and pierced belfries of Holland, decorative Gothic lacework of France and Germany, the broad golden fringe of the Italian Renaissance." But the real charm of the Spanish house "lies in its austere simplicity, its directness, its adaptability to site and exposure, its sturdy straightforwardness in construction, and its contrasts of materials, textures, and colours."[3] The American versions, observed as a whole, had characteristically shallow, overhanging, hipped and pitched tiled roofs, of either the half-cylinder Mission shape, or the S-curve shape of Spanish tiles, usually in some shade of terra-cotta. This color sometimes distinguished them from the green glazed-tile roof commonly used on Italian Renaissance style houses. About ten percent of Spanish style houses, especially the smaller and cheaper houses, had flat roofs with parapetted walls, token bits of tile on copings, or small shed roofs over doors.

The exteriors were typically of stucco, usually painted white, though sometimes cream or tan. The texture varied from a slightly uneven surface to more sculptural patterns, even to aggressively bold textures. The exteriors characteristically used wrought iron for balcony railings, window grills, gates, lanterns, and hardware. As in Spanish and Mexican architecture, colorful, decorative glazed ceramic tiles were used to adorn doors and windows, stair risers, niches, and wall plaques. Stucco bricks and tiles made wall vents and grills decorative. Heavy wooden doors were often elaborately paneled and set off by spiral columns and pilasters and surmounted with richly ribbed semicircular tympanums. Other popular features were square and cylindrical towers and playful chimneytops, often with their own little tile caps.

Many of these elements were also used for buildings in the Italian Renaissance style. Indeed the style of some houses, while clearly Mediterranean, was not purely "Italian" or "Spanish." The Thomas Hogg House had a Spanish exterior and an early Italian interior. Ayres himself lent to the confusion by calling it, his first clearly Spanish style exterior, "Italian," and calling his later house for the Robertses in Kansas City "Spanish," a house that both clients and Ayres believed to be Italian.[4] Perhaps he used the style designations interchangeably to humor specific clients or local tastes. Regardless, it was certainly not because he was ignorant of architectural styles. The most distinguishing feature of the Spanish style was asymmetry in the arrangement of the volumes and in the composition of their façades. Unlike the simple volume characteristic of the Italian Renaissance palazzo and villa with its unifying single great roof, the Spanish style house was composed asymmetrically of a number of parts, often with a mixture of hipped and shed roofs. The resulting multiplicity of various sized and shaped walls were lent further variety by windows and doors of many different sizes and shapes, irregularly spaced, and artfully placed to maximum dramatic effect in the large, bare stucco surfaces. Where the chimneys of the Italian villa were, as much as possible, evenly spaced or suppressed, the chimneys of the Spanish style house were deliberately eccentrically placed on corners or snaking up a wall. They were meant to be noticed, to be interesting, even amusing. Italian Renaissance style buildings were intended to be dignified, serious and correct, to appeal to the intellect through the abstract qualities of their proportions, the evidences of rational design, and a wealth of historically derived architectural detail and ornament, whereas the Spanish style houses were intended to delight the eye with their theatrical irregularity, their scenographic appeal, their relaxed and rambling compositions, and by the perfume of their exotic Mediterranean associations.[5] The Spanish style enjoyed its greatest popularity in the 1920s and early 1930s, but it soon faded thereafter. Perhaps the growing influence of Modernism made it seem hopelessly fake. Perhaps the Great Depression cast a pall over such a romantic attitude.

Atlee's first exposure to American Spanish style came in his trip with his wife to California in 1918. So smitten with the place and the architectural scene was he that he immediately thought to move there. As early as 1919, he was trying to induce his clients to construct their homes with hollow tile and finish outside with white stucco, carrying out an Italian and Spanish style. In May, 1919, he wrote the Los Angeles Pressed Brick Company asking for catalogues showing Spanish tile. He requested the March, 1919, issue of *The Western Architect,* which was beginning a twelve-issue series on "Spanish Colonial Architecture in America" by Rexford Newcomb. By 1921, Atlee decided to go to Spain to see the real thing. Although he was in the midst of his Italian houses, his itinerary began with a tour of Spain, starting in the south and moving north to Madrid and finally Barcelona before going along the south coast of France to Italy. There is little evidence of his first views of Spain. It was not until his 1928 trip that he made and bought the major collection of photographs previously described. In 1925 he canceled a planned trip to Italy and went instead for five weeks to Mexico, where he took and bought the photographs that illustrated his book, *Mexican Architecture, Domestic, Civil, and Ecclesiastical,* published in 1926. But, of all the inspirations for Atlee's Spanish style, the California examples came closest to the sort of American house that he envisioned for San Antonio. He was to return to California for sustained visits in 1923, 1926, and 1929, and others much later in life.

At first, Atlee was rather unclear about the differences between Italian and Spanish styles, which, after all, shared many characteristics, such as tiled roofs and stucco walls and in the more humble vernacular examples were remarkably similar. For Atlee, it was not only a matter of style per se. As he explained in a 1929 letter to *The Architectural Record* concerning the Carl Newton House, "The style of the house was determined principally by the locality as we felt that the contour of the ground and the shape of the lot called for an informal plan. As to the design, we feel that for this climate and atmosphere in general, the Spanish or the Italian type of house are the only ones suitable for this part of the country." The Spanish style permitted the irregularities and variety of plan and massing and detail that al-

lowed Atlee to bend and stretch the house to the cooling breezes, to preserve existing old trees, to afford views of the gardens and hills, and to delight in the bright sunlight and shadows on the white stucco walls.

Atlee's earliest attempt at Spanish style occurred in Del Rio, in southwestern Texas, in the residence of N. M. Abbey in 1920. Unlike the simple volumes, formal symmetry, and regular size and spacing of windows that characterized Ayres's Italian houses of the same years in San Antonio, the Abbey House had a variety of windows, including a pair of narrow, roundheaded windows in the stair landing, irregular, sloping, tiled roofs, a husky chimney placed boldly on one side of the front façade, and a vine-laden arbor beside the arched front door, all of which conspired to a picturesque effect distinctly different from the formality of his Italian houses. Also, the plan meandered more casually, even though most rooms still reflected the formal axial composition and local symmetries of Atlee's original Beaux-Arts training. The fireplace, so eccentrically placed on the outside, was, however, centered in the living room wall.

The Garret P. Robertson House at 129 East Summit (color plate 5), built two years later in 1922, was less convincingly one thing or another, though there were aspects that suggested both Italian and Spanish derivations. Although the façade was arranged symmetrically with shallowly projecting end wings—each distinguished by a tall door with a semicircular arch filled with open tile work and lined with several layers of rope moldings—only one of them was the actual front entrance, while the twin was merely a window in the sun room. The special doors, the flanking, wrought-iron lanterns, the meager, wrought-iron balconies above them, the tiny bit of tile above the French doors, and the tile roof offered a faint Mediterranean flavor without much Mediterranean charm. Indeed, the center of the composition was a blank wall between pairs of French doors and windows above. (Later owners disguised this forced symmetry with lush plantings that focused the entry on the true front door, while hiding the faux one.) The rooms, while spacious and functionally disposed, were arranged as compactly as Ayres's earlier houses, sensible and practical, but with little drama and few expressive allusions.

However, by 1924, Atlee created his first major success in the Spanish style. In the Thomas E. Hogg House (plan 6) at 202 Bushnell Avenue. Atlee was clearly inspired not only by his trip to Spain in 1921, but even more by the Spanish style houses, motels, commercial strips, and service stations that he saw and photographed extensively in and around Los Angeles on his 1923 motoring tour of Southern California. There, he had met, and seen the work of, prominent practitioners in the Italian-Spanish Mediterranean styles. He had also identified sources for the tiles and other decorative surface elements: the crests, plaques, scrolls, and shells that were essential to the Spanish style—both for roofs and floors, and for decorative panels and moldings. For the fifty-year-old Ayres, the California Spanish style was stimulating, and liberating, a way of doing some-

thing freshly artistic and expressive and, at the same time, appropriate to the heritage of San Antonio, where beginning in 1918 there were a series of events and celebrations that brought attention to the city's Spanish past.[6] The California Spanish style depended on irregular masses with shallow tiled roofs, massive thick walls with rounded corners, large wood beams, often with painted decoration, lovely handmade tiles, beautiful ironwork, deep-set windows with wooden sash and thick mullions and ashlar stone surrounds. The soft, pale-colored surfaces received the shadows of the lush vegetation and improved with the patina of weathering and age. Those visions offered Atlee exuberant and fresh freedom. His enthusiasm was kindled not only by his own observation, but was also fueled by hundreds of his own photographs and those of others that he collected from magazines or were sent to him by friends.

The Thomas Hogg House was the first of Atlee's houses to capture with full measure the romantic, scenographic quality of the California Spanish style, even when new—before gardens softened the original, naked suburban lot. Atlee's most significant innovation was to stretch and

Fig. 34. Thomas E. Hogg House, 1924, front exterior view. The Alexander Architectural Archives, UT–Austin

angle the plan at forty-five degrees at approximately the midpoint where he used a round tower as a circular hinge or pivot (fig. 34). Atlee had seen and photographed many round and octagonal towers on both residential and commercial buildings in California. Indeed, some of his photographs showed towers used to give character even to service stations. The large, round tower, with its low conical cap of radiating tiles and band of arched corbels, was not only a successful way to turn the corner, but also to create a unique and dramatic element facing the street. The tower was very picturesque with a pair of tall French doors with round arches, a delicate wrought-iron balcony and flower pot holders supported by molded, arched corbels. Ayres promoted the thinning and bending of the plan as a way of capturing the prevailing breezes for the through ventilation desirable in the hot climate of San Antonio. Regardless of the efficacy of this arrangement, the irregular plan served to make the mass of the house more interesting, to break the long tiled roof and to create some mystery. Further variety was provided by varying the outline of the plan with advancing and receding sections. The circular tower was flanked by an advancing section containing the asymmetrically placed front entrance. Cast-stone columns supported a high circular arch encrusted with moldings that cast a deep shadow on the recessed door behind its wrought-iron grill. Prominent in the wall above was a large cast-stone shield and crown, not an emblematic coat of arms of some distinguished grandee, but—like most of Ayres's ornament—merely an allusive selection from a catalogue of prefabricated ornament. Beside the front door, a sturdy wrought-iron grill covered the large window of the den. Flanking the entrance, a recessive wing containing the living room and its large loggia was enriched by a wide chimney. On the other side, beyond the tower, a recessive wing with triple, roundheaded French doors led to the projecting service wing. Atlee had discovered the beauty

of large expanses of stucco walls punctuated, with skillful restraint, with very large and very small openings that entertained, even discombobulated, by their great variety and intriguing eccentricity of size, shape, and placement. He had also discovered the picturesque charm of complex sets of low hipped, tile roofs that created the impression of an old house of additions and changes over time. The Spanish style also gave him a canvas on which he would exercise his love of color: the terra-cotta of roof tiles, pale rose, salmon, cream or white stucco walls, brown or blue-green painted wood sash and trim, black wrought-iron railings and flower boxes overflowing with bright blooms. The rear of the Hogg House was less dramatically composed except for the small projecting loggia at the acute joint of the wings and the tiled roof of the projecting bay window of the breakfast room. However, the rear loggia was given some attention, with its arched openings framed with twisted colonettes and perforated stone panels in the parapet of the balcony above. Otherwise, the windows were sized and placed as needed for bedrooms and bathrooms without much attention to scenographic effect.

Atlee had also come to understand that the thick, masonry walls of real Spanish buildings gave them a strong presence. They cast deep shadows in the window and door openings and created interiors well protected from the harsh light and climate of Spain.[7] American architects who wanted to create similar effects were faced with American materials and construction methods, which, in California usually involved a light wood structure, stuccoed on the outside and plastered within. The effect of thickness was achieved by creating hollow walls, furred out to whatever thickness was desired for effect. Usually this conceit, being costly, was used mainly in places that most greatly contributed to the Spanish impression, often limited to the entrance façade. For his Mediterranean houses, Atlee used walls of structural, hollow-masonry tiles, which, with exterior stucco and interior insulation and plaster, created a reasonably thick wall of 11 ½". However, for the living room of the Thomas Hogg House, he added an extra 2" x 6" layer of furring, to increase the thickness to 18". Set behind the rounded corners of the jambs, the casement windows—with their wide 1 ¾"—frames and splayed interior walls convincingly created a sense of the thick walls of Spain and Italy. Atlee continued the effect with a selective thickness of the interior partitions: deep openings for the main rooms on the ground floor but ordinary, thinner wood stud walls for the second floor and service areas.

Within the Thomas Hogg House, Atlee took a major step toward achieving an authentically Mediterranean character. For the first time, instead of his customary use of wood flooring, he used handsome paving tiles in all of the ground-floor rooms (fig. 35). The importance Atlee gave to this material so crucial to the Spanish style was clear in the persistence with which he pursued sources outside of San Antonio, especially in California. Having visited the studios of Joseph Musto Sons during his 1923 trip to Los Angeles, Atlee soon wrote to inquire of large, handmade, dark red or mahogany color floor and base tiles. At Atlee's suggestion, Mrs. Hogg herself went to the Musto company to select tiles for the living room, dining room, and breakfast room. She also sought tiles at R. F. Angulo Tile of Santa Barbara. Thus the floors of the Hogg House became rich carpets of fine tiles of a great variety of sizes and shapes. In the living room a field of elongated hexagons—each measuring 7 ½" x 16"—was surrounded by a border of smaller diamonds and triangles. The floor of the octagonal breakfast room was comprised of 10" octagons interspersed with 4" squares, while decorative, blue faience tiles lined the corner recesses. Ayres used a herringbone pattern in the reception hall and circular stair hall, and diagonal squares in the cloister that flanked the dining room, which had rectangular tiles of 16" x 22".

As Atlee enriched the floors, he simplified the interior walls by eschewing the elaborate aggre-gations of classical moldings of his Italian Renaissance style houses. Instead he concentrated on endowing each room sparingly, with significantly Mediterranean elements of both Italian and Spanish derivations. At the time, the interiors were thought to be Early Italian.[8] The reception hall set the tone with its shallow barrel vault and walls of handtroweled plaster topped by a 6" decorative frieze of plaster ornament. At the far end, wrought-iron gates opened to a small loggia, flagstone terrace, and fountain. The openings from the reception hall were relieved only by thin rope corners and small corner brackets. In the adjacent circular stair hall, the light cantilevered stair rose to a smooth shallow plaster dome. Its wood handrail was supported by balusters of thin, twisted wrought iron. Entered from the low-ceilinged reception hall through heavy draperies, the living room had a noble austerity. Its plain walls and ceiling—11'3" high—were relieved only by a deep cornice of semicircular vaults supported on small capitals. The large fireplace had a simple, sloping chimneybreast, and the mantel was supported by plain, stone corbels and twisted, engaged shafts. As originally furnished with sturdy, dark wood tables, cabinets, and chairs covered with leather and velvet—illuminated by pairs of wrought-iron wall sconces—the room had a convincingly Italian austere grandeur. A tall, heavy, wood-paneled door led to a small library with its deep bookcases.

Opposite the living room, the dining room was relatively plain with a flat ceiling above a small cove and rope molding. Beyond, the octagonal breakfast, or morning room was more fanciful, not only with its elaborately tiled floor but also with its coved ceiling and wood-paneled doors with inserts of bottle-green, leaded glass that separated it from the pantry. There was also a tile-lined lavabo with cement shelves, a basin, and a glazed water vase with a spigot and a connection to the Frigidaire in the kitchen.

Regardless of style, Atlee's houses were full of

Fig. 35. Thomas E. Hogg House, 1924, interior view of living room, photo taken shortly after completion in 1924. The UT Institute of Texan Cultures, no. 83-806, courtesy Florence Collett Ayres

thoughtful touches that made living in them more convenient and attractive. In the Hogg House, there was a little telephone room, a toilet in its own little space with a window, a telephone and pushbutton bells to the kitchen and servant's room, a three-way electrical switch from the house to the detached garage building and servants' quarters. In the kitchen, there were zinc-lined bins, marble tops and backsplash, and a tiled wainscot 5' high. There were also aesthetic niceties: a plaster, barrel-vaulted ceiling and arch in the passage to the master bedroom and subtle adjustments of proportions of ceiling heights to other dimensions—9'6" in the dressing room, 10' in the kitchen, and 8'6" over the sunken bathtub.

At 207 Laurel Heights Place, Atlee's son Robert's house was built in 1925. The Robert Ayres House (fig. 36), "described as a 'Spanish farmhouse' received the first place award for domestic structures given by the West Texas chapter, American Institute of Architects, in January, 1927."[9] According to one observer, "Severely plain, with only graceful arches, wrought iron grilles and a shell recessed mosaic to relieve its plain lines, this place is representative of the pure Spanish type." The editor of *Country Life* concurred in 1927: "I think the little Spanish house your son has just completed is one of the most charming I have seen for a great many months." Robert's house was of frame finished on the outside with metal lath and stucco. The roof was of red Mission tile manufactured by Ludowici Celadon Company of St. Louis, Missouri. Inside, the cream white walls had an uneven finish. The ceiling of the living room had exposed, stained, wood trusses and rafters. The floors throughout

the first story were red California handmade tiles of varying patterns, provided by the Alhambra Tile Company of Santa Monica.

Atlee's skill with the vernacular of southern Spain, the so-called "Andalusian" form of Spanish style, continued to evolve with the P. L. Mannen House (color plate 6) of 1926 at 323 Bushnell. Ayres gave this relatively modestly sized house a convincingly Spanish flavor, using many of the same devices that he had deployed in the Hogg House two years earlier and more recently in his son Robert's house. Atlee created an even more picturesque composition that quite casually joined a low arcaded one-story, pitched roof wing to a two-story block comprised of a frontal, pitched roof section and another part under a low hipped roof. The façade toward the street held deep pockets of shade behind the wide roundheaded arches of the living room terrace. Under the corbeled, bracketed overhang, the shade lingered in the deeply recessed front door

trimmed with colorful square tiles. The shaded, second-story porch of the Monterrey style wooden balcony protected dark, arched windows in the dining room below. Dramatic too was the contrast between the loggia's stocky square columns of uneven stucco rounded at the corners and the dark stained wood of the balcony railings and balusters and the delicate wrought-iron grill over the porch window. Atlee's attention to the telling detail extended to obtaining just the right light fixtures throughout the house, and especially the one beside the front door. He was very particular. Harold Russ Glick, his supplier in Pasadena, California, wanted to know, "Do you like a bit of antique brass used in conjunction with iron? Do you prefer the very rusty bronzy finish to the darker almost black finish? Do you like heavy beaten back plates plain or with chisel marking? . . . In your lanterns, do you like the frame enclosing the glass to be very thin or do you like more iron shown?" Mr. Glick suggested a glass that is "entirely handmade, has a particularly fine sparkle and comes from one of the oldest glass centers of Europe. It is said to be the finest glass made and only comes in small sheets. Also it is more than twice the price of American glass." As it turned out, Atlee sent Mr. Glick his preference for mottled, antique brass in connection with iron, and well-proportioned back plates in order to give a good substantial appearance. In the event, Ayres was well pleased although he found the lanterns as a rule to be a little too small in scale, preferring those made for his son Robert's house, which he found much better proportioned. He also sought ornamental tile for the front entrance and around the fountain of the Mannen House from the studio that had supplied tiles for Robert's house. Atlee specified a "good bright pattern" but no "$2.50 a piece peacock design."[10]

In 1927, Atlee's Spanish style was in full flood. In that year he completed three important houses in the style. The Carl Newton House (fig. 37) at 800 East Olmos Drive was in many ways similar to the Thomas Hogg House in its elongated, bent plan and tall, pivotal tower.

This particular lot was an irregularly shaped corner with quite a bit of slope towards both streets. The street to the right of the house is a winding one that is parallel to the garage at that end of the house, and swings around paralleling the dining room and kitchen wing. The street on the front of the house is parallel to the living room and east loggia, so you can see from this, that we were influenced somewhat by our irregular shaped property. We also had to take into consideration the preservation of some very old oak trees on the property. . . . The style of the house was determined principally by the locality as we felt the contour of the ground and the shape of the lot called for an informal plan. As to the design, we feel that for this climate and atmosphere in general, the Spanish or Italian type of houses are the only ones suitable for this part of the country.[11]

The house was judged by *House and Garden* a "distinguished expression of Spanish motifs. Colorful, yet restrained, it avoids the picturesque excesses generally committed in the name of

Fig. 37. Carl Newton House, 1927, front exterior view. The UT Institute of Texan Cultures, no. 83-794, courtesy Florence Collett Ayres. Photo by Atlee B. Ayres, 1929

Iberian architecture." The complex turnings of the plan and the several octagonal bays of the stair hall, the den, and the breakfast room required twenty-two separate planes of the rough, irregularly laid roofs at shallow slopes of 5½" in 12". The two chimneys had their own little tile pitched roofs. Besides the artful placing of the many windows—largely casements, many with wrought-iron grills and balconies and wood shutters—the principal focus of ornament was the molded plaster around the principal front door and a smaller entrance at the side. The first had a series of rectangular frames, the outer ones in modeled stucco with curious little hemispheres and an inner frame of decorative tiles. The opening to the deeply recessed door had a delicately curved top, like a widow's peak. The plaster frame of the side door, though smaller, had elegant baroque curves. By that time, Ayres felt free to exploit little "accidents," such as the curious bulge that contained a second-floor bathroom and a closet off the kitchen, as well as very small, circular windows to add dynamic variety to the façades. He could by then manage the charm of irregularity, asymmetry, and intriguing variety, achieved without theatrical excess, depending on the many contrasting shadows on the dead white stucco against the brilliant Texas sky.

Also in 1927 and close to the Carl Newton House in Park Hill Estates, Ayres completed one of his most picturesque Spanish style houses for Amye Bozarth (fig. 38; plan 7). Completely asymmetrical, the house meandered through a series of forty-degree angles, numerous changes of wall planes lively with a great variety of sizes and shapes of openings. Some had semicircular arches, some were screened by stucco grills, some had solid dark wood shutters, and a few led to wood balconies with holders for flower pots. The effect of an old house that had grown like topsy over time was enhanced by fifteen, low-pitched roof planes of clay tile plus several more flat roofs. Unusual for Atlee, there were purely decorative

conceits like the sculptural, non-structural stucco fin wall outside the corner of the dining room. The eaves were decorated with simply curved outriggers scabbed onto the rafters. As in the Newton and Hogg Houses, Atlee relied on a tower to give character to the street façade—in this case it was capped with an octagonal clerestory containing ventilating vents filled with wood louvers and copper mesh screening. Its little octagonal, tiled roof was lightly capped with a copper weathervane. Unexpected and eccentrically placed at one of the turns of the plan was the richly paneled wood front door, entered through the 2' thick arches of a deeply shaded porch, which was embroidered with corbeled arches and flanked by 2' wide, flat stucco pilasters with simple capitals and bases. Within the cool shade of the porch, there were tiled seats.

Once inside, one was in a curiously shaped wedge of space in the turning of the plan. To the right, glimpsed through a wooden grill, was a sun room and beyond, down a few steps, was the dining room. To the left of the entrance was the principal delight of the spacious living room (fig. 39), 30' long and 16' wide, and rising a full two stories in height to a dark wood ceiling with false beams. High on the front wall was a small circular window with amber glass. Pairs of French doors opened both to the front and to the brick, herringbone-floored rear porch. The plaster chimneybreast for the baronial fireplace rose to the ceiling of 15'2". At the far end of the room, beyond triple arches supported by square columns with chamfered corners, a wide stair wound its way up a circular tower to the second-floor balcony. The balcony that overlooked the living room below connected the master bedroom, up two steps, with its dressing room and bath to two further bedrooms and baths at the opposite end of the house. Both floors provided a charming series of pleasant surprises as one followed the turnings and twisting of the plan, whose angles Atlee often emphasized with little transitional plaster arches. Otherwise, the materials and

SOUTHEAST FRONT ELEVATION

·RESIDENCE FOR·
·MRS AMYE·BOZARTH·

details were rather plain: plain plaster walls and ceilings, a modest wood picture rail, oak strip floors. The service areas of the house were arranged unusually along the back of the house where a rear porch connected the garage, servant's room and bath on one end with the kitchen on the other. It all added up to an exceptionally intriguing house that greatly expanded the dynamic possibilities of the Spanish style and clearly related it to the vernacular, farmhouse tradition of Andalusia and southern Italy, rather than the more formal Renaissance traditions of those countries.

Although the turned and angled plan was one of the hallmarks of Atlee's Spanish style, the John B. Chadwick House of 1929 at 114 Park Hill Drive, in Olmos Park, demonstrated that it was not an absolute essential of the style. On the contrary, the Chadwick plan was strictly or-thogonal, a composition of linear axes and ninety-degree angles. The plan gave no clue to the house's Spanish flavor, which was achieved by a variety of other means, many of which were purely cosmetic and deployed principally on the street façade. The most conspicuous touch was a tower that had an entrance porch under a tiled shed roof supported by a pair of low square stuc-coed columns. In what might be taken for a stair tower, a pair of semicircular arched windows with fancy wrought-iron grills actually illuminated the toilet of the second-story master bath. Still higher the tower was punctuated with a pair of cast-stone grills above stucco corbels and moldings. Compared with the towers of the Hogg House, the Carl Newton House, and the Amye Bozarth House—all of which contained graceful circu-lar stairs—the Chadwick tower seemed only an applied, exterior decorative element.

*Fig. 39. Amye
Bozarth House,
1927, drawing of
interior elevation
of living room,
reproduced from
original working
drawings dated
1927. The
Alexander Archi-
tectural Archives,
UT–Austin*

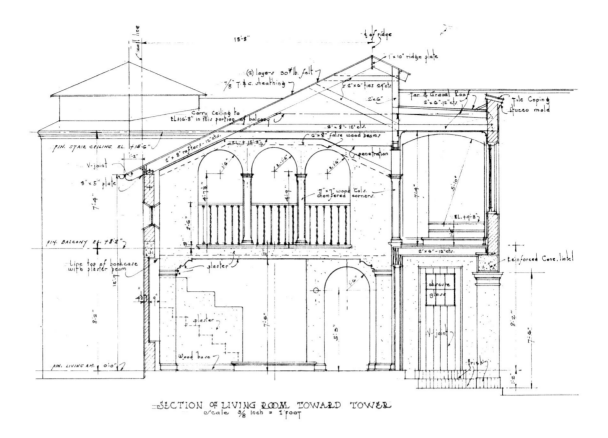

SECTION OF LIVING ROOM TOWARD TOWER
scale ⅜ inch = 1 foot

On January 3, 1926, Atlee wrote a letter to Mrs. D. F. Atkinson, the former Marion Koogler McNay, a vastly rich oil and property heiress who had recently come to live in San Antonio. As often when he got wind of a prospective client, Atlee wrote Mrs. Atkinson of his professional credentials, citing substantial houses he had done for a number of prominent San Antonians, including the English Tudor style house for Jesse Oppenheimer, the Italian Renaissance style house for David Robertson, and, most importantly as it turned out, the Spanish style house for Thomas Hogg. He suggested to Mrs. Atkinson, "If you would give us some idea of your requirements, we would be glad to send you some sketches together with photographs and plates for you to look over."[12]

His initiative bore fruit, for in the next year, the Atkinson-McNay House (plans 8 and 9) was started on a farm off the old highway leading north to Austin (color plates 7, 8, and 9). The pro-

gram of February 3, 1927, called for a two-story, hollow tile and stucco house with tile roof in the Spanish style, oriented to the south and east, with a west-facing dining room and a library of 19' x 32'. By April 12, 1927, Atlee wrote again to notify Mrs. Atkinson of the drilling of test holes for the foundations and to reassure her: "We are making very good progress with your house plans and will have something for you to look at very soon." Indeed on June 3, 1927, bids were received from six general contractors, ranging from a low bid of $111,947 to a high of $121,342. The Atkinsons chose the low bid of George W. Mitchell, Sr., to which they added $4,422 for extras that included imported Caen stone, a wall for the patio, and stone sills. Construction began in August, 1927. Sixteen months later, as the house neared completion, a statement for August 23, 1928, showed a cost of $138,348.48 plus Ayres's seven percent fee of $6,178.98, to total $144,527.46, or the approximate equivalent of

$4 million in 1998.[13] On July 20, 1927, the general contractor sent a list of subcontractors for tile work (Redondo & Company), cast stone, millwork, sheetmetal, roofing, weather stripping, lathing, plaster, and ironwork (San Antonio Foundry). At first, things moved quickly. On September 2, 1927, the engineer reported the completion of ninety-two of one hundred planned footings, straight piles, forty-seven of which were 40'–50' deep, thirty of them 30'–40' deep, and thirteen 10'–20' deep. The remaining eight were 36' deep.

Out beyond the expensive houses on suburban lots in Monte Vista and Laurel Heights, the Atkinson-McNay House was to be more a true estate whose crowning jewel was a sprawling hilltop mansion looking south over the city of San Antonio. The house was to be a Xanadu for Marion Atkinson who by 1927 was sole heir to a large fortune that was started ten years earlier with the discovery of oil on her father's farms in El Dorado, Kansas. The wells were abundantly productive throughout her life. Apart from Atlee's reputation, "knowing of your intimate knowledge of old Spanish and Mexican architecture, and of your high standing as an architect and a gentleman," Mrs. Atkinson's choice of Spanish style might have been influenced by the happy six months she had spent in Laredo in 1918 with her first husband, and the two years prior to moving to San Antonio that she and her mother spent in St. Petersburg, Florida, at a time when the vogue for Mediterranean style was at its height there.[14] Mrs. Atkinson was reputed to have been deeply involved in the planning, building, and furnishing of the mansion, and to have had a productive working relationship with her architects who were "frequently astonished and impressed by her flair for style, her accuracy of scale planning, her suggestions and insistence on small accents, and her general knowledge of technical problems."[15] Mrs. Atkinson, who had studied art at the Art Institute of Chicago in her late teens, was credited with designing, cutting the

stencils, and applying the decorative patterns on the beams of the ceiling and the archways of the entrance and dining rooms. Similarly, she personally designed, had made, and occasionally installed some of the tilework, as well as designing many of the iron gates and grills executed by local foundries. She also searched out appropriate antique lighting fixtures and hardware; supervised the development of the surrounding landscaped grounds of gardens, terraces, drives, and walks; and chose the imported palms and yuccas and exotic cacti, which were to transform the dusty caliche hill.

The house was furnished with an eclectic mixture that included elaborately carved Spanish and Italian style chairs and chests, Persian carpets, Chinese rugs, screens, faience jars, a Venetian *torchère,* high-backed Indian rattan chairs, a bulky, shiny, mahogany pedestal table, a Frenchified settee, and a pleasant clutter of curious objects and many books. Whatever Mrs. Atkinson's actual involvement, the house that greeted guests at the housewarming receptions in 1929 was a splendid example of the fruits of diligent labor, of scholarly knowledge, aesthetic judgment, and artistic sensibilities—on the part of the architects and the client—to create the inspired adaptation of the architecture of Spain and Mexico.

The house was at that time the largest and best of Ayres's houses in the Spanish style. Like his earlier Spanish houses, such as the Thomas Hogg House of 1923, the Atkinson-McNay was bent and angled in plan to expose the rooms to the prevailing Gulf breeze from the southeast. In previous houses, Ayres had used casement doors, giving onto stone and brick terraces with fountains, to connect the interiors of the houses to the grounds of their suburban lots. Exploiting the greater size of the Atkinson-McNay House, Ayres wrapped the two-story house around three sides of one end of a long patio that continued on, surrounded by a high wall around the fourth side (fig. 40). The secluded but very open patio had lush tropical vegetation, fountains, and pools, overlooked by wooden balconies and an upper terrace served by a tiled stair.

It was a patio much different from the traditional Mediterranean court totally enclosed within the house, which was designed to be a still well to capture the cool night air, protected from the sun and the hot air from the street or baking countryside, a completely inturned private domestic world that, with its circuitous entrances and sparsely windowed, blank exterior façade, discouraged the entrance of dust, noise, and prying eyes. Such a patio was unsuited to the hot, mostly humid, semitropical climate of San Antonio, nor was it representative of the more open and secular American society of 1929. The rough white stucco walls were adorned with a profusion of faience tiles, including a large, brilliant, blue, white, and yellow peacock panel. Tiles

lined the low walls of the many-fountained pool, and the bright risers—no two alike—of the stair to the upper terrace. The Atkinson patio was a magical place, with the soughing of the wind in the palms and the croaking of the specially imported Kansas bullfrogs.

When the guests arrived at the housewarming in 1929, they entered a reception hall whose double flights of sweeping stairs (fig. 41) bracketed a broad set of French doors wide open to the exotic court, there to be entertained by Spanish dancers amidst the spiky palms and twinkling lanterns. Entered from a flagstone terrace—via a stepped and recessed doorway that was 12' tall to the top of its arched transom, and through the tile-lined arches from the little cross vaulted vestibule—the reception hall itself was inviting enough. The spacious 30' x 25' room was paved with pleasantly uneven tiles in variegated soft

Fig. 40. Atkinson-McNay House, 1929, aerial view. The UT Institute of Texan Cultures, no. 83-808, courtesy Florence Collett Ayres

shades, as were the stairs with lacy iron railings that swept up on either side. The girders and cross-beams of the ceiling bore fanciful geometric patterns, originally in bright blues, greens, and yellows. Shallow white plaster barrel vaults spread like canvas awnings between the beams.

If the reception hall was an invitation to the patio and the point from which the whole house radiated, it was also the joint, the knuckle, for the wandering plan. On either side could be glimpsed the principal rooms, the library to the right, the dining room to the left, angled at forty-five degrees from the reception hall. The difficult, angled transitions from the reception room were solved with felicitous invention by means of intermediate passages—*entr'actes,* so to speak. One leading to the library was flanked by a small

office containing a city phone and house phone as well as a safe. The library was a spacious, but not overpowering room, 19' x 32', spanned with heavy cross-girders and beams (fig. 42). The focus of the room was a stately, composition stone chimneypiece with classical egg and dart moldings, wreathes, carved consoles, and an elaborately filigreed fire screen. Flanking the fireplace, deeply recessed pairs of doors led to the patio. Symmetrically placed on the opposite wall were doors leading to a tiled loggia open to the prevailing southeast breezes. Directly beyond the library and up a few steps there was a smaller sitting room with another fireplace and beyond that a private guest room and bath.

The passage from the reception hall to the dining room was flanked by a powder room and

a small room for flower arranging. Gates of wrought iron in an abstract pattern of peacock feathers opened to the dining room, which lay on the main long axis of the patio to which it opened through French doors and a triply arched porch. These were matched on the opposite side by similar French doors and filmy wrought-iron gates to a columned porch that overlooked broad stairs descending the terraced garden. Like the reception room and the library, the dining room had a sturdy beamed ceiling, this time of square coffers stenciled in a stylized peacock motif, which was echoed in a Chinese rug of deepest blue background. The peacock theme pervaded the house. It appeared in the patio in a large wall plaque of brilliant blue, green, yellow, and white Talavera tiles made from Mrs. Atkinson's sketches in Puebla, Mexico. The theme was reiterated in three smaller tile plaques of the arches of the loggia. There was a further peacock tile plaque on the inside wall of the library loggia, which also contained a tile with the image of a young woman who may well have been Marion Atkinson herself. The peacock theme continued in a wrought-iron fanlight over the carriage entrance.

Beyond the dining room there were the service rooms: the pantry, kitchen, laundry, back stairs down to a semibasement mechanical room, and a hall leading to a three-car garage via a two-story porch, called the "promenade," which also provided convenient shelter off the patio. Upstairs, the second floor held the owners' apartment, dressing rooms with carefully designed, cedar-lined closets, large tiled bath, sleeping porch, and roof terrace—all stretched out over the library below and similarly open to the prevailing southeast breezes. Next to the master suite, off the crossvaulted upper hall, there was a guest room and bath and an octagonal study above the entrance door. From the study, a narrow hidden stair led up to an open tower *mirador.* There, under the sturdy, wood, radiating beams and tile roof, Mrs. Atkinson could survey San Antonio, spread out beyond her hill.

The house clearly embodied the architect's careful concern for comfort in the semitropical climate of San Antonio, not only by proper orientation to facilitate air circulation, but also by integrating the rooms with the patio and the surrounding gardens through many doors, windows, loggias, and balconies. The attenuated plan lacked some of the convenience of a more compact arrangement, but at the same time encouraged and facilitated the flow of the Atkinsons' guests at their frequent entertainments. It also afforded a separation of the service areas from the owners' rooms. The kitchen was placed in the northeast corner to keep cooking odors away from the principal rooms and ventilated through an exterior grill under the sink that drew in make-up air to mitigate the heat of the stove. With its countertops of small white tiles and 5' high wainscot of larger, shiny, glazed white tiles, its plain wooden cabinets painted a soft green and trimmed with a continuous copper shoe mould, the kitchen was convenient, light, and airy. There, as in most of his houses, Atlee resolved practical and technical matters with care and ingenuity.

Like all of Atlee's houses, the Atkinson House lacked a full basement except for a small mechanical room under the service wing. That held a coal-fired boiler that generated steam to supply the radiators throughout the house. The pipes for the steam and those to return the condensate ran in a low space between the ground and the floor. Most of Ayres's houses were supported on low masonry piers that held the wood girders and beams several feet off the ground, creating a crawl space for utility access. The mechanical room also contained the water heater, an incinerator connected by a chute from the kitchen above, and, of course, the coal bin.

But it was not enough that the house be comfortable and useful—it required "style" of expression, and the choice had been made to be reminiscent of Spanish domestic buildings. This Ayres knew how to do. It was in part a matter of shape and composition, a rambling series of volumes under low pitched (5 ½" in 12") roofs of barrel clay tiles, punctuated by a three-story octagonal entrance tower. The effect depended upon stuccoed walls, textured with a palm relief to distribute the flickering light, white walls to capture the shadows of the tall palms, and walls punctuated by shaded recesses of arcaded loggias. The noble, arched front doorway, and dark wood framed windows of different sizes and shapes revealed the great thickness that conveyed a sense of permanence, of antiquity, of strength and security.

The Spanish style also depended heavily on the decorative use of two materials: ceramic tiles and wrought iron (color plates 8 and 9). The very plainness of thick walls invited adornment. Largely devoid of the ornament of classical architecture, the American Spanish style depended on decorative tile, individual tiles, and colorful plaques—sometimes of Mexican or Spanish manufacture—but more often made in the United States, mainly in California. The tiles provided abstract qualities of colors, sparkle, and vitality on the stair risers, and in and around the pool. They also were enjoyed for their imagery and narrative. More than twenty tiles over the outdoor fireplace and on the walls of the "promenade" illustrated the adventures of Don Quixote. In the dining room loggia, heraldic tiles with coats of arm suggested an aristocratic, albeit specious, provenance.

Wrought iron was also essential to the Spanish style. At the Atkinson-McNay House, the ground-floor windows were protected by a variety of lacey, black, wrought-iron grills. The upper floor doors opened onto wooden balconies with slatted railings overlooking the patio. To set the tone at the entrance, perhaps drawing on his collection of photographs of Spanish and Italian doorways, Ayres created a stepped, recessed door, 5' wide and 7' tall, flanked by twisted cast-stone columns, capitals, and bases. The door, paneled and studded, with a semicircular transom rose to 12'. Equally in character were the wooden garage doors of V-groove boards below and slated spindles above for ventilation. The theme continued outside in many small details: wrought-iron lanterns, terra-cotta pots, and the little tile hats on the chimneys.

Inside, the Spanish flavor depended on the slightly uneven, handtroweled, plaster walls; the plaster rope moldings; stenciled, beamed, and vaulted ceilings; leaded glass; tile floors; and the extensive use of wrought iron in lighting fixtures, stair railings, hardware, and drapery rods. Openings characteristically had small brackets to make the transition from the jamb to the head. Some of the Spanish flavor was a matter of artifice. The steel "I-beam," 20" deep, required by the wide span of the reception room was concealed as a deep wooden beam stenciled and painted like the rest of the wooden structure. The library ceiling also concealed two, 12" steel beams. Some of Ayres's greatest artifice was devoted to creating the illusion of the very thick stone and brick masonry walls of the Spanish prototypes he was trying to recall. Though Ayres used structural clay tile faced with exterior stucco and interior plaster to make a wall approximately 11" thick, he tried to give the impression of much thicker walls by furring out the interior walls, sometimes, as in the library, concealing heating radiators in the thick walls flanking the doors to the patio. The sense of thickness was further created by slightly rounding all corners, which also gave a sense of handcraft. Typically, rooms requiring modern equipment were less thematic and more frank about contemporary materials, the Atkinson kitchen having Vitrolite countertops, standard shiny, white tile wainscot, and plain wooden cabinets.

This judicious, free combining of ideas from other countries and times with the materials,

methods of construction, technological invention, changing ways of living, and—in the case of Ayres—a strong sensitivity to the qualities and character of San Antonio was really typical of eclectic architects of the first part of the twentieth century. Though disdained by more radical architects as rather reactionary, imitative, and dishonest to new materials and production, those eclectic architects could create a house of the stature of the Atkinson. It was quickly recognized as an exceptional house.[16]

In the succeeding years, the Atkinson–McNay House underwent several transformations, the first of those being the remodeling undertaken by Ayres and Ayres, Architects, to convert it to the Marion Koogler McNay Museum of Art. The changes, largely concerned with new equipment for climate control, did little to alter the house's essential Spanish character, which was, if anything, improved by the closing of some of the windows and doors. However, during the period of 1970 through 1987, the house was extended first in an extension of the dining room and later in a series of one-story gallery pavilions that entirely enclosed the patio to the east. They were designed by the San Antonio firm of Ford, Powell, and Carson. They comprised another stage of eclecticism, very different from, but sympathetic to, the original house. O'Neil Ford was a native Texan, whose scant formal architectural education left him free to draw on indigenous buildings for inspiration, rather than the icons of Beaux-Arts Europe. He created buildings that were "a symbiosis of the modern movement, unadorned geometric forms articulated in response to climate, site, and the potentials of the material: and his passion for the Mexican flavor of his adopted city." He was after "the essence rather than facile stylistic imitation."[17] The first addition to the McNay was a two-story, glass-enclosed box into which one descended from the original dining room. Recessive from the outside, shielded by trees and shrubbery, the room was a transparent setting for sculpture. The

Mexican tile floors and wood paneling of the ceiling gave a flavor unexpectedly compatible with the Spanish flavor of the original house. Successive additions by Ford, Powell, and Carson were equally simple with warm floors of tile or mesquite block inside. Outside were plain blank stucco walls, not as textured as the original surfaces, with simplified Mexican cornices and scuppers.

The McNay Museum acquired two further buildings: one built in 1974, the other in the late 1980s by the celebrated architect Charles Moore. Though not part of the museum when it was built, its very proximity made relationship of styles an issue. Arguably a foil or contrast to the McNay, the Moore building entrance was an oversized, flamboyantly theatrical, albeit whimsical, Post-Modern version of Ayres's original entrance to Mrs. McNay's house. The rest of the building was a metal-roofed and thin stucco wall affair with an occasional Texas lone star pasted on for symbolism.

Another chapter in the stages of eclecticism at the McNay began in 1994, when Overland Partners designed a new auditorium for concerts, films, educational programs, and special events. Overland chose to draw inspiration from the original Ayres building. The new auditorium—resembling a Spanish chapel, with its octagonal entrance tower recalling the original entrance, stucco walls, terra-cotta tile roof, and arched porticos—was more overtly Spanish than the Ford, Powell, and Carson additions it adjoined. Inside, cast-stone column designs from the original house were replicated for the construction of the auditorium. Similar tiles and hardwood floors were used to relate the new building to the old. None of these overt references were impediments to the current technology required by the auditorium.

In 1931, as the clouds of the Great Depression darkened, the firm of Ayres and Ayres was fortunate to have a new major commission for one of the largest and best of their Spanish houses.

The John Albert Brown House was to be in Nichols Country Club Estates, an exclusive, residential suburb of Oklahoma City where the owner was a principal of the Rorabaugh-Brown Drygoods Company with two stores in Oklahoma, five in Kansas, and offices in New York, London, Paris, and other European cities. Ayres was very happy to get this commission, as he wrote, "It is the first time in years that I have started the New Year without a single new job in the office."[18] Mr. Brown had hesitated to give the job to an "outside" architect, but he was persuaded by Atlee's insistence:"I know exactly how the local architects feel about the outside architects coming in . . . But they ought to realize that if [it involves] a certain type of work, like Spanish, that they are not accustomed to, they should not expect to be given the work." Atlee had shown the Browns photographs of the Carl Newton and Robert Straus Houses, and, above all, the Atkinson-McNay House, which became a major inspiration for the Browns' house. The documents relating to the Brown House are peppered with phrases such as "similar to Mrs. Atkinson's"; "Use column treatment like Mrs. Atkinson's"; "Cast stone balustrade perforated design similar to Mrs. Atkinson's";"Double stairs with wrought iron railing and tile treads and risers similar to Mrs. Atkinson's";"Stair to curve at corners . . . Niches on stair landing . . . Beam ceiling (stenciled)"—all like or similar to Mrs. Atkinson's. Mrs. Brown wanted to "reproduce exactly the standing lanterns that Mrs. Atkinson has at bottom of her stairway." Far from being offended by imitation, Mrs. Atkinson said it was alright to copy the entire house. However, the Browns' imitative desire posed problems for Atlee. "We . . . would not like to copy the Atkinson entrance and other features unless you absolutely want us to do so." Although the Browns wanted a copy of the Atkinson front door, they were dissuaded "because we are worn down with the matter rather than any real desire to have a front door other than appears in the Atkinson house."

The Browns did have their own independent ideas. Mrs. Brown had collected ideas from magazines and deferentially tried to express her thoughts. "We do not want the outside lines of the house to look stately and formal but a softer look. . . . The West corner and east wing seem a trifle formal. . . . Last night in looking over the plates Mr. Brown expressed himself as liking rooms that look attached rather than all under one roof." With admirable candor, she added, " It is hard for us to know what we want." Ayres tried to help the Browns visualize the house by sending them a small cardboard model as well as photographs from his collection. Atlee was sympathetic to their desire for a more informal, even though very large, house. He "didn't want tower to get too tall and stilted as we are trying to get a low rambling effect in keeping with Spanish style." And again, "We were carrying out the Spanish Colonial type as he [Wallace Neff] and other California architects do," suggesting a more relaxed, even picturesque, version of Spanish style.

As usual Atlee began the design with considerations of the relationship of the house and the site, the topography, and especially the prevailing breezes. A series of sketches explored the position and shape of the driveway, which swept up past the front terrace through an archway to a turnabout and main rear entrance sheltered by a marquise or awning. On the front of the house, a grand tower (fig. 43) faced directly down the center of the property toward the Capitol. The entrance itself, remarkably like the Atkinsons', was a tall, roundheaded opening embroidered with several rows of lacy, artificial-stone moldings and a delicately pierced transom over the wrought-iron gates of the front door. There were wrought-iron wall lanterns identical in design to the Atkinsons' but flanking the doorway more closely. The similar window above was covered with a wrought-iron grill slightly different from the Atkinson-McNay House. For the Browns, Atlee added stucco baroque scrolls that unified the lower and upper openings. The

long wings were turned forward at slight angles, their size and symmetrical placement producing a much more grandiose and formal effect than that supposedly desired by both the Browns and Ayres. This effect was further emphasized by the long balustraded terrace with an artificial stone made of concrete that was surfaced with ½" Atlas white cement and sand balustrade—similar to the Atkinsons'—that stretched entirely across the front. Guests could arrive across the terrace's colored and decorated tiles from the driveway. Ayres tried to dilute the formality of the long wings by varying the size and placements of the openings, by corbeling one portion of the second floor, and by adding a balcony at one end. Off the living room there was an arcade with triple arches. But the embracing wings were clearly unified by the heavy shadows of the continuous, deeply overhanging eaves. The angles were originally planned to sweep back from the tower, to converge views from the living room and dining room on statuary at the end of a swimming pool. Eventually the pool was built to the rear at an angle off the living room in an open-air, arcaded room with Moorish horseshoe arches and a tiled roof. Only at the far end of the dining room wing did the house dissolve into a series of smaller wings, individually roofed in tile. Here were the service quarters and the garages through the sort of picturesque round-headed archway favored by the California architect Wallace Neff, whom Atlee admired. The formality and sheer size of the Brown House was ameliorated by extensive application of Ayres's "Spanish" touches. The schedule for wrought iron showed sixty-two pieces completed by October 30, 1931. Outside, these were deployed in window grills, gates, lanterns, flower pot holders; and inside, for gates, stair railings, light fixtures, and hardware. Atlee also made use of pierced grills of tile and brick. Of course, the roofs were Mission tile, straight barrel tiles by Ludowici Celedon Company, in variegated shades of red. Atlee himself went to Mexico for

Fig. 43. John Albert Brown House, 1931, front exterior view from driveway. The Alexander Architectural Archives, UT–Austin

decorative tiles, to Puebla for *azulejos de Talavera* from the firm of Isauro Uriarte, also for picture plaques—twenty-one tiles for *gallos* (cocks) and twenty-eight tiles for *leones* (lions) and a yellow *pajarito* (parrot). (Atlee was compelled by the sleeping car conductor to pay for an upper berth for the tile trunk.) For the terraces, he found the Spanish, mosaic, art tile closer to home at Aztec Art Tile in San Antonio. Iron Crafts, Inc., was there on Laurel Street as well.

The interiors of the Brown House were exceptionally generous: the living room was 22' x 52'; the dining room, seating twenty-four persons, was 19' x 28'. The Browns wanted high ceilings, 13'6" in the main rooms, exceeding those of the Atkinson House by more than a foot. The entrance reception hall was virtually a replica of Mrs. Atkinson's. The walls were lined off in blocks of 14" x 8" to imitate Caen stone. The walls of the other major rooms had a handtextured plaster finish and dark-stained woodwork. The floors of the living room and dining room had originally been specified as terra-cotta tile but were changed to edgegrain oak from 6" to 14" wide.

The remaining floors were 2¼" flat grain oak. The servants' rooms had less expensive pine floors (as was Ayres's usual practice). The exterior loggia had a cement tile floor with cast-stone borders, sills, and columns supporting the deep arches. The house also included a music room, an office up two steps from the living room, a breakfast room to seat eight—which had indirect lighting and a place for an electric toaster, coffee pot, and waffle iron—and a powder room with "unusual lighting effects." As with his other clients, Atlee provided the Browns with numerous amenities: loudspeakers in the living room, dining room and master bedroom; telephone plugs for portable phones; an intercom and burglar alarm system controlled by a switch in the master bedroom; outside underground feed for Christmas tree lighting; sound deadening in the sleeping porch; an intake for blower air for the organ; an air compressor in the basement for the master bubble bath; ice water at the pantry sink, etc. The master bedroom suite was a model of luxury, a room 18' x 22' with an arched ceiling above a cove and rope molding, a screened loggia with a cement floor, a gymnasium with artificial electric sun bath, belt machine and bicycle, a 2'-thick oiled maple massage slab, electric steam bath, and special tub for the bubble bath with its airline to the basement compressor. There was also a kitchenette on the second floor. The tower was used for director board meetings or dancing. Service rooms were no less carefully considered. The linoleum-floored kitchen had a Monel metal sink and worktable top with outlets for mixers, a glazed tile hood over the stove, and a refrigerator 5' long, 36" deep. The extensive servants' quarters housed the cook, a butler, and gardener, as well as day help. In the basement were the boiler room, the water heater, water softener, the air compressor, incinerator, a drying room, and dressing rooms for the swimming pool.

The large house was built expeditiously, though Mr. Brown wrote in April, 1932: "The house has been such a task that Mrs. Brown and I are both completely exhausted and do not have any resistance left to fight any longer for the things that ought to be correct that are not correct about the place. There are so many things that I feel badly about that I could not begin to mention all of them." (The Browns had discovered like most clients, especially those building very large houses, that a house is not a Swiss watch.) However, one month later, Mrs. Brown wrote, "The house is very lovely and lawn looking better." But she also reported that the "Wind nearly drives us mad. Porch impossible during storms. Business poor." However, they weathered the Depression in style. In May, 1933, Atlee was advising Mrs. Brown on a Mexican program for her brother's wedding announcement, with ices, cake, and iced coffee, and "with Spanish dancers with two guitar players and super Spanish girl ride in burrow dressed in her bright colored native costume with a bridal veil." In 1934, the Browns mounted a bronze plaque on the stately piers of the wrought-iron entrance gates, displaying the Spanish name of their home, which, translated in English, was "Happy House."

Ayres and Ayres were to do one more Mediterranean style house before the Second World War. In 1938 they completed the H. L. Blackstock House (fig. 44; plans 12 and 13) on Alameda Circle in the Olmos Park section of San Antonio. With a little over 10,000 square feet of enclosed space, plus extensive loggias, porches, and a *porte cochere,* it was one of their largest houses, rivaled only by their roughly contemporaneous mansion for Frank and Merle Buttram in Oklahoma City. Unlike the Buttram House, which was an exceedingly formal, symmetrical exercise in Beaux-Arts classicism, the Blackstock House blended the dignified balance of Italian villas with the picturesque irregularity of the Spanish style. It directly addressed Alameda Circle with a symmetrical principal entrance façade centered on a stately front door surrounded by bold cast-stone moldings and an open loggia above (color plate 11). The entrance door was flanked by symmetrically balanced, cast-concrete grills protecting smaller windows to a closet and toilet room. In the front façade, there were wrought-iron grills in the window of the ladies powder room on the one side, and the window of the circular stair hall on the other. This skin-deep symmetry, revealing little of what lay behind, was especially telling in the deep, splayed window embrasures that concealed the major circular stair (fig. 45) that was "embedded" in the mass of the house, quite unlike the exuberant expression of the circular stairs in the bold towers of the Thomas Hogg, Carl Newton, and Amye Bozarth Houses. From the central façade, two-story wings splayed out on both sides toward the front and toward the rear, a "butterfly" plan that not only accommodated the irregular property lines that followed Broadmoor Drive and Hermosa Drive from Alameda Circle, but which allowed generous light and ventilation to fill the house. The entrance drive on Broadmoor passed by the front door to a motor entrance in the *porte cochere* and on to the parking court on the basement level and an exit on Hermosa, a very thoughtful and

*Fig. 44. H. L.
Blackstock House,
1938, front exterior
view. The
Alexander Archi-
tectural Archives,
UT–Austin*

commodious arrangement that left uncluttered the main façade directly in front of the circle. The impression from the streets was in great measure one of formal balance, not only in the symmetrical massing, but also in the symmetrical placement and proportions of the windows and their stucco surrounds, the suppression of all eccentricity. From the rear, away from the streets, the house sprawled away from a central arcaded loggia and sleeping porch above, extending along a large service wing where windows of more varied sizes and shapes were permitted. The overall impression of the house is one of enormous size: of large plain stucco wall surfaces, adorned only with a narrow string course below the second-story windows; wrought iron on the balconies off some of the bedrooms; square, cast-stone columns in the upstairs loggias; round columns of plaster over metal lath in the living room loggia—all very measured and reserved. Although different in style from either the 1935 Lutcher

Brown House or the Buttram House, the Blackstock House has a similar dry formality, relieved only slightly by the charm of what on the original model appear to be creamy stucco walls, deeply corrugated, orange, terra cotta roof tiles, pale yellow-green shutters, and some of the sparingly used Mediterranean details such as the little tiled roof over the bay window in the breakfast room.

Within, the house was all generosity of conventional spaces, serving an established pattern of formal living that involved the owners, their family and guests, and the staff in the wing that included three servants' bedrooms. Much of the luxurious living could be done on the large porch that extended from the central reception hall onto a broad, curved terrace from which one descended by flanking stairs to a lawn that fell away to an oval swimming pool and its triple-arched loggia reflected in the water. Other relaxed moments might be passed in the heated

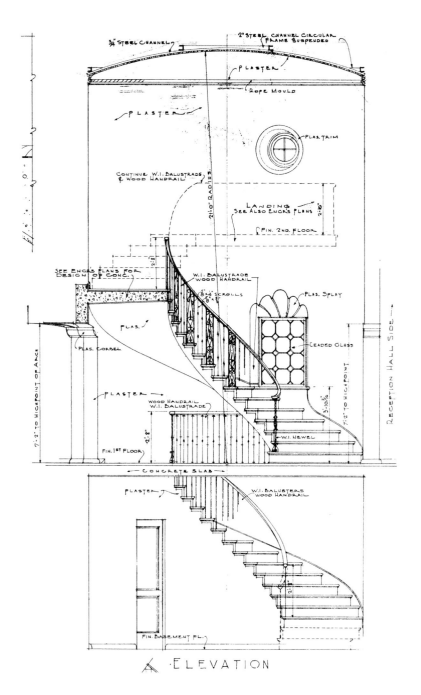

cabinet in the master bath or on the so-identi-fied "rub" table that let down from the wall. Convivial moments could be spent in the base-ment floor game room with its knotty white pine, vertically paneled walls, terrazzo floor, and brick fireplace flanked by a cabinet for twenty-one guns. At the other end of the room, a tile-fronted bar sparkled with opal glass shelves. The basement level also contained men's and women's dressing rooms, plaster over cork, insulated cold-storage room, the heating and air-conditioning room, and three-car garage with a large, circular car-washing device on the ceiling.

Fig. 45. H. L. Blackstock House, 1938, drawing of interior circular stair, reproduced from original working drawings dated 1937. The Alexander Architectural Archives, UT–Austin

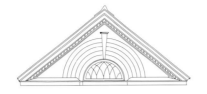

CHAPTER 12

Neoclassical Mansions, 1931–38

As most architectural firms, Ayres and Ayres felt the financial crisis of the Great Depression. As early as August, 1929, with the Atkinson-McNay House nearing completion, Atlee wrote to a friend in California that "Business has been absolutely rotten for a number of months." He wrote again in 1931, "I hope that I never experience another siege of depression as we are going through at the present time." Later in 1935, he was even more discouraged: "With everything uncertain, I cannot see why anyone with good judgement would think to trying to borrow money to build a house. How it is all going to terminate is more than anyone can definitely tell."[1] Fortunately, despite the economic hard times, the Ayreses' practice was kept afloat by two residential commissions: one completed in San Antonio in 1935, the other—begun in 1931 but not com-

pleted until 1938—in Oklahoma City. They were to be the last, and the grandest, of the firm's houses before the Second World War effectively put a stop to the building of luxury, architect-designed, single-family houses. When construction resumed after the war, residential building was focused largely on providing builder-designed housing for an expanding middle-class population. The post-war houses designed by Ayres and Ayres were to be much more modest, smaller, and more simply detailed—faint echoes of their rich eclecticism of the prewar period.

Even while Atlee was designing and, with Robert, overseeing the construction of the house for the John Browns in Oklahoma City, he was discretely, but persistently, angling to land another, even more promising, commission there from their friends, the Frank and Merle Buttram

House (plans 10 and 11). Buttram was a very successful oilman, civic leader, and philanthropist. His wife, professor of violin at the University of Oklahoma, was involved in local music programs and the Oklahoma City Symphony. In 1931, the Buttrams had acquired eighty-nine acres in the recently incorporated Nichols Hills suburb of Oklahoma City and had already hired the San Antonio landscape architect Homer L. Fry to begin landscaping the property.[2] At that time, they also engaged Ayres and Ayres to begin design work on a large mansion. However, the Buttrams were in no hurry to build the house. As the 1930s went on, the Ayres firm turned out many design studies for the large house. From the beginning, it was to be an imposing house in the Beaux-Arts style, popular from 1890 to 1930, a style characterized by grandiose axial formality in planning and composition, coupled columns, articulated stone walls, grand staircases, and rich decoration both inside and out—decorative swags, garlands, shields, cartouches, and

free-standing statuary. It was also closely related to the Neoclassical Revival style that began about the same time but that lasted, in one form or another, through the whole twentieth century. In the 1930s the Neoclassical style was less monumental than the full-fledged Beaux-Arts style: the decorative detail was more restrained, the walls smoother with shallow moldings, pilasters, and quoins. Treading the line between dignity and pomposity, the Neoclassical style still favored monumental scale, especially in the ubiquitous two-story porticos with classical columns and elaborate capitals that adorned the façades (fig. 46).

The Buttram House, though clearly possessing many of the qualities of the Beaux-Arts style—especially the paired columns of the rear façade, the axial planning and the great oval stair of the interior—was rather neoclassical in the smooth, pale ashlar of the exterior walls broken only by a thin belt course, without quoins, swags, cartouches, or other florid decorations. The neo-

Fig. 46. Frank and Merle Buttram House, 1937, rear exterior view. The Alexander Architectural Archives, UT–Austin

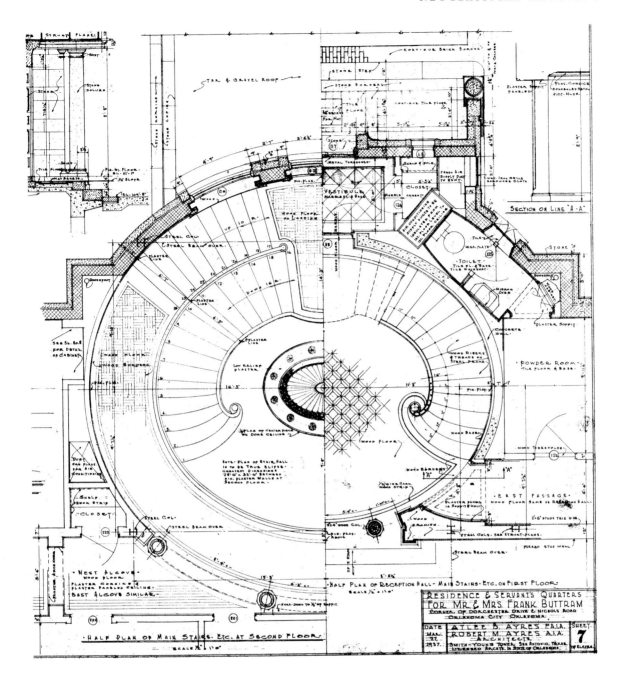

Fig. 47. Frank and Merle Buttram House, 1937, drawing of interior oval stair, reproduced from original working drawings dated 1937. The Alexander Architectural Archives, UT–Austin

classical character was especially strong on the entrance side, where the oval stair hall was capped by a balustraded flat roof and cornice with prominent modillions, and a flat-roofed *porte cochere* that was adorned with flat pilasters.

The interior of the Buttram House abided strictly to the Beaux-Arts tradition of axial arrangement. The house was entered by an elliptical hall, from which a double-rise, double-return stair (fig. 47) rose 28' to a domed ceiling subtly gradated in tone and decorated with a painted medallion. Three large, roundheaded, leaded-glass windows illuminated the stair. The hall led directly into the largest room, measuring 36' x 58' with a 14' ceiling. From the earliest designs, it was specified as the "art room," a magnificent hall with expansive walls and decorative, mirrored, and lighted niches for displaying the Buttrams' collections. Centered on the wall opposite the entrance was an impressive, imported, Carrara marble chimneypiece in high relief, surmounted by a Venetian scene, the largest painting in the house.

Predictably, the art room was flanked on one side by the large living room and, on the other, by the dining room, which had the most elaborate ceiling in the house. Barrel vaulted, heavily coffered in plaster octagons and circles, and painted by Italian and German artisans with robust colors, the ceiling had the richness of a Roman palace. The other major room on the ground floor, and likely the most lived-in, was the mahogany-paneled library with its fireplace of Verde Antico marble and oak mantel. The east wall had a large plate-glass window that overlooked the terraces of the formal gardens and the swimming pool. Reached by a circular stair was a small balcony that was connected by a concealed stair to the master bedroom above.

As logic would have it, the remaining corner of the house was devoted to the extensive service arrangements, utilitarian and without decoration but well equipped with the most modern commercial equipment. As in typical Beaux-Arts plans, the small spaces between the major rooms were cleverly filled with pantries, lavatories, and other servant functions. The upper floor contained seven bedrooms and private bathrooms, including the master suite and bathroom, which was elaborately equipped and decorated with a domed, handcolored turquoise ceiling.

An indication of the size of the nearly 30,000-square-foot house was its 7,500-square-foot full basement, which had a shooting gallery, a clubroom decorated as a medieval hall, a bar, bowling alley, card rooms, fully equipped showers and locker rooms for men and women, as well as the rooms for the laundry, storage, and the heating and air-conditioning equipment.

Unlike most of Ayres's residential projects, the Buttram project was as notable for the development of its extensive grounds as for the house

itself. The original landscape plan combined Italianate axial formality in the terraces and gardens near the house together with the French tradition of radiating avenues through the trees and the more English meanderings of the driveway, small ponds, and paths that wandered into private clearings and secret woods.

In 1935, Ayres built the H. Lutcher Brown House (fig. 48) at 636 Ivy Lane in Terrell Hills, San Antonio. Oak Court, as it was called, was similarly fortunate in having a very large site. It permitted a long alley leading from dignified brick gates, through a formal, symmetrically walled forecourt flanked by buildings for servants and the garages and terminating at the long front portico with its six, majestic, 21' Ionic columns— in all, a perfect neoclassical composition. The original columns were composites of five wood 2" x 8" planks, later replaced with brick and plaster in 1957. The 207' façade presented an almost obsessive symmetry that included rows of identical windows with louvered shutters, matching dependencies housing Lutcher Brown's office on one end, and the kitchen on the other, and a false chimney on one of the projecting wings to maintain the rigid balance. The recessed wall behind the columned portico was stucco, but all the other walls were Cordova Cream limestone in graded ashlar courses ranging from 8" to 18". With its green, purple, and red, mottled, Vermont slates of the hipped roof (the same slates used on the Marshall Field Estate by John Russell Pope), and crab orchard stone paving, the exterior of the house was of impressive quality.

Yet it was a marked change from Ayres's earlier Italian Renaissance style houses and even more so from the more informal, picturesque Spanish style houses, even the very large ones. The striking difference suggests that in the 1930s, with Atlee by then in his sixties, that his son and partner Robert—who had been trained at the Beaux-Arts-oriented architecture school of the University of Pennsylvania—was principally responsible for the Lutcher Brown House, and,

Fig. 48. Lutcher-Brown House, 1934, model of house and entrance forecourt. The Alexander Architectural Archives, UT–Austin

judging from its neoclassical similarities, perhaps for the Buttram House as well. In fact, the Lutcher Brown working drawings were done by an Ayres employee, Charles Webb, under Robert Ayres's design supervision. In any case, there is no doubt that Robert had been an active, important part of the firm since he entered it as partner in 1922, acting in his father's absences to deal with clients and supervise construction, as he had on the Lutcher Browns' House.

Despite the impressive, but rather rigid neoclassicism of the exterior, the true grandeur of the house lay in its superb interiors, which would justify Robert's claim to the house being of the "Georgian type . . . True Georgian in every respect."[3] Mr. Lutcher Brown's extensive timber holdings provided a spectacular wealth of fine woods: walnut for the walls of the library; mag-

nolia for the wainscoting in the dining room, sitting room, and office; a floor with a white oak pattern and border in the entrance hall; stairs with oak treads, magnolia risers, and walnut handrails; doors of walnut, birch, magnolia, and white pine. These adorned a series of well-proportioned formal rooms of English eighteenth-century, Georgian character. Although Robert had been desirous of obtaining an old pine-paneled room from a firm in London that specialized in parts of old English halls, priories and colleges,[4] his own designs in the Georgian manner were impeccable: well-scaled and beautifully detailed, scrolled and pedimented doorways; fireplaces with mantels carved with swags, acanthus leaves, egg and dart moldings, plaster cornices of bundled reeds. He had clearly gone to plates and detailed drawings in books on Georgian architecture and, in

Lutcher Brown, had a client with the means to execute such fine work even in the lingering Depression. English style gave way to the tastes of the ladies of the house upstairs, where French Rococo and Louis XVI crept into their bedrooms and baths.

By 1939, the grounds of the estate were adorned with a little brick octagonal summer house with stone pilasters and louvered doors. Facing the swimming pool there was the pedimented and columned porch of a square casino with a central dome. The rear façade had a roundheaded central window with a view of a fountain and balustraded stairs to the lawn. Else-where a cast-stone arch between tall hedges led to an oval dance floor and bandstand with fluted columns and a radiating latticed roof: an enchanting place to enjoy before the cataclysm of the Second World War, which was to bring to an end the eclectic odyssey on which Atlee had embarked forty years before. In 1935, even Atlee had sensed a change in the architectural wind. "I am considering purchasing some portfolios or books containing illustrations of good, not too radical Architectural modernistic designs."[5] The firm would continue after the war, but the era of residential eclecticism of the caliber of Atlee's houses was over for good.

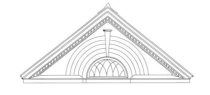

CHAPTER 13

Postscript

Post-1945 Varieties of Eclecticism

"Eclectic activity—selecting elements from preexisting
sources and applying them to a new context—is a constant
factor in architectural production at any time."

—Howard Barnstone, *The Architecture of John Staub*

Atlee Ayres's eclectic odyssey (fig. 49)—his effort to give character and expression to what would otherwise be merely buildings—followed a course similar to that of many architects in the mainstream of American architecture in the first forty years of the twentieth century. In San Antonio alone there were a number of Atlee's contemporaries skilled in eclectic uses of the past. In the first decade of Atlee's practice at the beginning of the century, Atlee was designing the 1908 Halff House at 601 Howard, whose "metal shingled roof, with its twin projections flanking the main entrance, seems almost Japanese in character," whose "arch framing the front door harkens back to the work of H. H. Richardson," and whose "most original details are the columns of the first floor, with their quasi-Art Nouveau foliate carving."[1] Henry T. Phelps had adorned the

1907 Franklin C. Davis house at 509 West French Place with an imposing neoclassical front portico of monumental two-story columns with elaborate Corinthian capitals. In that same year, Alfred Giles provided a friendlier array of commodious verandas, decks, and a *porte cochere* surrounding the asymmetrical block of the Floyd McGown House on the corner of French Place and San Pedro.

Later, in the 1920s and '30s, along the streets of Monte Vista, others of Atlee's contemporaries designed fine houses in a variety of styles. Like Atlee, many focused on the Mediterranean styles, Italian Renaissance, Spanish, and hybrids of the two. Robert B. Kelly's 1928 house for Harry Landa at 233 Bushnell Avenue, now a branch of the San Antonio Public Library, remains a robust example of Spanish style with its sculptural, columned

Fig. 49. Atlee
Ayres sketch for
a house based on
Greek Church
of St. Nicolas,
Karytena, n.d..
The Alexander
Architectural
Archives,
UT–Austin

KARYTAENA—THE CHURCH OF S. NICHOLAS

entrance door and a colorful tiled stair rising from the entrance hall within. More Italian in feeling was Kelwood Company's imposing 1926 house for Julius Seligmann at 106 Oakmont Court. With the beautiful white loggia of the 1930 Robertson House overlooking Devine Road, William McKnight Bowman convincingly re-called a true Palladian Venetian villa. Other ar-chitectural firms and builders accomplished in the Spanish and Italian styles included Robert H. H. Hugman, George Louis Walling, C. B. Schoeppl & Co., and Frost Carvel Co.

Equally adept in several manners was the ar-chitect Ralph Cameron who designed a Palla-dian style house for Dr. and Mrs. Oscar Hunt Judkins at 240 West Summit in 1920, another house inspired by the Villa Medici for Mr. and Mrs. Lee B. James at 241 West Lynwood, and the 1929 red brick Colonial house for Fred A. Hornaday at 1010 East Kings. Carlton Adams produced a number of Italian and Spanish de-signs but also an English Tudor house for Henry H. Bryant at 230 West Summit in 1925. In fact, the English styles of the smaller late-medieval and Elizabethan manor, and eighteenth-century Georgian house, were, along with a continuing use of American Colonial designs, the major ri-vals to the Mediterranean styles in the 1920s in San Antonio. Tall gables, patterned brick and ran-dom stone walls, and diamond-paned windows were used by Beverly Spillman, Albaugh and Henry Steinbomer, and Robert McGarraugh to create relatively authentic evocations of English country houses. In addition to San Antonio ar-chitects, there were others from Texas, including Houston's foremost eclectic architect John F. Staub who, in 1939, designed a monumental stone version of a French chateau for the Seeligsons at 835 Contour Drive in the Olmos section of San Antonio. Known from the epicen-ter of Spanish style in Santa Barbara–Montecito as one of the most accomplished practitioners of the Spanish style, George Washington Smith de-signed the lovely, courtyard Maverick-Zachry

House on Torcido Drive in Alamo Heights in 1929. These architects practiced as did Atlee, seek-ing inspiration from the architecture of the past, and by judicious selection and adaptation, creat-ing buildings appropriate to the present. This sort of eclecticism seemed utterly natural, and—with due consideration to the integration of the most up-to-date mechanical equipment for heating, plumbing, kitchen and bath equipment—"mod-ern" to most American architects of Atlee's gen-eration.

Of them all, Atlee had a special talent for un-derstanding what those who created the styles of the past found beautiful. By understanding and respecting the elements that constituted beauty for his predecessors, he avoided the dangers of pastiche, of skin-deep stylistic dressings applied promiscuously. Thus his Italian houses honored the essential Renaissance concern for symmetry, proportions, balance, simple massing, correctness in the choice, scale and placement of classical details, and a simplicity and clarity of plan ar-rangement. Similarly he grasped the essentials of Spanish style and celebrated complex massing, the picturesque juxtaposition of sculptural tow-ers and stairs, the deep shadows of a wealth of openings in thick, stucco walls, brilliant white in the sun and accented by blue-green shutters, and within, richly tiled floors like Cordovan leather and bright wall tiles decorating walls and niches. He understood both styles and used them with discretion, eschewing the overtly theatrical and the flashy that would have satisfied neither his clients' nor his tastes.

However, Atlee was not a mere stylist. In many ways he was a rationalist. He shaped his build-ings with considerations of climate, site, the na-ture of materials, the requirements of sound con-struction, and the influence of economics. His houses were very well planned for lifestyles that he understood and shared. At the same time, he believed in himself deeply as an artist and in his houses as artistic expressions. Indeed, his restless-ness and desire to move to California after the

First World War was motivated as much by the desire for new artistic stimuli and freedom, as for professional and economic reasons.

Atlee's houses are only one window on the eclecticism of the twentieth century. In a century of cultural pluralism, it is expected to find a proliferation of many kinds of eclecticism. The predominant posture of Ayres, and most American residential architects of his time, was a mixture of nostalgic referencing of the past, especially the rich heritage of western Europe and England adapted to American technology and relatively casual lifestyles. Atlee and others believed that cultural allusion through inventive uses of historical styles provided a richness of meaning and expression that a purely functional, technologically advanced house did not. Even if in the hard times of the Great Depression it became a matter of stylistic touches giving recognizable style to indifferent carcasses—thereby creating severely undernourished versions that lacked the details and expensive materials of their predecessors— it was still possible through careful proportions and expressive use of materials to strike authentic chords of meaning and enjoyment. Indeed, after the Second World War the Ayreses themselves responded to new conditions of the economy and construction with much smaller and simpler Colonial houses with touches of New Orleans grillwork on the second-story balcony, a kind of southern regionalism much favored by John Staub in Houston as well.

Atlee's houses stand in contrast to the course of eclecticism in the latter half of the twentieth century, which has seen a fast-changing proliferation of sources of inspiration and attitudes toward their practical and expressive uses. After the Second World War, although there were Modern designs sponsored by the *Ladies Home Journal* and exhibited at the Museum of Modern Art, *Good Housekeeping* was more prescient in claiming that sentiment and familiar architectural styles were preferred by most people, albeit with every modern functional convenience.

Significantly, the hundreds and then thousands of almost identical houses built by the developer William J. Levitt were "The model-T equivalent of the rose-covered cottage—or Cape Coddage [*sic*] . . . It is meant to look like the Little Home of One's Own that was a subsidiary myth of the American Dream long before Charlie Chaplin put it into 'Modern Times.'"[2] In the interior, two styles predominated: Early American, which recalled the past; and Modern, which was "new," practical, and cheap.

In the 1960s suburbs, traditional designs lingered on, much reduced in size and, for the most part, one story. Character was supplied by touches of decorative detailing drawn from traditional sources: a bit of New Orleans—stock, wrought-iron grill, a pair of small, louvered shutters nailed to the walls beside wide picture windows. The twin desires of convenience and recognizable "style" pervaded the captions in the building magazines: "The Charm of French Country style plus the advantages of practical, present-day living"; "Familiar adobe design includes an unusual master suite"; "Popular split-level living in the traditional guise of the Old Southwest."[3]

The minimally traditional houses were in fact close kin to houses in the Ranch style, which became the dominant residential style in the 1950s and '60s. Emulating the ranch houses of California, they spread even lower and wider under their broad, shallow pitched or hipped roofs. Aside from modest bits of Spanish, English Colonial, or Craftsman detail, the character of the house derived from the exterior materials— stone, brick (often thin stone and nail-on brick), wood clapboards or shingles—often freely used in combination on a single house. Their residents and those of the popular and very practical type known as the "split level" were content with fewer, fainter, and often unrelated references.[4]

The frank emphasis on functional concerns as the basis of design and the willingness to relegate traditional forms to a minor role, was, during the same postwar decades, favored by the architects and clients of custom-designed houses. One strain derived from the flat-roofed European International style, usually adapted to American regional building materials and methods of construction. The example had been given in the houses designed by the architects of the Bauhaus who had come to teach at the Harvard Graduate School of Design in the late 1930s: Walter Gropius's use of white vertical siding in Massachusetts; Marcel Breuer's field stone, in Connecticut. But their ornament was strictly limited to the expression of integral structural and constructional necessities, exposed wood or steel beams, and the hardware of connectors, bolts, and rivets. A second approach, less rigorously European, favored gabled, pitched roofs that suggested the earlier Prairie and Craftsman houses of the Middle West, and even the Ranch houses that were so popular, but they too eschewed applied traditional ornament and other than regional historical references.

The year 1965 was a watershed for architects as it was for many Americans in a time of serious economic recession and the traumatic experience of a losing war in Viet Nam. The catalysts for change in the architectural world were the buildings of Sea Ranch, a group of condominium second homes designed by Charles Moore and William Turnbull for the rugged coast of Northern California, and the 1966 publication of Robert Venturi's book *Complexity and Contradiction in Architecture* (The Museum of Modern Art Papers on Architecture, Number 1). Both Venturi and Moore argued in their own ways for an inclusive architecture that considered many things ignored or deliberately excluded by European modernists and their American advocates in what appeared to most Americans to be rather severe, functionally fixated, highly abstract designs. Sea Ranch dipped back into the California vernacular, to the traditional forms of barns and sheds. With the help of the landscape architect Lawrence Halprin it was sensitive to the native qualities of its spectacular and fragile coastal site. Appearing as a weather-beaten cluster of indeterminate vintage, Sea Ranch was a brilliant antidote to the Modernism and strained structural exhibitionism of other major American architects, whose work often seemed oblivious of place and tradition. Within, the units at Sea Ranch were charming, homey, and adaptable to many forms of personal expression.

Venturi similarly was not intimidated by the narrow rules of orthodox Modernism. He was for "messy vitality over obvious unity." He looked for richness of meaning. Although Venturi's intellectual posture was too sophisticated for most, his desire to make buildings more accessible and meaningful to their inhabitants, more accommodating to the "messy vitality" of their lives, was in the mainstream of Post-Modernism that was superceding the belief in any overarching metanarratives, any one "valid" architecture. Of the two, Moore was the more easily understood and influential, largely because of the playful and unpretentious quality of many of his houses. Ironically, clusters of new shed roof, wooden houses reminiscent of old barns and sheds were built in places far from their regional roots. Regardless, they had "the vitality of the contemporary," and offered "old-fashioned luxury within a bold exterior."[5] Elsewhere, regionally inspired houses settled happily into their environments. Turner Brooks built houses evocative of New England farmhouses. In the hands of architects such as these, a comfortable regionalism and an unaffected historicism developed.

In the decade of the 1970s, houses designed by architects represented rival camps within the profession, as well as an even greater than usual schism between architect-designed houses and those designed for and by builders and contractors. The schism had not been particularly noticeable until the 1930s. It was more apparent after the Second World War, when professional efforts and taste were directed toward a sleek modernist aesthetic for the buildings of commercial capitalism, and some architects had tried to use the same aesthetic and functionalist rationale in the design of houses. In 1972, a small group of architects—the so-called "New York Five"—published a book of their recent houses, which, though bearing as many differences as similarities, were in one way or another derived from the 1910–29 work of European modernists, especially Le Corbusier. The retreat to a largely formal, purist, exclusivist position soon invited retort from inclusivists like Charles Moore and Robert Stern. Concurrently, traditional styles still continued to capture the popular imagination of those who were extorted, "If you like half-timbering and stone, turrets and gables, mullioned casements, think English Tudor," whose façades were "unhampered by demands for symmetry, are charming outside and convenient inside."[6]

By 1980, one of the "New York Five," Michael Graves, sensed that Modernism was a stylistic straight-jacket that limited his painterly interest in color and his new-found pleasure in historic Italian architecture rekindled during his stay on a Prix de Rome at the American Academy. As Graves said, "I thought it was going to be a pretty lonely world out there for me, if I continued to speak what seemed to be a more or less private language."[7] Graves's rediscovery of the classical language of column and beam; of base, middle, and top; of typically Renaissance sequences of screens, exedras, aedicules, galleries, and loggias; of symmetry and axes; and of clearly defined and carefully proportioned rooms that had not melted into the amorphous spaces of informal American living heralded a Post-Modernism that drew inspiration from the classical past, a source already much dredged in American architecture. However, the eclecticism of Post-Modernism had its own distinctive flavor. From a variety of positions that included scholarly fundamentalist sincerity, sophisticated and mannerist intellectual play, and sheer ignorance of the past, the designers of the houses of the 1980s were engaged in a battle of styles. The dike of Modernism that was founded on functional usefulness and expression of contemporary materials and methods of construction was breached and there emerged a delta of approaches that included new versions of classicism. Some conscientiously furthered the essence of classicism, but the majority were highly decorative, often ironic and superficial applications of stylized classical motifs that narrowed the gap between educated professional architectural taste and fashion-driven popular taste. Post-Modern eclecticism was essentially Mannerist, using the past with irony, humor, and a decorative superficiality that reflected social and ideological uncertainty and confusion. Modernist fondness for high technology found a few advocates who were willing to live in glass, steel, and concrete, and the burgeoning array of synthetic materials. Other new streams flowed from the art world into the innovatively sculptural creations of Frank Gehry, and from the world of contemporary philosophy, from semiology and structuralism, and from the ideas of Levi-Strauss, Desaussure, Derrida and Lacan, which were turned into difficult, and usually unlivable, houses designed by Peter Eisenman and others. From 1978 to 1987, the energy of American architects, as that in other professions, was "expended on private pursuits rather than public ones, and this movement away from earlier architectural ideals parallels a redirection of resources in the broader society. The ecology movement, feminism, the new historicism, the electronic and computer revolution, and the peace movement were all to find proponents as societal influences on the art and science of architecture."[8] Charles Moore opined, "might architecture schools inaugurate programs for critic-poets or critic-dreamers?"

Despite this ferment in the professional world of architects, architectural magazines and critics, and the few clients who could afford their experiments, most Americans still preferred houses that, although traditionally dressed, had evolved to accommodate increasingly informal lifestyles, a fulminating technology, and by the 1990s a spectacular growth in personal wealth toward the upper end of the scale. The new eclecticism was realized in a sixteen thousand-square-foot villa in California, whose owner researched the grand palazzos of Italy to lend to the design of her "ancient" Italian villa. "Three years in the making, the residence beautifully replicates a villa of centuries-old artisanship: handcrafted Vicenza stonework, arched windows and French doors of leaded glass, true-to-the-order columns, and a plethora of exquisite wrought iron, marble, adoquin stone, cupolas, and custom moldings." The gardens contained a picnic and dance pavilion designed as classical ruins. "We had some cast columns left over, knocked a few of them down, and grouped them at the base of the property. . . . Voila . . . instant ruins."⁹ Embedded in the mansion, offered at $8.9 million, were fiber-optic lighting and advanced systems for communications, stereo sound, and security.

In the 1990s, new houses were described by phrases such as "French Elegance and Luxury," "Contemporary Mediterranean," "exuding Spanish elegance and charm," "Old World European," and "New Tuscan Contemporary" (Aspen, Colorado). Houses take their place in developments "Just like the fabled forest that was home to Robin Hood and Maid Marian, Houston's own Sherwood Forest is characterized by tall pine forests and quiet country lanes. . . . this two-story redwood Country French residence features traditional elegance masterfully blended with contemporary elements" along with six and one-half baths. Elsewhere in America, new houses include other allusions: a widow's walk recalling Nantucket's whaling days, a minstrel gallery overlooking the soaring great room with fireplaces at either end; beamed cathedral ceiling and secret panel door leading to the wine tasting room. The "magnificent stone and brick English manor has a media room and relaxed family room which opens to the wonderful kitchen with tray ceiling." The house is approached through a gate and "picturesque winding lanes past bucolic paddocks with white

fences, the essence of this sought-after association with private security." Interiors sport vaulted and coved ceilings, handtroweled and faux-painted walls, Palladian windows, mosaic-trimmed floors, marble and granite countertops.¹⁰

A similar eclecticism is still found today at the beginning of the twenty-first century. Although houses are described as "English Georgian," "Mediterranean Style," "Spanish Mission," or "Queen Anne," it is no longer important that the eclectic reference be used consistently. Indeed, the fashion is for an eclectic collection of pieces, of "touches." The past is valued as a treasure chest of costumes to suit ephemeral moods and deployed without deep knowledge of, or respect for, its original existence. What is required in a house is curb appeal. Preferably, it should look as impressive as possible, must seem old and new at the same time, and have some eye-catching features. Inside, it should have history without inconvenience. Alas, what is obvious in late-twentieth-century residential building is a shabbiness of construction, a skimpiness and coarseness of architectural detail, and a fondness for ersatz and "faux." The interior of the house is another collection of "features"—of his and hers wardrobes, double lavatories, whirlpool baths, kitchens with central islands and tray ceilings. "There's nothing that tops gracious Southern hospitality—unless it's offered in Southern farmhouse style. The entry hall soars two stories, opening through an archway on the right to a banquet-sized formal dining room." This in a 1,770 square-foot house with plans for sale.¹¹

Despite the efforts of some architects well grounded in the history of architecture such as Robert A. M. Stern and Michael Graves who have brought a refined eclecticism to the house-plan business, the fact remains that the majority of late-twentieth-century American houses across the economic spectrum are largely image-driven collections of architectural non-sequiturs, with infusions of aesthetic touches of nostalgia for a little known or truly appreciated past. For the architecturally educated and knowledgeable, these create a haunting feeling of uneasiness, of sham, of something unhealthy, or at least stale about the dressing of the present with promiscuous borrowings from other times and places—a kind of "hybrid" eclecticism. A more pure Modernism lives on in the architectural journals' coverage of buildings by Frank Gehry, Rem Koolhaus, Herzog and deMeuron, Stephen Holl, and others in whose buildings style is not "applied," but "integral," as it was in a Greek temple, the Roman Pantheon, and the Gothic cathedrals.

Theirs are valuable explorations of new possibilities of form, structure, and materials and new aesthetic qualities that can touch one directly without allusions to previous buildings. But the abstractions of Modernism, without the overt signs and symbols of traditional architecture, without the support of the past, are difficult for most people to understand or desire for the more personal world of their own homes. In no other part of our environment is eclecticism—the matter of choice—so valued, so viscerally felt. It was in Atlee Ayres's day, and it is today.

SELECTED LIST OF AYRES HOUSES

All in San Antonio unless otherwise noted
★ designates those discussed in chapters 8–12

1900
J. Bruce Martindale, 237 West Magnolia★

1901
William Negley, 421 Howard★

1903
David K. Furnish, 501 West French Place
John W. and Rachel Z. Furnish, 515 Belknap★

1904
D. J. Woodward, 1717 San Pedro

1905
L. J. Hart, Cray Place
E. B. Chandler, 124 French Place

1906
Winchester Kelso, 107 West Craig

1907
Christopher H. Surkamp, 105 West Kings
    Highway
Armand and Hattie Halff, 105 Madison★

1908
Louis Hartung, 124 West Woodlawn
Alex H. Halff, 601 Howard

1909
Nicholson/Furnish/Smith, 1015 West
    Woodlawn★
Charles Bertrand, 134–136 East Mistletoe
Carrie A. Bonner, 145 East Agarita
Atlee B. Ayres, 201 Belknap★

1910
Roy Hearne, 300 West French Place
George W. Brackenridge, French and Belknap
John W. Kokernot, 119 East Kings Highway★

1911
Bishop and Mrs. W. T. Capers, 108 West

1913
Frank Winerich. (later John J. Kuntz), 118
    Kings Highway★
Charles Zilker, San Pedro and Ashby

1914
Robert N. Martindale, 108 West Kings High-
    way
Marshall Terrell, 213 West Agarita★
Lonnie Wright, Wilkins and Roosevelt
L. E. Cartwright, Uvalde, Texas★

1915
Graham Hamilton, Cuero, Texas★
Alexander Hamilton, Cuero, Texas★

1916
J. A. Browne, Brownsville, Texas★

1918
Atlee B. Ayres, Jr., 224 West Mulberry
Jack W. Neal, 228 West Mulberry
Ira Havans, 222 West Mulberry

1919
Hiram Partee, 695 Belknap★

1920
W. G. Rigsby, Grove Place and Arcadia★
N. M. Abbey, Del Rio, Texas★

1921
Dr. F. L. Thomson, 302 West Mulberry★

1922
David J. Straus, 315 West Linwood★
Norville Chittin, 501 Elizabeth Road
Garret P. Robertson, 129 East Summit★

1923
J. D. Oppenheimer, Burr Duval and Arcadia★

1924
Thomas E. Hogg, 202 Bushnell★
Joseph Rosenfeld, 109 West Hollywood

1925
Joe Seldon, 331 West Kings Highway
Joe Lentz, 215 Bushnell

1926
Gustave Pagenstretcher, 502 Elizabeth Road
Percy L. Mannen, 323 Bushnell★

1927
Robert M. Ayres, 207 Laurel Heights Place★
Amye Bozarth, Park Hill Estates★
Edward B. Carruth, Jr., 218 Laurel Heights Place
Mrs. Wallace Newton, Park Hill Drive
Carl Newton, 800 East Olmos Drive★

1928
Mrs. William Tobin, 235 East Huisache

1929
Dr. And Mrs. Sam Roberts, Kansas City★
D. J. Atkinson–Marion Koogler McNay, Sunset
   Hills★
Ward W. Kelley, 199 Wickham Rise
John B. Chadwick, 114 Park Hill Drive★

1930
A. J. McKenzie, 138 Oakmont

1931
John Albert Brown, Oklahoma City, Oklahoma★

1934
Lutcher Brown, Ivy Lane★

1937
Frank and Merle Buttram, Oklahoma City, Okla-
   homa★

1938
H. L. Blackstock, Alameda Circle★

REPRESENTATIVE PLANS
OF AYRES HOUSES

The floor plans of eleven houses were chosen to illustrate their development from the early, compact, four-square plans (1900–1908)—Atlee's own Arts and Crafts style house (1909), and his later remodeling along more sophisticated Tudor lines (1920s)—to his experiment with the spreading, flowing spaces of the Frank Lloyd Wright–inspired Prairie School (1914), the symmetrical clarity of the Italian Renaissance (1922), the asymmetrical, angled plans of the Spanish style (1923–28), and, lastly, the elaborate, formal neoclassical arrangements of the mansions (1930s). The plans are printed all to the same scale to illustrate the differences in real size as the houses progress from the relatively small early houses to the later spacious mansions. All the plans are based on the original working draw-ings—in the Alexander Architectural Archive at the University of Texas, Austin—and were drawn by the author.

KEY TO PLAN ABBREVIATIONS

Br (bedroom), Brk (breakfast room), Dr (dining room), Drs (dressing room), Fr (fountain room), G (garage), Gbr (guest bedroom), K (kitchen), Lib (library), Lo (loggia), Lr (living room), Mus (music room), Mbr (master bedroom), P (porch), Pa (pantry), Pc (*porte cochere*), R (reception hall–entry), S (service rooms), Sbr (servant bedroom), Sit (sitting room), Sp (sleeping porch), Sr (sun room), V (vestibule). *Note:* Unless noted on the plan, the garage or carriage house, usually with servants quarters, was separate from the house.

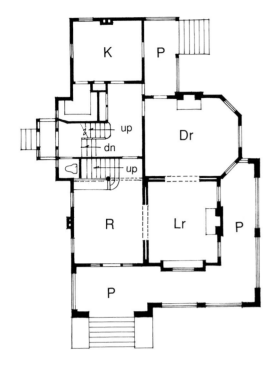

first floor

Nicholson/Furnish 1903

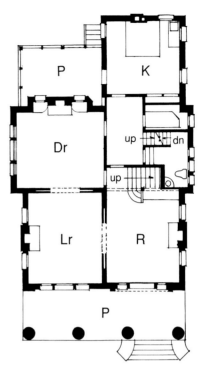

first floor

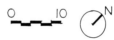

Armand & Hattie Halff 1907

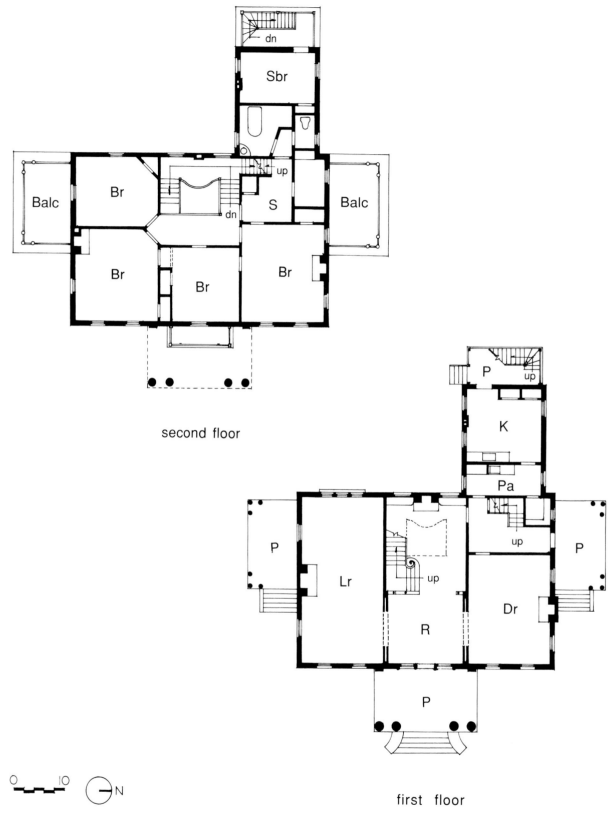

second floor

first floor

William Negley 1903

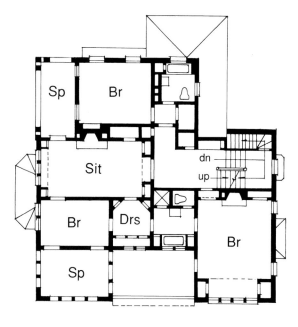

second floor

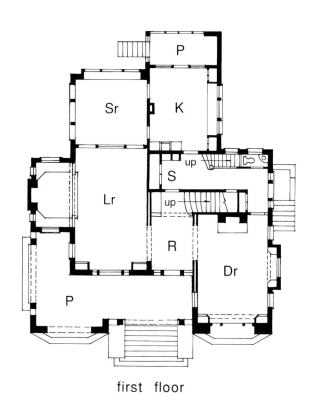

first floor

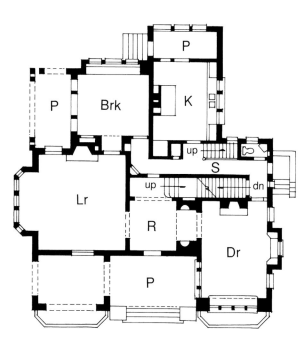

first floor

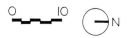

Atlee B. Ayres   1909

1922

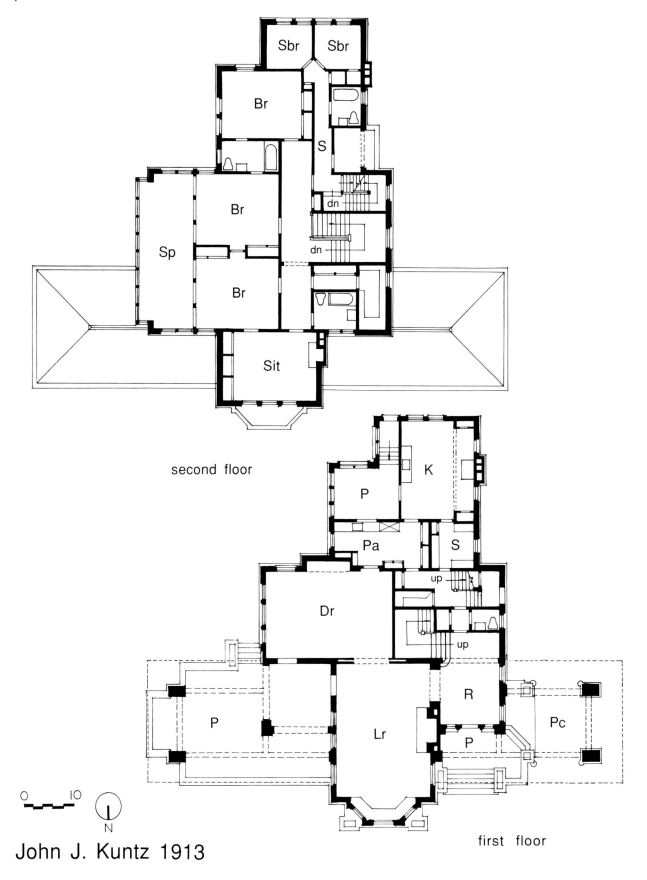

second floor

0 ___ 10

John J. Kuntz 1913

first floor

PLAN 4

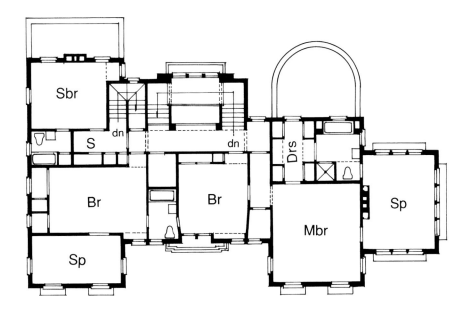

second floor

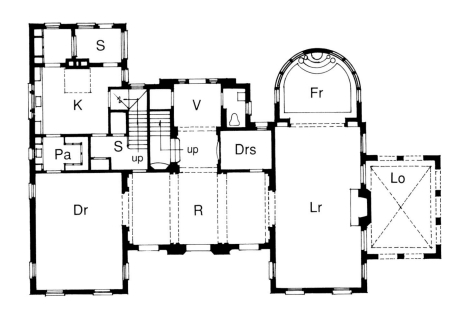

first floor

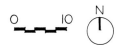

N

David J. Straus 1922

PLAN 5

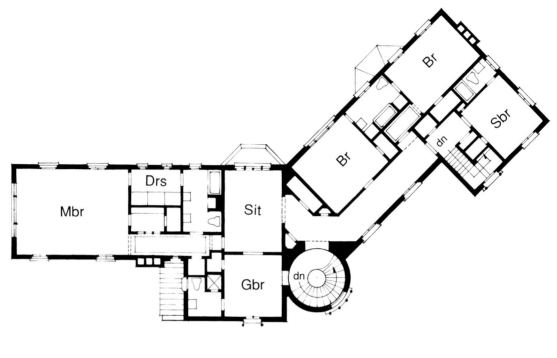

second floor

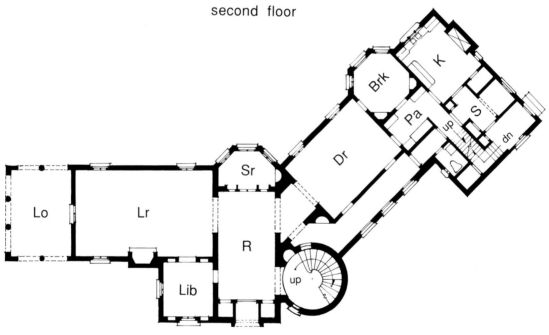

first floor

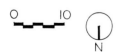

Thomas E. Hogg 1924

PLAN 6

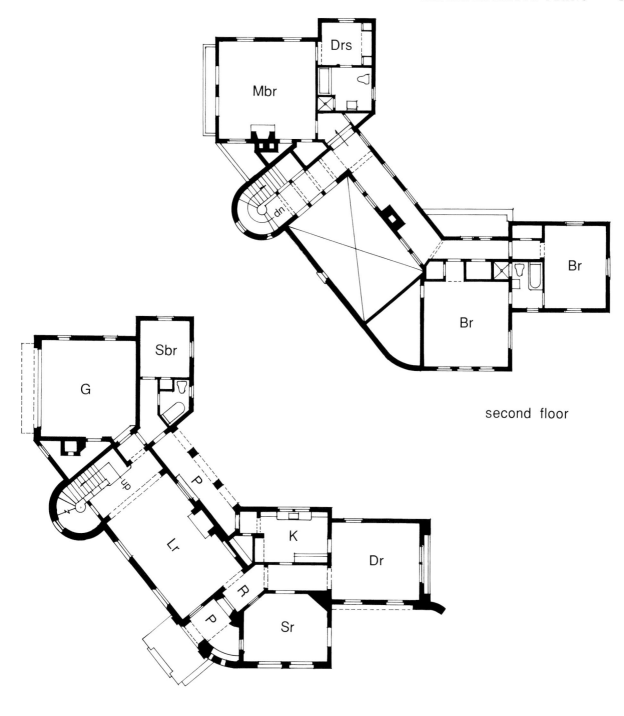

Drs

Mbr

dn

Br

Br

second floor

G

Sbr

up

P

Lr

K

Dr

R

P

Sr

first floor

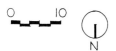

Amye Bozarth 1927

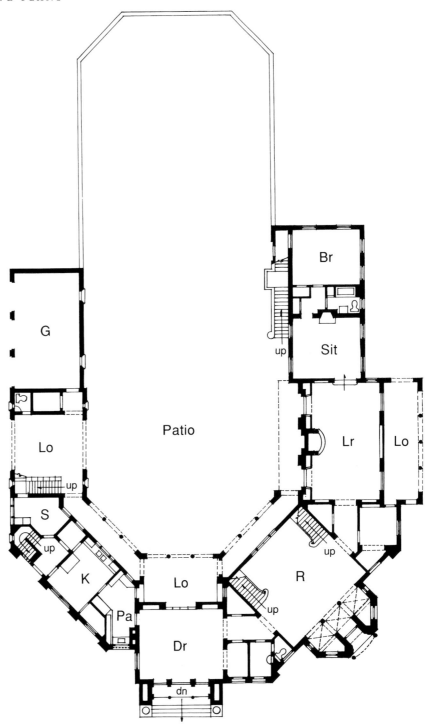

G

Br

Sit

up

Lo

Patio

Lr

Lo

S

up

up

R

K

up

Lo

Pa

Dr

dn

first floor

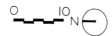

Atkinson-McNay 1927

PLAN 8

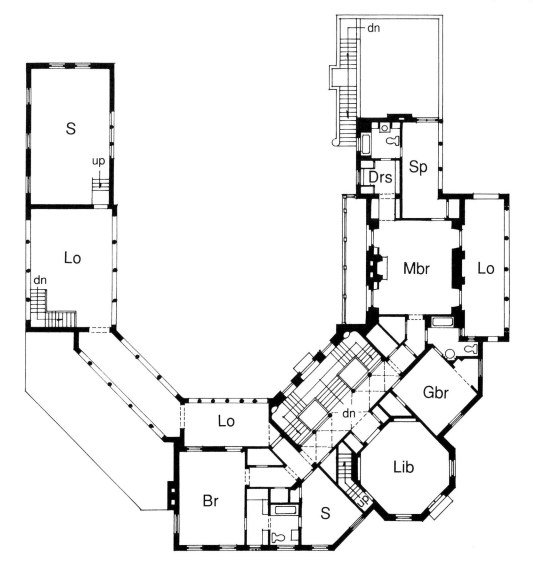

dn

S

up

Lo

dn

Sp

Drs

Mbr

Lo

Lo

Gbr

dn

Lib

Br

S

second floor

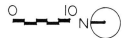

Atkinson-McNay 1927

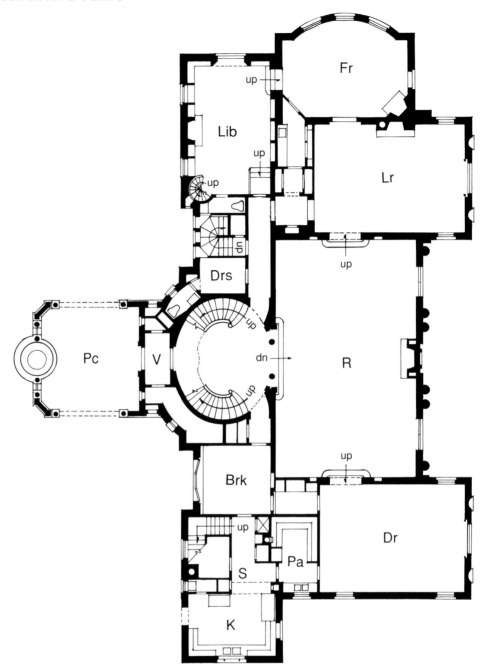

first floor

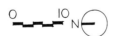

Frank & Merle Buttram 1937

PLAN IO

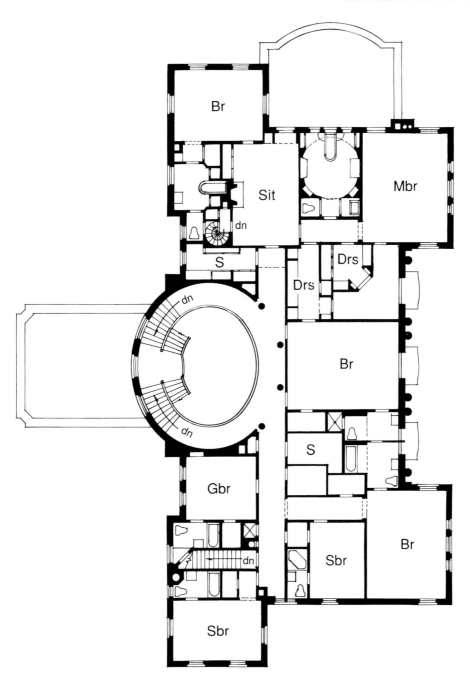

second floor

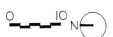

Frank & Merle Buttram 1937

PLAN II

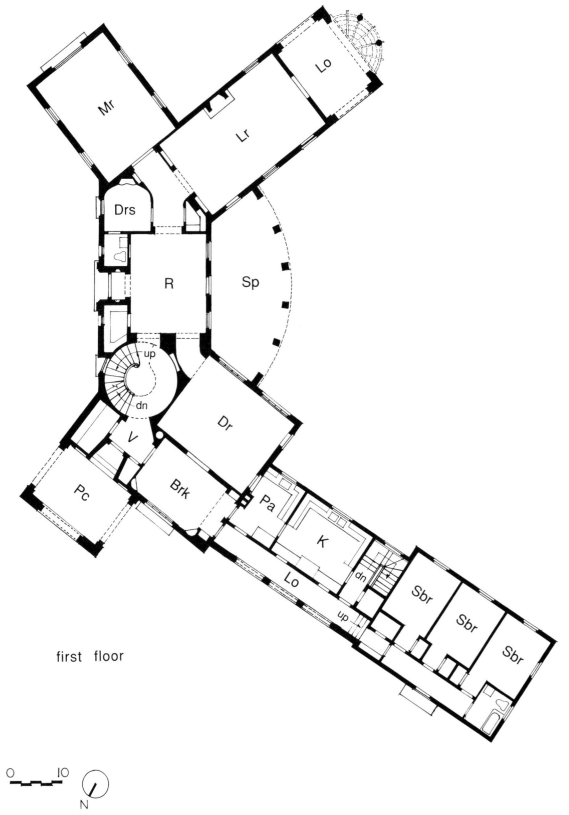

first floor

0   10

N

H. L. Blackstock 1938

PLAN 12

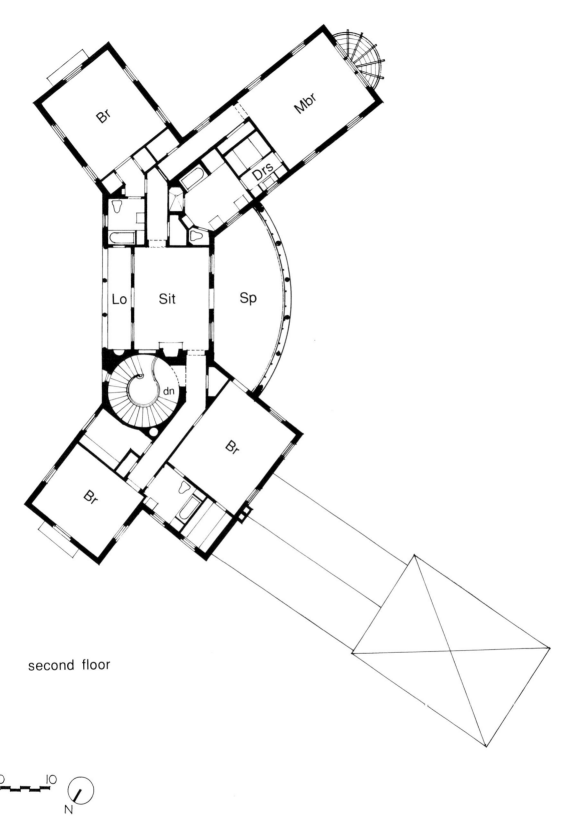

second floor

H. L. Blackstock 1938

NOTES

★ UT-AAA is an abbreviation for The University of Texas, Austin, Alexander Architectural Archive

CHAPTER I. AN ECLECTIC INHERITANCE

1. For an overview of American architecture in the nineteenth and early twentieth centuries, see John Burchard and Albert Bush-Brown, *The Architecture of America* abridged, and James Marston Fitch, *American Building: The Historical Forces That Shaped It.*

2. Clifford Edward Clark, Jr., *The American Family Home 1800–1960,* p. 74.

3. Lewis Mumford, *Roots of Contemporary American Architecture,* p. 124.

4. This statement by the architect Bruce Price comes from Frederich Platt, *America's Gilded Age,* p. 105, an excellent source of illustrations.

5. Wayne Andrews, *Architecture, Ambition and Americans,* p. 231.

6. Refer David Gebhard's foreword to Elizabeth McMillan, *Casa California: Spanish Style Houses from Santa Barbara to San Clemente,* p. 7. Gebhard also quotes Lewis Mumford who wrote in 1925, "Not being able to humanize 'business' we become gods when we get outside its domain; with a little architectural hocus-pocus we transport ourselves to another age, another climate, another social regime, and best of all, to another aesthetic system."

7. Louis Le Beaume, "The Manly Art of Architecture," *The Octagon,* Jan., 1929, p. 7.

8. Harry F. Cunningham, "Panacea or Poison," *Journal of the American Institute of Architects* 16, no. 9 (Sept., 1928): 371–72.

9. Le Beaume, "The Picturesque," pp. 345–46.

10. Atlee Ayres, Correspondence, June 22, 1935, UT-AAA.

11. *The Octagon,* Feb., 1933, p. 14.

12. In the 1930s the Ayreses designed a number of simplified but still traditional houses. These included the Robert Goodrich House in Fort Worth, the second Robert Ayres house, the Willard Berman House, the William Thomas House, and a concrete house in a modified Regency style, one of five designed for the builder H. B. Zachry in 1936. While the Ayreses, residential work continued along traditional lines, some of their commercial work of the 1930s adopted some forms of Modernism. Grayson's store sported Art Deco stylized letters, octagonal medallions, and abstracted pediments over steel windows. The Meador Packard Building with its long strip windows had the vertically grooved pilasters and plaques of the stripped down classicism with which many 1930s designers tried to meld Traditional style with International Modernism. By 1942, for the Zachry Company Office Building, the Ayreses designed a sweeping curved entrance with glass block and the tiniest of decorative grills in the fascia.

13. Walter Kidney, *The Architecture of Choice: Eclecticism in America 1880–1930,* illustration p. 149.

CHAPTER 2. AN ARCHITECTURAL
EDUCATION: NEW YORK, 1892–94

1. Biographical Information Folder UT-AAA.
2. Chris Carson and William McDonald, *A Guide to San Antonio Architecture.*
3. Atlee Ayres, narration at the annual meeting of the American Institute of Architects, San Antonio, Mar. 14, 1968.
4. Robert A. M. Stern, Gregory Gilmartin, and John Montague Massendale, *New York 1900,* pp. 88, 92.
5. "Prospectus" of the Metropolitan Museum of Art School, 1893–94 and exhibition catalogue, Folder UT-AAA.
6. Atlee B. Ayres sketchbook—student work at the Metropolitan Museum of Art, Folder UT-AAA.
7. Atlee B. Ayres student work, Drawings Folder UT-AAA.
8. Atlee B. Ayres notes from "History of Ancient Ornament" lecture delivered by Seth Justin Temple, Feb., 1894, UT-AAA.
9. First Annual Exhibition of the Metropolitan Art Students Association, 1893, Folder: UT-AAA.
10. John Burchard, Albert Bush-Brown, *The Architecture of America,* abridged, p. 183.
11. Stern, *New York 1900,* p. 13.
12. Wayne Andrews, *Architecture, Ambition, and Americans,* p. 197.
13. This picture of New York during Atlee's student days was fashioned largely from Stern, *New York 1900,* and Walter C. Kidney, *The Architecture of Choice: Eclecticism in America 1880–1930.*
14. Atlee Ayres to George D. Bartholomew, New York, Aug. 25, 1920, Correspondence File UT-AAA.

CHAPTER 3. FOREIGN TRAVELS

1. Trip to Europe 1911, UT-AAA.
2. As quoted from *The San Antonio Light,* July 12, 1914, in Donald E. Everett, *Monte Vista: The Gilded Age of an Historic District 1890–1930,* Supplement to *The North San Antonio Times* and the *Alamo Heights Recorder-Times,* Jan. 28, 1988, p. 37.
3. "Trip Around the World 1914," Travel Folder UT-AAA.

4. Four 13" x 16" albums, UT-AAA. (Atlee recycled these from their original use in displaying personal greeting cards, especially Christmas cards for sale mainly in bookstores. The faux leather covers were elaborated with scrolls, shields, armored helmets, or large gilded wood-cuts of wintry scenes. Within the albums, there is no identifying text other than that occasionally on the photographs themselves, and except for grouping by general subject, there seems to be no particular order.
5. Atlee Ayres, letter to John Mullin, Fox Foto Supply Company, Mexico City, June 1, 1925, and subsequent letters in Sept. and Oct., 1925; Ayres, letter to Mrs. J. H. Southerland, Mexico City, June 1, 1925; Ayres, letter to the Chamber of Commerce, Chihuahua, Mexico, Aug. 1, 1925.
6. For negotiations with Helburn and other publishers, refer Ayres Correspondence 1925–27, UT-AAA.
7. Atlee Ayres, letter to the secretary of the American Institute of Architects, Feb. 10, 1928.
8. Atlee Ayres described his photographic equipment in letters to Bausch and Lomb Optical, Rochester, New York, May 30, 1929. UT-AAA.
9. Two hundred eighty-four black and white photographs (4 ¾" x 7") in photographic album titled "Spanish," UT-AAA.
10. One hundred seventy-one black and white photographs (6 ⅜" x 8 ⅞"), mounted on cardboards, purchased from AR XIV "MAS." Barcelona, boxed collection UT-AAA.
11. Atlee Ayres, letter, Apr. 4, 1933, Correspondence UT-AAA.

CHAPTER 4. "IN LOVE
WITH CALIFORNIA"

1. For an Englishman's very perceptive overview of Los Angeles, see Reyner Banham, *Los Angeles of Four Ecologies.*
2. Atlee Ayres, letter to M. W. D. Syres, Los Angeles, May 12, 1924, Correspondence UT-AAA.
3. Atlee Ayres, letter to Hugh Knight, Riverside, Calif., 1919, Correspondence UT-AAA.
4. Hugh Knight, letter to Atlee Ayres, San Antonio, Nov. 8, 1919, Correspondence UT-AAA.

5. Atlee Ayres, letter to George B. Bartholomew, New York, Aug. 25, 1920, Correspondence UT-AAA.

6. Atlee Ayres, letter to George Kelham, San Francisco, Calif., Jan. 30, 1924, Correspondence UT-AAA.

7. Atlee Ayres, letters to George Washington Smith, Santa Barbara, Calif., Dec. 26, 1923, and Feb. 12, 1924, Correspondence UT-AAA.

8. Atlee Ayres, letter to Harry A. Reuter, Pasadena, Calif., Mar. 29, 1924, Correspondence UT-AAA.

9. Atlee Ayres, letter to Roy Seldon C. Price, Beverley Hills, Calif., Jan. 9, 1925, Correspondence UT-AAA.

10. Atlee Ayres, letter to John Byers, Santa Monica, Calif., June 4, 1925, Correspondence UT-AAA.

11. It is currently thought that 67 (3 ⅝" x 5 ½") of these are from the 1923 trip. The majority seem to be from the 1926 trip: 442 (4" x 5") and 108 (3 ⅝" x 5 1/2"). There are also 83 (4" x 5") negatives, perhaps from another trip in 1930, and a large number from a trip in 1932–33, including 44 (3 ⅝" x 5 ½") and 22 (2 ½" x 4 ½").

12. For houses of George Washington Smith and others in Santa Barbara and Montecito refer Herb Andree, *Santa Barbara Architecture: From Spanish Colonial to Modern.*

13. From the foreword by David Gebhard in Alson Clark, *Wallace Neff: Architect of California's Golden Age.*

14. Ayres Clippings Files UT-AAA.

CHAPTER 5. FLORIDA

1. Ayres Correspondence 1925–26, UT-AAA.

2. Hap Hatton, *Tropical Splendor,* chapter 2.

3. Donald W. Curl, *Mizner's Florida, American Resort Architecture,* p. 42.

4. Ibid., p. 68.

5. Ibid., p. 215: Endnote 51, Steven A. Seider, "The Mizner Touch," senior thesis, Yale University, 1958, pp. 35–40.

6. Christina Orr, *Addison Mizner, Architect of Dreams and Realities 1872–1933,* p. 23. Quoted from "Spanish Architecture," *Palm Beach Life,* Feb. 17, 1925.

7. James T. Maher, *The Twilight of Splendor, Chronicles of the Age of American Palaces,* p. 208.

8. Ibid., p. 200.

9. Curl, *Mizner's Florida,* p. 150.

10. Ayres Clipping Files, Folders 3, 9, 10, 16, UT-AAA.

CHAPTER 6. AYRES'S LIBRARY

1. Atlee Ayres, letter to Mrs. Herbert Kokernot, San Antonio, Aug. 10, 1925, Correspondence UT-AAA.

2. Atlee Ayres, letter to Mr. McIntosh, September 8, 1926. The year before, Atlee had claimed to have 350 books plus more technical ones. Beginning in 1938, 398 volumes of the Ayreses' library were given to the University of Texas in Austin. Of those, 173 are kept in the Special Collections of the Architecture Library in Battle Hall.

3. As quoted from Magonigle, one of Stanford White's assistants, in Leland Roth, *McKim, Mead & White, Architects,* p. 11.

4. Atlee Ayres, letters to publishers concerning acquisition of books, Correspondence UT-AAA.

5. Howard Barnstone, *The Architecture of John F. Staub: Houston and the South,* pp. 338–40.

CHAPTER 7. AYRES AND THE MAGAZINES

1. Unprocessed collection of clippings from architecture and decoration magazines.

2. By way of comparison, the Avery Index lists 772 entries, including 44 residences for the well-known New York architect Dwight James Baum in the 1920s and 1930s.

CHAPTER 8. AYRES HOUSES

1. All quotations and the descriptions of the early San Antonio suburbs are largely derived from Donald E. Everett, "Monte Vista: The Gilded Age of an Historic District, 1890–1930," Supplement to the *North San Antonio Times* and the *Alamo Heights Recorder-Times,* Jan. 2, 1988.

2. Everett, "Monte Vista," p. 24.

3. Ibid., p. 37.

4. Henry Russell Hitchcock, *The Architecture of H. H. Richardson and His Times.*

5. See Roderick Graddige, *Edwin Lutyens: Architect Laureate,* also Daniel O'Neil, *Lutyens: Country Houses.*

6. Robert MacLeod, *Charles Rennie Mackintosh: Architect and Artist.*

7. Benedetto Gravagnuolo, *Adolf Loos, Theory and Works,* also Mihaly Kubinsky, *Adolf Loos.*

8. For a discussion of the Queen Anne style, see Andrew Saint, *Richard Norman Shaw,* Chapters 2, 3, and 5.

9. For the characteristics of Frank Lloyd Wright's early houses and the Prairie school see H. Allen Brooks, *The Prairie School.*

10. For Louis Sullivan's approach to ornament, see William H. Jordy, *American Buildings and Their Architects: Progressive and Academic Ideals at the Turn of the Twentieth Century,* Chapter 2, pp. 83–179.

11. Henry L. Wilson, *The Bungalow Book;* Robert Wilson, *The California Bungalow;* and William Dana, *The Swiss Chalet.*

12. Edgar Kaufman, Jr., *Frank Lloyd Wright: The Early Work.* See in particular the Hickox and Bradley Houses.

CHAPTER 9. MEDITERRANEAN STYLE I, 1918–31: ITALIAN RENAISSANCE STYLE

1. The architecture of Italy had already inspired three closely related styles in America between 1845 and 1875. The earliest was the Italian Renaissance Revival, derived from Sir Charles Barry's Reform and Travelers Clubs in London. The buildings were simple, imposing rectangular blocks with smooth limestone or stucco façades, restrained decorative features, string courses, tall windows, and assertive cornices. Similar, but less imposing, usually with shallow-pitched, hip roofs and often with a crowning cupola or lantern, and likely clad in wood siding, were houses called Italianate, Tuscan, or Lombard. The most romantic version was based on the English picturesque villa, which had been popularized in America by Andrew Jackson Downing. It was recognized by complex, informal massing, a high tower, loggias and verandahs, a shallow, pitched roof with broad overhangs and carved brackets, and varied windows often with rounded tops. The Norton-

Polk-Mathis House on King William Street in San Antonio is a good example. Ayres's work was part of the second Italian Renaissance Revival of 1890–1930, which, unlike the previous Italian styles that had depended largely on secondary sources from pattern books, looked directly to the originals in Italy to produce more academically correct, scholarly buildings.

2. Everett, "Monte Vista," p. 31.

3. The Rigsby House had disappeared entirely by the 1980s, but twenty-seven detailed working drawings remain in the UT-AAA.

4. Ayres had a number of catalogues that were used to specify on the working drawings prefabricated decorative elements and details. Two of the most frequently used were *The General Catalogue of Jacobson & Co., New York,* 1923 and 1929, and the 1931 *Catalogue of Interior and Exterior Decorative Ornament* of the Fischer and Jirouch Co. in Cleveland, Ohio.

5. For the vocabulary of the classical architecture of ancient Greece and Rome, see Robert Adam, *Classical Architecture: A Complete Handbook,* especially Chapter 3 "The Orders," and Chapter 5 "Mouldings."

6. The opulence of Renaissance style for American houses had its critics. "But it remained essentially a pretentious style. These Renaissance revivals always seem like a visiting grandee who never adapts to the American scene—who manages to keep his accent and clings to the security of his European manner. He is perhaps always a little suspect . . . ." James Milnes Baker, *American House Styles,* p. 102.

7. On February 24, 1920, while working on a $25,000 Italian style house, Atlee requested illustrations of cement stone materials in that style from Schwartz-Eustis Co. Ltd. in New Orleans. On October 18, 1920, he wrote to Sarti G. Luchesi and Co. New York for exterior "Della Robbias." In 1919 he had sought illustrated books on Italian architecture from Scribner's Sons, Correspondence UT-AAA.

8. Peggy Roberts Browning, "On Living in A Mansion," unpublished memoir, June, 1988, in possession of Robert Ulhman, Kansas City, Kans.

CHAPTER 10. ENGLISH INTERLUDE, 1923

1. The best coverage of the English house between 1860 and 1900 is still that by the German architect Hermann Muthesius, attached by his government to its embassy in London about 1900. *Das englische Haus* was published in Berlin in 1904. The first English edition was published by Granada Publishing Ltd. in 1979.
2. Refer Nathaniel Lloyd, *A History of the English House: from Primitive Times to the Victorian Period,* and Maurice Howard, *The Early Tudor Country House, Architecture and Politics 1490–1550.*
3. Illustrated in Kidney, *The Architecture of Choice,* p. 81.
4. For illustrations, see Virginia and Lee McAlester, *A Field Guide to American Houses,* in particular "Eclectic Houses" Tudor 1890–1940, pp. 355–71.
5. This note and the specification from the Jacobsen and Co. Catalogue are on the working drawings for the Oppenheimer House, UT-AAA.

CHAPTER 11. MEDITERRANEAN STYLE II, 1924-31: SPANISH STYLE

1. For Spanish Renaissance and Baroque architecture, see Sir Banister Fletcher, *A History of Architecture on the Comparative Method,* Chapter 24.
2. Refer John D. Hoag, *Islamic Architecture.*
3. Rexford Newcomb, *Mediterranean Domestic Architecture in the United States.* This book included Ayres's Thomas Hogg House, pp. 157–60.
4. The Thomas Hogg House caused some confusion with its Spanish exterior and Italian interior. The Roberts House, however, was clearly Italian inspired both outside and in. Refer Everett, "Monte Vista," p. 54, and Atlee Ayres's letter to Joseph Rosenbloom, Correspondence UT-AAA.
5. Refer Rexford Newcomb, *The Spanish House for America: Its Design Furnishing and Garden.*
6. See Stephanie Cocke, *Texas Architect,* Sept./Oct., 1996.
7. Refer Suzi Moore, *Under the Sun,* pp. 55–58 (southern Spain).

8. Refer Sophie Bajard and Raffaello Bencini, *Villas and Gardens of Tuscany.*
9. Everett, "Monte Vista," p. 55.
10. Mannen Job Files, Correspondence UT-AAA.
11. Atlee Ayres, letter to T. S. Larson, Editor's Department, *The Architectural Record,* Sept. 4, 1929, UT-AAA.
12. Excerpts from the correspondence between Atlee and Mrs. Atkinson, as well as information about the builders and the construction of the house, are from the Atkinson-McNay Job Files, UT-AAA.
13. This figure was derived from Historical Statistics of the U.S. Department of Commerce for 1990, adjusted to 1928.
14. Adina De Zavala, letter to Atlee Ayres, Correspondence UT-AAA.
15. Mrs. Atkinson's involvement in the design and making of the house, as well as the descriptions of the original interior, are derived from Lois Wood Burkhalter, *Marion Koogler McKay: A Biography 1883–1950.* This scantily documented, slim volume presents Mrs. Atkinson in an uncritical, admiring light, but the historic photographs of the recently finished house are informative.
16. For the reception of the Atkinson house in the architectural publications, see Chapter 6, "Ayres and the Magazines."
17. Mary Carolyn Hollers George, *O'Neil Ford, Architect.*
18. For Atlee's correspondence with the Browns, refer to the Job Files in UT-AAA, in particular the letters of January 2 and 5 and April 23 and 30, 1931.

CHAPTER 12. NEOCLASSICAL MANSIONS, 1931-38

1. Atlee Ayres, letter to Benjamin F. Betts, editor of *American Architect,* New York, May 22, 1935.
2. Much of the information on the Buttrams and their house and grounds came from the nomination form submitted by the Oklahoma Historical Society to the National Register of Historic Places at the National Park Service, the U.S. Department of the Interior, July 27, 1990. The

form included detailed descriptions of the exterior and interior of the mansion and the extensive grounds. The original design studies and working drawings are in the UT-AAA.

3. Lutcher Brown Job Files, Mar. 12, 1935.

4. White Allom and Charles Roberson, London, reply to Robert M. Ayres, San Antonio, July 6, 1934.

5. Atlee B. Ayres, letter to Vincent, Freal & Cie, June 22, 1935, Correspondence UT-AAA.

CHAPTER 13. POSTSCRIPT

1. *A Guide to San Antonio Architecture,* The San Antonio Chapter of the American Institute of Architects, p. 104.

2. Eric Larabee, quoted from *Harpers* in Russell Lynes, *The Tastemakers: The Shaping of American Popular Taste,* p. 251.

3. *House and Garden Building Guide* 12 (fall/winter, 1965–66): 119.

4. Refer Virginia and Lee McAlester, *A Field Guide to American Houses,* pp. 476–86.

5. *House and Garden Building Guide,* fall/winter, 1965–66.

6. *Plans: A House and Garden Guide,* 1977, p. 101.

7. Barbara Diamond, *American Architecture Now,* p. 51.

8. Denise Scott Brown, "Looking from the Future into the Immediate Past," *Architecture,* May, 1997, p. 18.

9. *Christie's Great Estates,* 1997, p. 18.

10. Ibid.

11. Ibid.

GLOSSARY

Adamesque: characteristic of the work of Robert Adam, an eighteenth-century Scots-born English architect renowned for the delicacy and richness of his ornament, inspired by ancient Rome and Greece.

acanthus: a wild Mediterranean plant with deeply serrated and scalloped leaves. It is represented in stylized form on the Corinthian column **capital** and other classical decorative designs.

anthemion: an ornamental figure of Greek derivation based on a flower, perhaps honeysuckle, from which long slender leaves radiate in a formalized palmette.

arabesque: surface decoration using combinations of flowing lines, tendrils, and scrolls, and fanciful combinations of vases, figures, animals, flowers, and fruit.

arch: a curved span across an opening; arches common in twentieth-century traditional styles were semicircular, segmental with a curvature of less than 180 degrees, Gothic pointed, and Tudor low curved and pointed.

attic: the space, wall or story above an **entablature,** the horizontal elements supported by columns.

awning window: outswinging, hinged along the top.

baluster: small pillar or column, a series of which comprise a balustrade supporting a handrail on staircase, terrace, or balcony.

bay window: a volume that projects beyond the face of an exterior wall.

bracket: any strut or angled support of a shelf, beam, overhang, or projecting roof.

buttress: a masonry projection from a wall to add strength and resist the outward thrust of a roof or vault above.

cantilever: a projecting or overhanging beam, slab, or portion of a building with no visible means of support.

capital: a carved or decorated block at the top of a column.

cartouche: an oval or oblong decorative device usually embellished with swags or garlands.

casement window: hinged along the vertical edge, inswinging or outswinging.

classical: of, pertaining to, or derived from the architecture of Greek or Roman antiquity.

coffer: a variously shaped recess, often square or polygonal, in a compartmented ceiling, vault, or dome.

colonnade: a gallery, portico, or porch, supported on a line of columns.

console: bracket with a compound curved outline.

coping: a protective band of brick, stone, or metal weatherproofing the exposed top edge of a parapet or top of a wall.

corbel: to project forward from the face of a wall by superimposing elements in an oversailing configuration.

cornice: the upper section of the **entablature** in classical architecture, also a projecting feature in wood or plaster along the top of a wall outside or within a room.

course: a horizontal row of brick or stone in a wall. A **belt course** is one articulated to emphasize horizontality. A **soldier course** is a type of brick course in which individual bricks are laid up vertically on their heads.

cove: a curved connection between the cornice and ceiling of a room.

crenellation: the notched parapet or battlements at the top of a wall.

cyma: a molding taking its name from its contour or profile, resembling that of a wave. Consisting of two joined curves, the **cyma recta,** which is concave above and swelling or convex below; the **cyma reversa** reverses the contours. Also called an **ogee.**

dado: the lower portion of an interior wall, usually differentiated from the field above by a decorative horizontal band, paneling, or other decorative device; also called a **wainscot.**

dormer: a glazed structure with its own roof that projects from the main roof.

double-hung window: a pair of superimposed sashes that are offset so as to slide up and down within the same frame. Only one of them is moveable in a **single-hung window.** A **triple-hung window** has three sashes.

dentil: a toothlike, rectangular block that projects beneath a cornice.

eaves: the underside of a roof that projects beyond the face of an exterior wall.

Elizabethan: referring to the architecture of the sixteenth-century reign of Elizabeth I of England, also the early-seventeenth-century **Jacobean,** both characterized by Italian Renaissance elements used on buildings of medieval character.

engaged: an element conjoined with, but visually differentiated from, another element, such as an engaged column.

entablature: in architecture of classical derivation, the articulation of the transition between roof and vertical support in a horizontal band composed of three elements: **architrave, frieze, and cornice.**

fanlight: a semicircular or elliptical transom window above a doorway.

fascia: a flat-surfaced band and finish board that covers the ends of roof rafters.

fenestration: pertaining to windows.

festoon: carved, suspended, garland of flowers and fruits, also a **garland.**

fillet: a small flat projecting **molding.**

finial: the top-most ornamented feature of a gable, roof, or parapet.

fluting: vertical grooves with a concave profile or channels running up the face of columns or pilasters.

four-square: the name given to the simple, square-shaped house built in profusion as middle-class housing between 1900 and 1930.

French doors: pairs of double doors usually inswinging and with glass panes.

frieze: middle division of the entablature, also a horizontal fascia on a wall, located just below the eaves.

furred out: increasing the apparent thickness of a wall by nonstructural additions, common in twentieth-century eclectic Mediterranean styles.

gable: the triangular piece of wall between the two sloping sides of a pitched roof.

groin: the line formed along the points of intersection of vaults.

Georgian: referring to the eighteenth and early nineteenth century reigns of the four King Georges of England and the architectural styles of Neoclassicism, Palladianism, and Regency. **American Georgian** was a colonial adaptation of early- and mid-eighteenth-century English architecture, which became a principal inspiration for the "Georgian" architecture of the twentieth century.

Greek key: an ornamental pattern (fret), consisting of repeating right-angle spirals.

guilloche: a decorative pattern resembling interlaced ribbons, generally linear in form.

half-timbering: an exposed heavy timber frame, infilled with plaster, brick, or some other material; originally structural, later decorative.

head: the horizontal member framing the top of an opening. Also called a **lintel.**

hipped roof: one comprised of four or more sloping planes that all start at the same level.

jamb: the side of a doorway, window, or archway.

jib-headed window: a sash window that slides into a cavity above the head of the window frame, leaving a clear opening.

loggia: a recessed colonnade.

mansard roof: one having two slopes on all four sides, the lower closer to vertical, the upper closer to horizontal.

molding: the profile or contour of a continuous vertical or horizontal detail.

medallion: a round or oval-shaped decorative device used in plastered ceilings.

mullion: vertical post or upright bar dividing a window into two or more panes of glass or "lights."

muntin: the cross-pieces dividing the panes of glass within a window sash.

newel: central post in a circular or winding stair, also the principal post.

order: the five Greek and Roman formal, proportional systems of pedestals, columns, and horizontal entablatures that form the basis of all classical architecture. The five orders are Tuscan, Doric, Ionic, Corinthian, and Composite.

ovolo: a convex molding with a profile resembling half an egg, sometimes carved with a pattern of alternating eggs and arrowheads or darts.

Palladian window: an arched opening flanked by narrower openings.

pediment: a triangular gable used above a portico and over doors and windows. Can be of broken form when the center portion or the base is open, or **open** form when the center portion of the sloping sides is left out.

pergola: a garden arbor or open slat-work structure usually serving as a framework for vines.

pilaster: a flat pier or column attached to and projecting from a wall. When the projection exceeds half the width of the column it is an **engaged** column.

pitch: the slope of a roof. A **pitched roof** has two slopes from a common ridgeline. A **crosspitched roof** has two or more intersecting pitched roofs.

porte cochere: a roofed porch providing covered passage for a vehicle and access to a building.

portico: a porch with columns, often surmounted by a pediment and used as the centerpiece of a façade.

quoin: block or simulated block of stone, used in vertical series, on the corner of a building, usually in alternating long and short courses, sometimes rusticated to contrast with the smooth wall.

rafter: a sloping roof beam.

soffit: the underside of any projecting or overhang feature, such as the roof.

spindle: a turned vertical member supporting a railing.

stretcher: the long face of a brick. The short face is the **header.**

stringer: a sloping support for a stair.

terra cotta: a baked clay material usually shaped in the form of tiles, decorative panels, or sculptural features.

terrazzo: a cement surface with integral polished marble chips, usually used for floors.

transom: a panel, often operable, sometimes glazed, above a door or window.

voussoir: the wedge-shaped stone or brick that with others radiates from the center of an arch and forms its structure.

BIBLIOGRAPHY

Adam, Robert. *Classical Architecture: A Complete Handbook.* London: Viking-Penguin, 1992.

American Country Houses of Today. 8 vols. New York: Architectural Book Publishing, 1912–35.

Andrea, Herb, Noel Young, and Patricia Halloran. *Santa Barbara Architecture.* Santa Barbara: Capra Press, 1975.

Andrews, Wayne. *Architecture, Ambition, and Americans.* New York: Harper & Brothers, 1947.

Ayres, Atlee B. *Mexican Architecture, Ecclesiastical, Civil, Domestic.* New York, Helburn, 1926.

———. "A House of Distinction in San Antonio." *House and Garden.* August, 1929.

———. "Thomas E. Hogg House." *The American Architect* 134 (August 20, 1928).

———. "House of P. L. Mannen, San Antonio, Texas." *The American Architect* 135 (January 20, 1929).

———. "E. B. Carruth House." *Architectural Forum* 60, no. 42 (January, 1934).

———. "Essay on Eclecticism." *Master Detail Series No. 7* 55 (March, 1934).

———. "A House of Distinction" (Atkinson-McNay House). *San Antonio House and Garden* 54 (August, 1929).

Bajard, Sophie, and Raffaello Bencini. *Villas and Gardens of Tuscany.* Paris: Finest S.A./Editions Pierre Terrail, 1993.

Baker, James Milnes. *American House Styles: A Concise Guide.* New York: W. W. Norton & Company, 1994.

Baker, Paul R. *Richard Morris Hunt.* Cambridge, Mass., 1983.

Banham, Reyner. *Los Angeles: The Architecture of Four Ecologies.* New York: Harper & Row, 1971.

Barnstone, Howard. *The Architecture of John F. Staub.* Austin: University of Texas Press, 1977.

Boyd, John Taylor. "The Home as the American Architect Sees It." *Architecture and Decoration* (1929–31): 31–35.

———. "What Style for the Country House?" *A and D* 15 (October, 1921).

Brooks, H. Allen. *The Prairie School.* New York: W. W. Norton & Company, 1976.

Bunting, Bainbridge. "John Gaw Meem." *Southwestern Architect,* 1983.

Burchard, John, and Albert Bush-Brown. *The Architecture of America,* abridged. Boston: Little Brown and Company, 1961.

Burkhalter, Lois Wood. *Marion Koogler McNay: A Biography 1883–1950.* San Antonio: Marion Koogler McNay Museum of Art, 1968.

Byne, Arthur, and Mildred Stapley. *Provincial Houses in Spain.* New York: William Helburn, Inc., 1925.

———. *Majorcan Houses and Gardens.* New York: William Helburn, Inc., 1928.

———. *Spanish Gardens and Patios.* Philadelphia: J. B. Lippincott Co., 1924.

Calvert, Albert Frederick. *Spain: An Historical and Descriptive Account of its Architecture, Landscape, and Arts.* 2 vols. London: J. M. Dent & Sons, Ltd., 1911.

Carley, Rachel. *The Visual Dictionary of American Domestic Architecture.* New York: Henry Holt & Co., 1994.

Carson, Chris, and William McDonald, eds. *A Guide to San Antonio Architecture.* San Antonio: San Antonio Chapter of the American Institute of Architects (AIA), 1986.

Clark, Alson, ed. *Myron Hunt 1868–1952: The Search for a Regional Architecture.* Los Angeles: Hennesey and Ingalls, 1984.

———. *Wallace Neff: Architect of California's Golden Age.* Santa Barbara: Capra Press, 1986.

Cocke, Stephanie H. "Golden Age." *Texas Architect,* September/October, 1996.

Crook, J. Mordaunt. *The Dilemma of Style.* Chicago: University of Chicago Press, 1987.

Curl, Donald W. *Mizner's Florida, American Resort Architecture.* Cambridge, Mass.: MIT Press, 1984.

Dana, William. *The Swiss Chalet Book.* New York: William T. Comstock Co., 1913.

"The Earliest Mission Buildings of San Antonio." *The American Architect* 126 (August, 1924).

Eaton, Leonard K. *Frank Lloyd Wright and Howard Van Doren Shaw: Two Chicago Architects and Their Clients.* Cambridge, Mass.: MIT Press, 1969.

Edgell, G. H. *The American Architecture of Today.* New York: Charles Scribner's Sons, 1928.

Everett, Donald E. "Monte Vista; The Gilded Age of an Historic District 1890–1930." Supplement to the *North San Antonio Times* and the *Alamo Heights Recorder Times,* January 28, 1988.

Ferguson, John C. "The Country Houses of Atlee B. Ayres and Robert M. Ayres." *CITE The Architecture and Design Review of Houston* (spring, 1986).

Flagg, Ernest. *Small Houses: Their Economic Design and Construction.* New York: Scribner's, 1922.

Fletcher, Sir Banister. *A History of Architecture on the Comparative Method.* New York: Charles Scribner's Sons, 1961.

Foley, Mary Mix. *The American House.* New York: Harper & Row, 1980.

Gebhard, David. "The Mediterranean Villa in America: Three Episodes." *CENTER* (Center for the Study of American Architecture, The University of Texas, Austin). New York: Rizzoli, 1985.

———. *George Washington Smith.* The Art Museum, University of California at Santa Barbara, 1964.

George, Mary Carolyn Hollers. *O'Neil Ford, Architect.* College Station: Texas A&M University Press, 1992.

Gowans, Alan. *Styles and Types of North American Architecture.* New York: Harper Collins, 1992.

———. *The Comfortable House: North American Suburban Architecture* Cambridge Mass.: MIT Press, 1987.

Graddige, Roderick. *Edwin Lutyens: Architect Laureate.* London: George Allen & Unwin, 1981.

Gravagnolo, Benedetto. *Adolf Loos, theory and works.* New York: Rizzoli, 1982.

Grizzard, Mary. *Spanish Colonial Art and Architecture*

Guerra, Mary Ann Noonan. *The Missions of San Antonio.* San Antonio: The Alamo Press, 1982.

Hamlin, Talbot. *The American Spirit in Architecture.* New Haven: Yale University Press, 1926.

Handlin, Davis. *The American Home: Architecture and Society 1815–1915.* Boston: Little Brown, 1979.

Hatton, Hap. *Tropical Splendor.* New York: Alfred A. Knopf, 1987.

Henderson, Anne. "Revival Modes and Regionalism in the Early Twentieth Century: Atlee B. Ayres's Residential Designs for Suburban San Antonio." Master's thesis, art history, University of Texas, Austin, 1968.

Hewitt, Mark. *The Architect and the American Country House 1890–1940.* New Haven: Yale University Press, 1990.

Hielscher, Kurt. *Picturesque Spain.* New York: Brentano's, 1922.

Hitchcock, Henry Russell. *The Architecture of H. H. Richardson and his times.* Cambridge, Mass.: MIT Press, 1966.

Hoag, John D. *Islamic Architecture.* New York: Electa Rizzoli, 1987.

Howard, Maurice. *The Early Tudor Country House, Architecture and Politics 1490–1550.* London: George Philip, 1987.

Hudson, Karen E. *Paul R. Williams, Architect.* New York: Rizzoli, 1993.

Johnston, Alva M. *The Legendary Mizners.* London: Rupert Hart Davis, 1953.

Jordy, William H. *American Buildings and Their Architects: Progressive and Academic Ideals at the Turn of the Twentieth Century.* Garden City, N.Y.: Anchor Press Doubleday, 1976.

Jutson, Mary Carolyn Hollers. *Alfred Giles: An English Architect in Texas and Mexico.* San Antonio: Trinity University Press, 1972.

Kaufman, Edgar, Jr., ed. *Frank Lloyd Wright: The Early Work.* New York: Horizon Press, 1968.

Kidney, Walter C. *The Architecture of Choice: Eclecticism in America 1880–1930.* New York: George Braziller, 1974.

Kubinsky, Mihaly. *Adolf Loos.* Zurich: Kurt Lusten-
berger, 1994.

Lloyd, Nathaniel. *A History of the English House from
Primitive Times to the Victorian Period.* London: The
Architectural Press, 1931.

Lynes, Russell. *The Tastemakers.* New York: Harper and
Brothers, 1949.

Maher, James T. *The Twilight of Splendor.* Toronto:
Brown and Company, 1975.

Maass, John. "Where Architectural Historians Fear to
Tread." *JSAH,* March, 1969.

MacLeod, Robert. *Charles Rennie Mackintosh: Architect
and Artist.* London and Glasgow: Collins, 1968.

Massey, James C., and Shirley Maxwell. *House Styles in
America.* New York: Penguin Studio, 1996.

McAlester, Virginia and Lee. *A Field Guide to American
Houses.* New York: Alfred Knopf, 1984.

McCoy, Esther. *Five California Architects.* New York:
Holt, Rinehart and Winston, 1975.

McMillian, Elizabeth. *Casa California.* New York:
Rizzoli, 1996.

Moore, Suzi. *Under the Sun.* New York: Bulfinch Press,
1995.

Morrison, Hugh S. *Louis Sullivan: Prophet of Modern
Architecture.* New York: W. W. Norton, 1962.

Muthesius, Hermann. *The English House.* Ed. Dennis
Sharp. London: Lockwood Staples, 1979.

Neff, Wallace H., and Alson Clark. *Wallace Neff, Architect
of California's Golden Age.* Santa Barbara: Capra
Press, 1986.

Newcomb, Rexford. *Mediterranean Domestic Architecture
in the United States.* Cleveland: J. H. Jansen, 1928.

————. *The Spanish House for America: Its Design,
Furnishing, and Garden.* Philadelphia: Lippincott,
1927.

————. *Spanish Colonial Architecture in the United
States.* New York: J. J. Augustin, 1937.

Oliver, Richard. *Bertram Grosvenor Goodhue.* Cambridge: MIT Press and The Architectural History
Foundation, 1983.

Orr, Christina. *Addison Mizner, Architect of Dreams and
Realities 1872–1933.* Palm Beach Florida: Norton
Gallery and School of Art, 1977.

O'Neil, Daniel. *Lutyens: Country Houses.* New York:
Watson-Guptill Publications, 1981.

Patterson, Augusta Owen. *American Homes Today.* New
York: Macmillan Company, 1924.

Reilly, Charles Herbert. *McKim, Mead and White.* New
York: Benjamin Bloom, 1922.

Roth, Leland. *McKim, Mead and White Architects.* New
York: Harper & Row, 1983.

Saint, Andrew. *Richard Norman Shaw.* New Haven and
London: Yale University Press, 1976.

Saylor, Henry Hodgman. *Architectural Style for Country
Houses.* New York, R. M. McBride, 1912. Reprint,
1919.

Sexton, R. W., and Arthur C. Holden. *American
Country Houses of Today.* New York: Architectural
Book Publishing Co., 1930.

"The Small House in Spanish Style." *Southern Architect
and Building News* (December, 1927): 53.

"Small Italian and Spanish Houses as a Basis of
Design." *Architectural Forum* 126 (August, 1924).

Soule, Winson. *Spanish Farmhouses and Minor Public
Buildings.* New York: Architectural Book Publishing, 1924.

Staats, H. Philip. *California Architecture in Santa Barbara.*
New York: Architectural Book Publishing, 1929.

Steiner, Francis. *Frank Lloyd Wright in Oak Park and
River Forest.* Chicago: Sigma Press, 1903.

Stern, Robert A. M., Gregory Gilmartin, and John
Massengale. *New York 1900: Metropolitan Architecture
and Urbanism 1890–1915.* New York: Rizzoli, 1983.

Tarbell, Ida M. *The Florida Architecture of Addison
Mizner.* New York: Helburn, 1928.

Turner, Martha Anne. *Clara Driscoll.* Austin: Madrone
Press, 1979.

Ware, Dora, and Maureen Stafford. *An Illustrated
Dictionary of Ornament.* New York: St. Martin's
Press, 1974.

Whiffen, Marcus. *American Architecture Since 1780: A
Guide to the Styles,* rev. ed. Cambridge, Mass.: MIT
Press, 1992

Wilson, Henry L. *The Bungalow Book,* fifth ed.
Chicago: Henry L. Wilson, 1910.

INDEX

ISBN 1-58544-122-8

90000